D1297337

METHOD OF MAKING "CAPER" TEA.

A RESIDENCE

AMONG

THE CHINESE:

INLAND, ON THE COAST, AND AT SEA.

BEING A NARRATIVE OF SCENES AND ADVENTURES DURING A
THIRD VISIT TO CHINA, FROM 1853 TO 1856.

INCLUDING NOTICES OF MANY NATURAL PRODUCTIONS AND WORKS OF ART,
THE CULTURE OF SILK, &c.;

WITH SUGGESTIONS ON THE PRESENT WAR.

By ROBERT FORTUNE,

HONORARY MEMBER OF THE AGRI-HORT. SOCIETY OF INDIA, AUTHOR OF
" THREE YEARS' WANDERINGS IN CHINA," " A JOURNEY TO THE TEA COUNTRIES," ETC.

WITH ILLUSTRATIONS.

SR Scholarly Resources Inc.
Wilmington, Delaware

DS 709
F 76
1972

915
F745

SCHOLARLY RESOURCES, INC.
1508 Pennsylvania Avenue
Wilmington, Delaware 19806

Reprint edition published in 1972
First published in 1857 by John Murray, London

Library of Congress Catalog Card Number: 72-79821
ISBN: 0-8420-1363-6

Manufactured in the United States of America

PREFACE.

It is now nearly fourteen years since I landed in China for the first time, in the capacity of Botanical Collector to the Horticultural Society of London. From 1848 to the beginning of 1851 I was engaged by the Honourable Court of Directors of the East India Company in procuring supplies of tea-plants, seeds, implements, and green-tea makers, for the government plantations in the Himalayas. In the end of 1852 I was deputed a second time by the East India Company for the purpose of adding to the collections already formed, and particularly of procuring some first-rate black-tea makers for the experimental tea-farms in India.

The present volume gives an account of my last travels amongst the Chinese—from 1852 to 1856 —which it is hoped will be found as interesting as my former 'Three Years' Wanderings,' and ' Journey to the Tea Countries.'

During my first visit my investigations were chiefly confined to the coast near the five ports at which foreigners are permitted to trade. In my second book I described some long journeys to the green and black tea countries; and in this one I have endeavoured to give the reader a minute account of some extensive districts of country which lie between the coast-line and the points formerly reached. For the talented sketches which illustrate the work I am indebted to my friend Mr. Scarth.

In keeping a journal of the ever-varying scenes which passed daily in review before me, I have not been unmindful of a friendly hint which I received from some reviewers of my former works. I have, therefore, endeavoured to describe more minutely the characters, manners, and customs of the Chinese in those districts in which I lived for a length of time almost like one of themselves. And with regard to this part of the performance I can only say that the figures on my canvas are such as I daily met with in the course of my travels, and are true to nature. The reader is left to draw his own conclusions; but it is hoped that those who have been inclined to form their estimate of the Chinese character from what has been written about the low rabble of Canton, will, after the perusal of these pages, look with a more favourable eye upon the inhabitants of China when seen from other points of view.

The natural productions of the country which came under my notice, whether simply ornamental in their character, or articles of commercial value, have been fully described. During a sojourn of some months in the heart of the great silk country I had an opportunity of seeing the cultivation of the mulberry, the feeding and rearing of the silk-worms, and the reeling of the silk; and these in-

teresting operations are now described, I believe,
for the first time by an English eye-witness.

The concluding chapter gives the author's views
upon the late disturbances at Canton. It shows
how these might have been avoided, and suggests
a line of policy by which our future relations with
the Chinese may be placed on a more firm and
satisfactory basis. These suggestions are of importance, not to England only, but to all civilized
nations in the West who trade with China, or
who may be interested in her future welfare and
progress.

The remarks on the climate of China, with
reference to the health of our troops, are the results of long experience, and, in the event of our
going to war with that country, ought to be carefully considered by those who have the direction
of the expedition.

Having thus given a general idea of the scope
of the work, I have only to express a hope that,
while it may add to our knowledge of the people
and productions of China, it may, at the same time,
enable us to look with more kindly feelings on a
large portion of the human family, far more
ancient as a nation, and as industrious, if not so
civilized, as ourselves.

Brompton, April, 1857.

CONTENTS.

CHAPTER I.

Arrival at Shanghae — Kindness of Mr. Beale — An earthquake — Chinese superstitions — Hairs said to come out of the ground — An examination and the result — Reports of a sunken village — Preparations to visit it — Contradictory statements — The truth at last ! — The Chinese rebellion—Its rise and progress—Taking of Nanking — Alarm at Shanghae — Means taken for protection — Taoutai's request for foreign aid — Sir George Bonham proceeds to Nanking — Arrogance of the insurgents — War-vessels of America and France visit them — The religion of the insurgents fanaticism — An extraordinary official statement — Future prospects as regards Christianity   ..   ..   ..   Page 1

CHAPTER II.

Objects in visiting China — My boat and boatmen — A groundless alarm — Chinese pilgrims — Chair-bearers — Road to Ayuka's temple — Crowds by the way — Shyness of ladies — Description of scenery — Wild flowers — Tea-farms — Approaches to temple — Ancient tree — Hawkers and their stalls — Scene in temple — Visit to high priest — Shay-le or precious relic — Its history and traditions — A picnic — Character of the people for sobriety — An evening stroll — The temple at night — Huge idols — Queen of Heaven and child — Superstitions of Chinese women   ..   22

CHAPTER III.

Tea-gatherers and their wages — Food of Chinese labourers compared with the food of the same class in England — Old city of Tse-kee — Streets and shops — Market — Mode of skinning frogs

—Temple on hill and fine scenery — Lake near north gate — Temples and priests — My servant's mode of answering questions — Chesnut-trees discovered — Introduced to India — Chinese tombs and ceremonies — A widow comes to worship — Beggars and coffins — Different customs in different countries — Reflections .. .. Page 41

CHAPTER IV.

Entomology — Chinese ideas respecting my collections — My sanity doubtful — Mode of employing natives to assist me — A scene on returning to my boat — Curious tree — Visit from a mandarin — An endeavour to explain my objects in making collections of natural history — Crowds of natives — Their quietness and civility — Return mandarin's visit — My reception — Example of Chinese politeness — Our conversation — Inquisitiveness of his ladies and its consequences — Beauty of ladies at Tse-kee — Our luncheon and adieu 59

CHAPTER V.

Visit a collector of ancient works of art — His house and garden — Inspect his collections of old crackle china and other vases, &c. — Fondness of Chinese for their own ancient works of art — Description of ancient porcelain most prized by them — Ancient enamels — Foo-chow enamels — Jade-stone — Rock crystal — Magnetic iron and other minerals — Gold-stone — Red lacquer and gold japan — Porcelain bottles found in Egyptian tombs — Found also in China at the present day — Age of these — Mr. Medhurst's remarks 78

CHAPTER VI.

Boat-travelling — Unsettled state of the country — A midnight alarm — Old quarters at Tein-tung — A good Buddhist priest — Chinese farmers — Their wives and families — Chinese women's passion, and its effects — Woman's curse — The author is seized with fever — A native doctor and his mode of treatment — Method of taking honey from bees — Mosquito tobacco — Its composition and manufacture 93

CHAPTER VII.

Difficulty in procuring black-tea manufacturers — Return to Shanghae — City taken by a band of rebels — Chief magistrate murdered — Strange prejudices of foreign residents — Their professions of neutrality — Chinese warfare — Dr. Lockhart's hospital
and patients — Value of medical missions — Public opinion
changes — Shanghae evacuated by the rebels — Entered by the
Imperialists — Cruelty of soldiers — Effects of the rebellion on
the face of the country .. .. Page 116

CHAPTER VIII.

Return to the tea-districts of Chekiang — Mode of making collections
of seeds amongst Chinese peasantry — Messengers sent to Moo-
yuen and Ping-shuy — Ping-shuy teas — Agricultural and Horticultural Society of India — Varnish-tree — Wax-insect tree —
Soap-tree — Death and funeral of a Buddhist priest — New blue
dye — Its cultivation and manufacture — " Green indigo " — Its
introduction to India and Europe 142

CHAPTER IX.

Journey to the Snowy Valley and waterfalls — Kong-k'how pagoda
— Adventure with a blind man — Elaborate carving — A new
acquaintance, Mr. Achang — Iron-ore — Mountain stream — Its
rafts and cormorants — The temple of the Snowy Valley — Description of the falls — Our dinner and guests — How Mr. Achang
enjoys it — His lecture on medical botany and lucky spots for
graves — A Buddhist recluse — Continue our journey across the
mountains — Natural productions — Fine variety of bamboo —
Its introduction to India — Romantic glen — Arrive at our boats
and bid adieu to Mr. Achang 171

CHAPTER X.

Collections shipped for India — Success attending this year's im-
portations — Visit Canton — Method of scenting teas described

— Flowers used in the operation — Their scientific and Chinese
names — Their relative value — Prices paid for them — Manufacture of "caper" described — Inferior ditto — "Lie capers" —
Orange pekoe — High character of foreign merchants in China —
Howqua's garden described — Its plants, ornamental doors,
and alcoves, &c. — Polite notices to visitors worthy of imitation   ..   .. Page 195

CHAPTER XI.

Visit the port of Foo-chow-foo — Its foreign trade — The advantages
and disadvantages of the port — Steamer "Confucius" — Sail for
Formosa — An amateur watch kept — Sea-sickness of mandarins
— Appearance of Formosa from sea — Land on the island —
Rice-paper plant — The natives — Productions of the island —
Suggestions to the navy in these seas — Sail for Shanghae —
Spring and spring flowers   219

CHAPTER XII.

Return to Chekiang — A journey to the interior — Chinese country
fair — Small feet of women — How formed, and the results —
Stalls at the fair — Ancient porcelain seal same as found in the
bogs of Ireland — Theatricals — Chinese actors — Natural productions of the country — Liliaceous medicinal plant — "Cold
water temple" — Start for Tsan-tsin — Mountain scenery and
productions — Astonishment of the people — A little boy's
opinion of my habits   245

CHAPTER XIII.

A dinner audience — Adventure with a priest — Sanatarium for
Ningpo missionaries and others — Abies Kæmpferi — Journey
to Quan-ting — Bamboo woods and their value — Magnificent
scenery — Natives of Poo-in-chee — Golden bell at Quan-ting —
Chinese traditions — Cold of the mountains — Journey with
Mr. Wang — A disappointment — Adventure with pirates —
Strange but satisfactory signal — Results 268

CHAPTER XIV.

Season's collections shipped for India — Ancient porcelain vase — Chinese dealers — Joined by two friends — Inland journey — City of Yu-yaou — Fine rice district — Appearance and conduct of natives — Laughable occurrence with an avaricious boatman — Soil and rocks of district — Village of Ne-ka-loo and Chinese inn — Shores of the bay of Hang-chow — Salt and its manufacture — Curious moonlight journey — Rapid tides — Passage junk — Voyage across the bay — Chinese sailors — Arrive at Kan-poo .. .. Page 294

CHAPTER XV.

The Tsien-tang river — Its eagre or "bore" — Appearance it presents — Effects it produces — Superstitions of the natives — City of Kan-poo — Mentioned by Marco Polo — Its decay as a maritime port — Another source of wealth — Its inhabitants — Village of Luh-le-heen — Engage canal boats — Pass through borders of silk country — City of Yuen-hwa — Supposed emporium for " Yuen-fa " silk — Geology of isolated hills — City of Ping-hoo — Way to manage Chinese crowds — Shops and gardens — A dangerous position — Arrive at Shanghae 316

CHAPTER XVI.

Leave Shanghae for the silk country — Melancholy results of the Shanghae rebellion — Country and productions about Cading — Indigo and safflower — Bamboo paper-making—Insects — Lakes and marshy country — Visit the town of Nan-tsin in the silk districts — Its shops and inhabitants — Producers of raw silk and silk merchants — Description of silk country — Soil — Method of cultivating the mulberry—Valuable varieties—Increased by grafting and not by seeds — Method of gathering the leaves — Hills near Hoo-chow-foo — Temples and priests 331

CHAPTER XVII.

Enter the city of Hoo-chow-foo — Chinese crowds — Description of the city — Richness of the shops — Fans and silks — Rich dresses of the people — Raw silk and hongs — Flowered crapes

— Chinese play and audience — How I perform my part! — Leave the city — Charming scenes in the country — Thrown silk — Silk villages and their inhabitants — Temple of Wan-shew-si and its priests — Taou-chang-shan pagoda — Glorious views from the pagoda hill .. .. Page 350

CHAPTER XVIII.

Ascend the Lun-ke river — A musical Buddhist high priest — Hoo-shan monastery — Its silk-worms — Mode of feeding them — General treatment — Their aversion to noise and bright light — The country embanked in all directions — A farmer's explanation of this — Town of Mei-che — Silk-worms begin to spin — Method of putting them on straw — Artificial heat employed — Reeling process — Machine described — Work-people — Silk scenes in a monastery — Industrious Buddhist priests — Novel mode of catching fish — End of silk season — Price of raw silk where it is produced 365

CHAPTER XIX.

Leave the silk country — Adventure at Nanziang — A visit from thieves — I am robbed of everything — Unsuccessful efforts to trace the robbers — Astonished by another visit from them — Its objects — My clothes and papers returned — Their motives for this — A visit to the Nanziang mandarin — Means taken to catch the robbers — Two are caught and bambooed — My visit to the mandarin returned — Arrive at Shanghae — Report the robbery to Her Majesty's Consul — A portion of the money recovered — The remainder supposed to be kept by the mandarins 379

CHAPTER XX.

Tea-makers from Fokien and Kiangse engaged for India — Ning-chow tea country — Formerly produced green teas — Now produces black — How this change took place — Difficulty in getting the men off — One of them arrested for debt — All on board at last and sent on to Calcutta — Coast infested with pirates — Ningpo missionaries robbed — Politeness of the pirates — Their rendezvous discovered — Attacked and destroyed by the 'Bittern' — A mandarin in difficulty — The English "don't fight fair" — Liberality of the Chinese and English merchants — Captain Vansittart's reward .. .. Page 392

CHAPTER XXI.

Return to the interior — Curious superstition — Adventures with a priest — Journey in search of new trees — Mountain scenery — New Rhododendron — Valley of the Nine Stones — Fine trees — Yew and golden pine — Curiosity of the natives — A dark and stormy night — We lose ourselves amongst the mountains — Seek shelter in a hut — Alarm of the inmates — Morning after the storm — Return to Ningpo — A fine new plant discovered — Adieu to the north of China — Engage scented-tea makers, &c., at Canton — Sail for India — Complimentary letter from Lord Dalhousie — Ordered to visit the tea-plantations in the Himalayas and Punjab — Return to England 405

CHAPTER XXII.

ON THE PRESENT WAR.

Dispute with the Chinese about the lorcha "Arrow" — Lorchas and their crews — Abuse of the English flag — Right of entrance into the city of Canton — The Chinese outwit us in diplomacy — True causes of our position in Canton — We have ourselves to blame — The policy which ought to be pursued — The city of Canton must be opened — Foolish restrictions on foreigners and their trade ought to be abolished — Direct communication with the court of Peking — Method of carrying out these views — Remarks on the climate with reference to the health of our troops — Conclusion 423

LIST OF ILLUSTRATIONS.

PAGE

1. Method of making "Caper" Tea .. .. .. *Frontispiece.*

2. Boats used on the rivers in China 22

3. Ladies and Children on a Pilgrimage to Ayuka's Temple.. 25

4. Remarkable Tree 65

5. Curious pilgrim-shaped Bottle, enamelled with butterflies 79

6. Porcelain Vase enamelled with figures of animals and plants 81

7. Vase of sea-green crackle 84

8. Oviform Bottle of rare turquoise colour 85

9. Gourd-shaped Bottle of yellowish stone colour crackle .. 85

10. Ancient porcelain vessel 87

11. Ancient Vase enamelled on metal.. 88

12. Bottle, same as found in Egyptian tombs 92

13. Rain Cloak—Hemp palm 145

14. Wax Tree 147

15. Tea-Picker—Canton 207

16. Foo-chow Countrywoman 249

17. Ancient porcelain Seals 254

18. Larch Tree 274

19. View on the Grand Canal, with mulberry trees on its banks 339

20. Mulberry Tree 345

21. Mulberry Tree 347

22. Curious method of Fishing 375

THE CHINESE:

INLAND, ON THE COAST, AND AT SEA.

CHAPTER I.

Arrival at Shanghae — Kindness of Mr. Beale — An earthquake — Chinese superstitions — Hairs said to come out of the ground — An examination and the result — Reports of a sunken village — Preparations to visit it — Contradictory statements —The truth at last! — The Chinese rebellion — Its rise and progress — Taking of Nanking — Alarm at Shanghae — Means taken for protection — Taoutai's request for foreign aid — Sir George Bonham proceeds to Nanking — Arrogance of the insurgents — War-vessels of America and France visit them — The religion of the insurgents fanaticism — An extraordinary official statement — Future prospects as regards Christianity.

ON the 14th of March, 1853, the Peninsular and Oriental steam-ship " Ganges," in which I was a passenger, sailed from Hong-kong for the port of Shanghae—the most northerly of the five at which foreigners are permitted to trade. The wind for the most part of the way was "right a-head," and sometimes it blew almost a gale; but the good ship, being powerful for her size, and well found in everything, ploughed the ocean "like a thing of life," and notwithstanding head winds and heavy seas we anchored in the Shanghae river four days

B

after leaving Hong-kong, having run in that time somewhere about nine hundred miles.

As on former occasions, I determined to make this port my head-quarters during my travels in the interior owing to the facilities it afforded for the despatch of my collections to India or to England. I was lucky enough to find my friend Mr. Beale, to whom I was so much indebted during my former "journey to the tea districts," still in Shanghae, and as kind and hospitable as ever. He again invited me to make his house my home whenever I should visit this port, an invitation of which I availed myself frequently during the three years I have been in the country. His large and interesting garden I found of the greatest value, as in it I could store my various collections until an opportunity occurred of having them shipped for their destination.

During the few days of my stay in Shanghae I experienced for the first time in my life the shock of an earthquake, a phenomenon which is not unusual in this part of the world. It was about eleven o'clock at night, one of those beautiful nights which one finds only in the sunny lands of the East. The stars were shining brightly in the sky, but a slight haze seemed to spread itself over the ground and the river; and the atmosphere, although perfectly calm, was warmer than is usual at this early period of the spring. I had been dining out, and had just returned home, and was sitting with Mr. Beale at the drawing-room fire.

In an instant I experienced an extraordinary and unaccountable sensation, which was perfectly new, and which I could neither understand nor explain. At the same moment the pheasants in the aviary began to scream, and the chandelier which hung from the ceiling swung slowly from side to side. " It is an earthquake," said Mr. Beale ; " let us go out on the lawn in front of the house." I confess I did not require a second bidding, but rushed out of the house forthwith. Mr. Beale, who seemed to have become accustomed to such things, quietly went to look for his hat in the lobby and then followed me. In the mean time his Excellency Sir George Bonham, her Majesty's Plenipotentiary and Governor of Hong-kong, who was staying at this time with Mr. Beale, came down stairs, and all the other gentlemen in the house made their appearance also, most of them in their night-dresses, as they had retired to rest before the occurrence took place. All this happened in much less time than I take to write it. When we reached the lawn the ground seemed moving and swaying to and fro under our feet, and I experienced a slight sickening sensation not unlike sea-sickness. At the same time the whole scene was rendered more striking by the ringing of bells in the adjoining houses, the screams of birds, and the crash of a falling house as we thought, but which turned out afterwards to be a slimly-built wall. The first shock lasted for a few minutes only, but several were felt afterwards, although less severe than the first.

When daylight dawned on the following morning it was found that the damage done was not very great. The wall I have already noticed had fallen, some beams in one of the houses had come through the ceiling, and a quantity of goods had tumbled down in one of the godowns. Most of the clocks had stopped, and some few lamps and glasses were broken, but upon the whole the damage done was very inconsiderable. Groups of Chinese were seen in the gardens, road-sides, and fields, engaged in gathering hairs which are said to make their appearance on the surface of the ground after an earthquake takes place. This proceeding attracted a great deal of attention from some of the foreign residents in Shanghae, and the Chinese were closely examined upon the subject. Most of them fully believed that these hairs made their appearance only after an earthquake had occurred, but could give no satisfactory explanation of the phenomenon, while some more wise than their neighbours did not hesitate to affirm that they belonged to some huge subterraneous animal whose slightest shake was sufficient to move the world.

I must confess, at the risk of being laughed at, that I was one of those who took an interest in this curious subject, and that I joined several groups who were searching for these hairs. In the course of my travels I have ever found it unwise to laugh at what I conceived to be the prejudices of a people simply because I could not understand them. In this instance, however, I must confess the results were not worth the trouble I took. The hairs, such as I picked up, and such as were shown me by the Chinese, had certainly been produced above the earth and not below it. In some instances they might readily be traced to horses, dogs, and cats, while in others they were evidently of vegetable origin. The north-eastern part of China produces a very valuable tree known by the name of the hemp-palm, from the quantity of fibrous bracts it produces on the stem just under its blossoms. Many of these fibres were shown to me by the Chinese as a portion of the hairs in question ; and when I pointed out the source from which such had come, and which it was impossible to dispute, my friends laughed, and with true Chinese politeness acknowledged I was right, and yet I have no doubt they still held their former opinions concerning the origin of such hairs. The whole matter simply resolves itself into this,—if the hairs pointed out to me were the *true* ones, then such things may be gathered not only after earthquakes but at any other time. But if, after all, these were not the real things, and if some vegetable (I shall not say animal) production was formed, owing to the peculiar condition of the atmosphere and from other causes, I can only say that such production did not come under my observation.*

* During a recent visit to the north-west provinces of India, where earthquakes are not unfrequent, I could find no traditions such as that I have alluded to.

A day or two after the earthquake took place a report was current amongst the natives that a large tract of ground, on which a populous village stood, had sunk down into the bowels of the earth, carrying with it the whole of the people, and that the spot was now marked by a large pool of water. This report was repeated to me in the country at a considerable distance from Shanghae, and seemed to be generally believed by the inhabitants. An old nursery-gardener, from whom I was in the habit of purchasing plants, informed me the village in question had been full of bad people, and that this was no doubt a judgment from heaven on account of their sins. I hinted that there might be some danger to his own property and to the city of Shanghae; but the old man told me my fears were groundless.

Being anxious to verify the reports of the Chinese by a personal examination of the place, I determined to pay it a visit. Mr. Forbes, American Consul at Canton, and Mr. Shortrede, editor of the 'China Mail,' agreed to accompany me. I had been told the spot was distant from Shanghae some thirty miles up the river, and in a south-westerly direction, but the more minute my inquiries were the greater difficulty I had in finding out the exact locality. In the mean time all our arrangements had been made except the hiring of boats, and we had agreed to start on the following morning. I had an excellent servant, a man who had travelled with me for several years, and whose

duty it was to engage the boats we required for
the journey. Before he left me for this purpose
I desired him to take care the boatman knew
the road, as it would never do to find out after we
had started that no one knew which way to go.
He left me on this mission, and was absent about
two hours. When he returned he informed me
that he had made the requisite inquiries about the
sunken village, that such an occurrence had taken
place, but instead of the spot being *up* the river we
must go *down* in an opposite direction in order to
find it. At the same time he told me candidly he
did not think the boatman knew anything about
the matter, and said I had better not go until
something more satisfactory could be ascertained
concerning it. I was reluctantly compelled to
admit that his advice was good, and wrote to the
others saying we had better put off the journey.
And now it is worth while to mark the result of
all this in order to get an idea of the extraordinary
character of the people of China. A few days
afterwards we were told with the greatest coolness,
by the same parties who had formerly given the
information about the sunken village, that " it was
quite true such an occurrence had taken place, but
that it had happened about two hundred years
ago ! "

While these events were going forward the
rebellion in the interior of the country was causing the greatest excitement, not only amongst the
natives, but also amongst foreign residents. The

rebels were known as the Kwang-si men, as they
belonged to the province of that name, which had
been for several years in a state of great disorder.
In 1850, three years before the time of which
I write, a memorial, presented to the government
by a number of gentlemen in the province, shows
that fully two-thirds of it was overrun by robbers,
who committed great violence upon the inhabitants.
" At the time the petition was written hundreds and
thousands of fields were lying uncultivated; the
communications were in the hands of the outlaws,
so that the supplies of government could not
travel." About the close of 1850 the well-known
Commissioner Lin was summoned from his retire-
ment in Fokien in order to put down the insurgents, but he died on the way. Sundry other high
officers, civil and military, were sent against them,
but apparently with but little success. In August,
1851, Hung-sew-tseuen, subsequently known as
Tai-ping-wang, seized Yung-ngan, a city of a sub-
prefecture in the east of the province, and held it
until April, 1852. The insurgent force, of which
he was the chief, advancing slowly at first, then
commenced its northern march by moving upon
the provincial capital Kwei-lin. The rebels soon
left this city behind them, and, after seizing and
abandoning various places in the south of Hoo-nan,
in the middle of December took Yohchau, a city
on the river Yang-tse-kiang. Before the end of
the month they had crossed this river, and stormed
Wu-chang, the capital of Hu-peh; then descending

the stream, they captured every city of note on or near its banks, both in Kiang-si and Ngan-hwui, until they arrived at Nanking, the ancient southern capital, in Kiang-su, which they stormed in March, 1853.*

When the news of the success of the rebels at Nanking and Chinkiang reached Shanghae, the alarm amongst all classes of the community was very great. Some persons were of opinion that the insurgents would march straight upon Shanghae, attracted thither by the reported wealth of the foreign merchants; and while the better informed did not apprehend much danger from this source, nearly all agreed in the propriety of taking some precautionary measures for the protection of the settlement. Meetings were held at the British Consulate, parties of sailors and marines were landed from our men-of-war, some rude fortifications were hastily thrown up, and every precaution was taken to prevent a surprise. It turned out afterwards that, however prudent these measures were at the time, they were quite uncalled for, as it does not seem to have been the intention of the insurgents to molest foreigners in any way whatever.

The Taoutai of Shanghae — a native of the Canton province, and a man of reputed wealth— had been making great exertions in order to put down the rebellion. He had chartered a number of Portuguese lorchas and other vessels, and sent

* T. F. Wade, in 'China Mail,' Sept. 12, 1855.

them up to Nanking to arrest the progress of the now victorious and successful insurgents. In addition to this, he applied to Mr. Alcock, her Majesty's Consul at the port, to request Captain Saunderson, of H. M. brig "Lily," to proceed with that vessel to Nanking, and exterminate the rebels. Captain Saunderson very properly refused to comply with this *modest* request, stating at the same time that a small sailing-vessel like the "Lily" would be useless in a river where the tides were rapid.

Her Majesty's Plenipotentiary, Sir George Bonham, having in the mean time arrived at Shanghae in the "Hermes," accompanied by the "Salamander," both war-steamers, the Taoutai renewed his application. After giving an account of the progress of the rebels received from the governor of Kiangsoo, which concluded by stating that, "if they are not speedily cut off, commerce will be interrupted, and the business of Chinese and foreign merchants will be totally ruined," he goes on as follows :—

"I have to request that you will, in the first place, despatch the vessels of war which may have already arrived at Shanghae, together with that stationed there, to Nanking, that they may, with the lorchas under their command, make a combined attack, solemnly binding themselves to extirpate the rebels, in order to gratify the public mind and open the path of commerce. I have also to request that you will urge by letter the speedy advance of the vessels which have not yet arrived, and their successive departure for Nanking, in order to sweep away every remnant of rebellion, and give tranquillity to the country, to the great happiness of myself, the Chinese officials, and people. For this I earnestly pray and earnestly entreat."

A polite answer was sent to this "earnest" communication; but as Sir George Bonham had made up his mind to remain strictly neutral in the affair, the poor Taoutai's request for foreign aid was not complied with, and Nanking, with Ching-kiang-foo, soon fell into the hands of the insurgents.

About this time the United States steam-frigate "Susquehanna," with his Excellency Colonel Marshall on board, made an attempt to reach Nanking by the Yang-tse-kiang, but, finding some difficulty, owing, it was said, to the shallowness of the river and the numerous sandbanks, returned to Shanghae without having accomplished the end in view. Afterwards this vessel was more successful.

Meanwhile the excitement amongst all classes of the community at Shanghae daily increased, and all sorts of exaggerated reports were promulgated. At one time it was reported that the insurgents were within thirty miles of us, and might be upon us at any moment. In addition to the means we had taken for the protection of the foreign settlement, the Taoutai, after his own manner, was most indefatigable in taking measures for the safety of the city. He purchased large supplies of gunpowder and guns from foreigners, enlisted soldiers, and called out the militia. But evidently being rather doubtful of the results, and perhaps not having much confidence in the bravery of his troops, he removed his treasure from the Imperial treasury in the city, and placed it on board of H.M. brig "Lily."

Captain Fishbourne, in his 'Impressions of China,' gives us an anecdote which shows plainly that the old man was in a great state of alarm :—"About this time I asked him how it was that, with such large and well-appointed armies as the Imperialists investing Nanking were said to be, they did not recapture it? He answered, these thieves were not men, they were devils; that they had undermined all the ground inside the walls; that the Imperialists had effected a breach in the walls, but, anticipating an ambuscade, they had driven a large number of buffaloes in through the breach, and that these had all disappeared into a dreadful gulf which the insurgents had made."

Things were in this state when Mr. Meadows, Interpreter to the Consulate, volunteered to try and reach the insurgent camp, and obtain some definite information with regard to their position, their numbers, and particularly their views with regard to Shanghae. He left Shanghae on the 9th of April in his own boat, with a picked crew, and, having a fair southerly wind, reached Soo-

chow on the following day. On the 13th he
passed the city of Chang-chow, and on the 14th
he arrived at a place called Tan-yang. At this
place his boatmen and servants seem to have
objected to proceed, and, meeting a man whom he
had previously despatched to procure information,
he returned to Shanghae in order to communicate
to Sir George Bonham the information he had
been enabled to gather during his journey connected with the movements of the insurgents.

Mr. Meadows was led to believe that the army
of the insurgents numbered from thirty to forty
thousand of "trusted and voluntary adherents,"
and in addition they had from eighty to one hundred thousand of pressed men and other adherents.
"The strangest," says Mr. Meadows, "and what
will probably prove by far the most important fact
connected with them, is, that they have got a
sacred book, which the chiefs and the older members of the army not only peruse and repeat
diligently themselves, but earnestly admonish all
new comers to learn."

The information communicated by Mr.. Meadows, and the well-known fact that the Chinese
authorities in Shanghae had been endeavouring,
by every means in their power, to make the insurgents believe that foreigners were to take the part
of the Imperialists in the quarrel, induced Sir
George Bonham to proceed himself to Nanking in
the " Hermes."

From a careful perusal of the published account

of this expedition it appears to have been useful in setting the insurgents right as to our determination to remain strictly neutral, and at the same time, if their statements were to be relied upon, it was ascertained that they had no intention of molesting us in any way at Shanghae. But the officials amongst the insurgents appear to have been full to the brim with Canton ideas of their superiority over all the nations of the earth, which augurs ill for our future connection should they be successful in upsetting the present dynasty and establishing one of their own. Listen to the modesty of the " Northern Prince :"—" The Lord of China is the lord of the whole world; he is the second son of God, and all the people in the whole world must obey and follow him. . . . . The true Lord is not merely the Lord of China; he is not only *our* lord, *but he is your lord also.*"

In order to show their views more fully, I must quote from another extraordinary document received by Her Majesty's Plenipotentiary at the time :—" But now that you distant English have not deemed myriads of miles too far to come *and acknowledge our sovereignty*, not only are the soldiers and officers of our celestial dynasty delighted and gratified thereby, but even in high heaven itself our Celestial Father and Elder Brother will also admire this manifestation of your fidelity and truth. . . . . We therefore promulgate this new decree " [permitting us to carry on commercial relations as usual, &c.] " of Tai-ping for the information of you English, so that all the human race may learn to worship our Heavenly Father and Celestial Elder Brother, and that all may know that, wherever our Royal Master is, there men unite in congratulating him on having obtained the decree to rule." Sir George Bonham says in his despatch,—" To this extraordinary document I returned the accompanying reply, which I deemed, under all circumstances, necessary, as, the sooner the minds of these men are disabused in regard to their universal supremacy, the better for all parties :—' I have received your communication, part of which I am unable to understand,' [no wonder] 'and especially that portion which implies that the English are subordinate to your sovereign.'" . . .

In the month of December, 1853, the French war-steamer "Cassini" paid a short visit to the insurgents at Nanking; in May, 1854, the American Minister, Mr. McLane, visited them in the "Susquehanna," and a short time afterwards H.M. steamers "Rattler" and "Styx" renewed the visit on the part of the English. These interviews with the leaders of the insurgents do not seem to have led to any results of importance, if we can judge from the statements which have been published from time to time in the newspapers. While the Chinese have treated the western officials with a certain amount of studied politeness, they have not failed, on all occasions, to assert their own superiority and to demand

that we should acknowledge their universal supremacy.   It therefore appears that these visits from
officials and ships of war belonging to western
nations have not only done no good, but have had
a tendency to foster that pride and self-conceit of
which the Chinese as a nation have rather more
than their fair share.

The religious character of the movement has
attracted, as might be expected, much notice from
the Christian nations of the West. At one time,
during our early acquaintance with the insurgents,
it was believed by the more sanguine amongst us
that nothing short of a miracle had been performed
by the Almighty, and that the millions of China,
for ages sunk in idolatry, were now " stretching
out their hand to God."   But our information on
this point was always crude and indefinite.   There
was, however, no doubt of one thing, namely, that
they were busily employed in printing and dis-
tributing copies of the Scriptures, that they appeared to be worshipping the same God whom we
worship, that they were keeping holy one day in
seven, and that their moral code was strict and
severe.   And it was not to be wondered at if, in
many instances, they were induced to put a literal
interpretation to certain passages of the sacred
writings which they had no one to explain.

But notwithstanding all this, there were many
persons amongst the foreign residents in China,
and I must confess myself as one of the number,
who viewed the religious character of the move-

ment with considerable doubt. This is not the age of miracles, and certainly nothing less than a miracle could account for many thousands of the Chinese being all at once converted to Christianity.

Mr. W. H. Medhurst, Chinese Secretary to the English Government at Hong-kong, who visited Nanking with the "Rattler" and "Styx," put us in possession of an official statement professing to be a few of the tenets of the so-called Chinese Christians. The document in question is certainly an extraordinary one. If we understand it aright, and if it really be what it professes, and an exposition of the religious belief of the insurgents, we must conclude their Christianity to be a sham, and their leaders fanatics or knaves.

In this document, one of the leaders of the insurgents, styled the Eastern Prince, professes to have direct communication with the Supreme Being. He pretends to fall into a trance in the presence of the females of the court, and in that state assumes that he is the Heavenly Father, and gives instructions to be communicated to himself, and also summons the Northern Prince to his presence. The instructions given to himself are afterwards communicated to him by the females, and are to this effect : he is desired to go to court, and reprove the Celestial King, Hung-sew-tseuen, the leader of the insurgents, for harshness to the females of his court and for over-indulgence to his son. When the Northern Prince arrives, the

c

Heavenly Father has ascended again to heaven, that is, the Eastern Prince is no longer under divine influence, and the whole party get into their sedan-chairs to communicate the divine commands to the Celestial King, Hung-sew-tseuen. Before they start, however, the Heavenly Father descends a second time, and the Eastern Prince falls again into a trance. The Heavenly Father now issues his commands by the lips of the Eastern Prince to the Northern Prince, who kneels reverently in the street to receive them. These are to the effect that He, the Heavenly Father, is to be conveyed to the Hall of Audience in the Celestial King's palace. When they arrive there, the Celestial King is summoned; he with the Northern Prince kneels before the Heavenly Father (the Eastern Prince) to hear his commands. The Heavenly Father now reproved the King in the following words :— " Sew-tseuen, you are very much in fault ; are you aware of it ? " Sew-tseuen, with the other officers of his court, kneels down before the Heavenly Father and says, " Your unworthy son knows he is in fault, and begs the Heavenly Father graciously to forgive him." The Heavenly Father then said with a loud voice, " Since you acknowledge your fault, you must be beaten with forty blows." When this judgment is pronounced, the Northern Prince and all the officers of the court prostrate themselves on the ground, and, weeping, implore the Heavenly Father to remit the punishment which their master had deserved, and offer at the same time to receive the blows in his stead. But the Celestial King will not hear of this, and insists on receiving the blows on his own person, prostrating himself for the purpose. The Heavenly Father now relents, and says, " Since you have obeyed the requisition, I shall not inflict the blows." The Heavenly Father then returns again to heaven, and the Eastern Prince is himself once more.

And now it becomes the duty of the Northern Prince to report to the Eastern Prince what the Heavenly Father had communicated, the latter pretending to be profoundly ignorant on the matter. " My fourth Elder Brother," said he, " the Heavenly Father has again troubled himself to come down into the world." The Eastern Prince appeared much pleased and said, " Has he indeed taken the trouble to come down again ? Truly he gives himself a great deal of trouble on our account."

The Eastern Prince, having been thus informed of the nature of the divine commands, hastens to communicate them to the Celestial King—a portion of them, however, appear to have been communicated before, during the interview at the palace. The Celestial King receives the heavenly commands with respect and gratitude, and then gives expression to an idea which, if we understand aright, is nothing else than blasphemy. And be it remembered that this is uttered by Hung-sew-tseuen, the leader of this so-called Christian

rebellion, and pupil of our Christian missionaries. The Celestial King then said, " When our
Celestial Elder Brother Jesus, in obedience to the
commands of our Heavenly Father, came down into
the world, in the country of Judea, he addressed
his disciples saying, ' At some future day the Comforter will come into the world.' Now I, your
second Elder Brother, considering what you, Brother Tsing, have reported to me, and observing
what you have done, must conclude that the Comforter, even the Holy Ghost, spoken of by our
Celestial Elder Brother, *is none other than yourself.*"
" Brother Tsing " readily agrees with Hung-sew-
tseuen, and now assumes the title of the Comforter
or Holy Ghost, and has his name included in the
hymn of praise which is chanted morning and
evening by the so-called Christian army.

Another of these worthies, styled the Western
Prince, pretends to personate our Saviour, "the
Heavenly Elder Brother," and utters his exhorta-
tions and commands as if they came direct from
heaven.

It must be confessed that such professions
amongst the leaders of this movement incline us
to pause before we can bring our minds to admit
them to be Christians. Those who are desirous of
obtaining a further account of these men may consult with advantage Captain Fishbourne's ' Impressions of China,' and Mr. Meadows's ' Chinese
and their Rebellions.' Foreigners, however, have
had no opportunity of making themselves fully

acquainted with this strange people, and I for one am content to suspend my judgment until we have the means of seeing and judging for ourselves. Any change, however, from Buddhism, Taouism, and the apathy with which the Chinese people have shrouded themselves for ages past in so far as religion is concerned, would seem to be desirable. And surely the thousands of copies of the Sacred Scriptures which are not only printed and circulated, but read by the insurgents, will bear fruit at last, although it is much to be feared the precious seed is still sown on stony ground.

Having these views, I fully agree with the following remarks made by a writer in 'The Times' upon this subject :—" It cannot be said at present that the Chinese have learnt the Gospel : but they have at any rate been taught to abandon a system of idolatry, to profess themselves believers in something better, and to appeal to this new law for the correction of social evils. . . . It will, probably, be long before this extraordinary revolution is consummated, but we do not see that the hopes entertained of the eventual conversion of China need be despondingly abandoned."

CHAPTER II.

Objects in visiting China — My boat and boatmen — A groundless
alarm — Chinese pilgrims — Chair-bearers — Road to Ayuka's temple
— Crowds by the way — Shyness of ladies — Description of scenery
— Wild flowers — Tea-farms — Approaches to temple — Ancient
tree — Hawkers and their stalls — Scene in temple — Visit to high
priest — Shay-le or precious relic — Its history and traditions — A
picnic — Character of the people for sobriety — An evening stroll
— The temple at night — Huge idols — Queen of Heaven and child
— Superstitions of Chinese women.

MY chief object in coming to China at this time
was to procure a number of first-rate black-tea
manufacturers, with large supplies of tea-seeds,
plants, and implements, such as were used in the
best districts, for the Government plantations in
the north-west provinces of India. Leaving Tai-
ping-Wang to fight his battles in the province of
Kiang-su and elsewhere, I sailed for the town of
Ningpo in the province of Chekiang, and on my
arrival at that port started immediately for the tea
districts in the interior. I had engaged a small
covered boat, such as is used on the canals in this
part of the country. It was divided into three
compartments : that in the stern was occupied
by the boatmen, who propelled the boat by a
powerful scull, which worked on a small pivot;
the centre was occupied by myself, and the fore-

BOATS USED ON THE RIVERS IN CHINA.

Page 22.

part by my servants. The length of time these boatmen are able to work this scull is very extra-ordinary. It is customary with them to go on continually both day and night, from the commencement of a journey until its end. When working in rivers, when it is calm, or when the wind is a-head, they have to anchor when the tide is against them, and in this way rest for six hours at a time; but in canals, when the tide is not felt, they go on always both night and day. And what is more wonderful still, the greater part of the work is done by one, and that one is oftentimes a mere boy. The boatman in each boat is generally the owner, and the boy is engaged by him to assist in the working of the boat. Hence the former is the master and the latter the *man*; and as a matter of course the man has to do the greater part of the work. But these boys are well fed and kindly treated by their masters, and they seem happy and contented with their lot in life. This continual working with the scull seems to unfit them for any other kind of work; when on shore they walk badly with a sort of rolling motion, much worse than that of a common sailor, and seem altogether like a " fish out of water."

The distance from the city of Ningpo to the end of the canal and foot of the hills to which I was bound was about ten or twelve miles. As we had travelled all night we reached the end of the canal some time before daybreak. I had slept pretty well on the way, but was now awakened by the sounds of hundreds of voices, some talking, others screaming at their loudest pitch, and the shrill tones of the women were heard far above those of the men. Half-awake as I was at first, I almost thought I had fallen in with a party of Tai-ping-Wang's army; but my servants and the boatmen soon set me right on that point, by informing me the multitudes in question were on their way to Ah-yuh-Wang, or Ayuka's temple, to worship and burn incense at its shrines. To fall asleep again was now out of the question, owing to the noise and excitement by which I was surrounded. I therefore got up and dressed, and took a seat on the roof of my boat, when I had a moonlight view of what was going on around me. Every boat seemed crowded with pilgrims, the greater part by far consisting of well-dressed females, all in their holiday attire. As daylight dawned the view became more distinct. Each boat was now brought close to the banks of the canal, in order that the passengers might be able to get on shore. I pitied the ladies, poor things! with their small cramped feet, for it was with great difficulty they could walk along the narrow plank which connected the boat with the bank of the canal. But the boatmen and other attendants were most gallant in rendering all the assistance in their power, and the fair sex were for the most part successful in reaching " terra firma" without any accident worth relating. Numerous chair-bearers and chairs lined the banks of the

LADIES AND CHILDREN ON A PILGRIMAGE TO AYUKA'S TEMPLE.

canal, all anxious for hire ; and if the more wealthy-
looking did not get conveyances of this kind, it
certainly was not the fault of the owners of these
vehicles, for they were most importunate in their
offers.   Indeed so much was this the case, that in
many instances under my observation the waver-
ing pilgrim was almost lifted into the chair before
he was aware of it.   These chairs are extremely
light and simple in their construction.   They are
formed of two long bamboo poles, with a small
piece of wood slung between them, on which the
traveller sits, and another smaller piece slung
lower and more forward, on which he rests his
feet.   Sometimes, when ladies and children were
to be carried, and the weight consequently light, I
observed two or three of these seats slung between
the poles, and this number of persons carried by
two stout coolies with the greatest ease.

After taking my morning cup of tea within
sight of numerous plantations of the " herb" itself,
which are dotted on the sides of the hills here, I
joined the motley crowd, and proceeded with them
to Ayuka's temple.   When I got outside of the
little village at the end of the canal, and on a
little eminence beyond it, I obtained a long view of
the mountain-road which leads to the temple.   And
a curious and strange view this was.   Whether
I looked before or behind me, I beheld crowds of
people of both sexes and of all ages, wending their
way to worship at the altars of the " unknown
God."   They were generally divided into small

groups—little families or parties—as they had left
their native villages, and most of these parties had
a servant or two walking behind them, and carrying some food to refresh them by the way, and a
bundle of umbrellas to protect them from the rain.
Each of the ladies—young and old—who were not
in chairs, walked with a long stick, which was
used partly to prevent her from stumbling, and
partly to help her along the road. Most of them
were dressed gaily in silks, satins, and crapes of
various colours, but blue seemed the favourite and
predominating one. As I walked onward and
passed group after group on the way, the ladies,
as etiquette required, looked demure and shy, as if
they could neither speak nor smile. Sometimes
one past the middle age would condescend to
answer me goodhumouredly; but this was even
rare. The men on the contrary were chatty
enough, and so were the ladies too as soon as I
had passed them and joined other groups farther
a-head. Oftentimes I heard a clear ringing laugh,
after I had passed, from the lips of some fair one
who but a minute before had looked as if she had
never given way to such frivolity in her life.

But while I am still on a little eminence from
which I have been viewing man, let me turn to
the other and not less beautiful works of nature.
Behind me lay a large and fertile valley, the same
through which I had passed during the night,
intersected in all directions with navigable canals,
and teeming with an industrious and happy

people. As it was now "the bonnie month of
May," the rice crops had been some time in the
ground, and the valley was consequently covered
with dense masses of the loveliest green. Water-
wheels were observed in all directions, some
worked by men, and other and larger ones by
bullocks, and all pouring streams of water upon
the rice crops from the various canals which intersect the valley. At the foot of the hills near
where I stood were numerous small tea-farms,
formed on the slopes, while groups of junipers and
other sombre-looking pines marked the last resting-
places of the wealthy. The ancient tombs of the
Ming dynasty are also common here, but they are
generally in a ruinous condition; and had it not
been for the huge blocks of granite cut into the
forms of men and other animals, of which they are
composed, there would have been long ago no
marks to point out the last resting-places of these
ancient rulers of China. So much for human
greatness! Higher up on the hill-sides the ground
was cultivated and ready to receive the summer
crops of sweet potatoes and Indian corn. Beyond
that again were barren mountains covered with
long grass and brushwood, which the industry of
the Chinese is never likely to bring under cultivation. Both below and above, on the roadsides,
in the hedges, and on every spot not under cultivation, wild flowers were blooming in the greatest
profusion. In the hedges the last fading blossoms
of the beautiful spring-flowering *Forsythia viridis-*

sima were still hanging on the bushes, while several species of wild roses, *Spiræa Reevesiana*, clematises, and *Glycine sinensis*, were just coming into bloom. But look a little higher up to that gorgeously painted hill-side, and see those masses of yellow and white flowers; what are they? The yellow is the lovely *Azalea sinensis*, with its colours far more brilliant, and its trusses of flowers much larger, than they are ever seen in any of our exhibitions in Europe. The white is the little-known *Amelanchier racemosa*. Amongst these, and scattered over the hill-sides, are other azaleas, having flowers of many different hues, and all very beautiful. It is still early morning; the sun is just appearing on the tops of the eastern mountains; the globules of heavy dew sparkle on the grass and flowers; the lark and other sweet songsters of the feathered race are pouring out of their little mouths sweet and melodious songs. I looked with delight on the beautiful scene spread out before me, and thought within myself, if Nature is so beautiful now, what must it have been before the Fall, when man was holy!

As I approached Ayuka's temple I observed other roads leading to the same point, crowded with people such as I have already described, all hurrying on to pay their vows at the altars of Buddha. The scenery in front of the temple, although in a ruinous condition now, at some former time was no doubt very pretty. Entering through an ancient gateway, a paved path led

straight up to the edifice, over an ornamental
bridge, which at one time probably spanned the
neck of a small lake, in which was cultivated the
sacred lotus (*Nelumbium speciosum*), but which was
now in these degenerate days allowed to get choked
up with weeds. Near this bridge a noble specimen
of the camphor-tree (*Laurus camphora*) lay prostrate on the ground, having been blown down by
a typhoon many years ago. The curious gnarled
and angular branches for which this tree is remarkable when it is alive and standing, seemed more
striking in its prostrate and withered condition.
For many years this relic of former days had been
carefully preserved by the priests, and was now
looked upon by them and the visitors as nearly as
holy as the temple itself. From the gateway up
to the doors of the temple numerous stalls were
erected for the sale of candles, joss-sticks, sycee
paper, and such things as are used in the worship
of Buddha. Others were of a less holy character,
and contained cakes and sweetmeats, toys, curiosities, and things likely to attract the notice of
the country people. It was curious to mark the
enthusiasm with which these pedlers endeavoured to
get off their goods. Every passer-by was pressed
to buy, and particularly those who had not their
hands full of candles, incenses, and other articles
which they were supposed to require. In many
instances I observed the venders actually laid hold
of the people, and almost forced them to spend
money on some articles ere they would allow them

to go on. Of course this was done in the most perfect good humour. These pedlers are first-rate physiognomists; they know at a glance those who are likely to become customers, and, should the slightest hesitation be visible on any countenance, that man is doomed to spend his money ere he passes the stall.

I now entered the temple itself, and found it crowded with idolaters. The female sex seemed much more numerous than the male, and apparently more devout. They were kneeling on cushions placed in front of the altars, and bowing low to the huge images which stood before them. This prostration they repeated many times, and when they had finished this part of their devotions they lighted candles and incense, and placed them on the altars. Returning again to the cushion, they continued their prostrations for a few seconds, and then gave way to other devotees, who went through the same forms. Some were appealing directly to the deity for an answer to their petitions by means of two small pieces of wood, rounded on the one side and flat on the other. If on being thrown into the air the sticks fell on the flat side, they had then an assurance of a favourable answer to their prayers; but owing to the laws of gravitation these stubborn little bits of wood fell much oftener on the rounder and heavier side than on the other, and gave the poor heathen a world of anxiety and trouble. Other devotees were busily engaged in shaking a hollow bamboo tube which

contained a number of small sticks, each having a
Chinese character upon it. An adept in shaking
can easily detach one of these sticks from the
others, and when it falls upon the floor it is picked
up and taken to a priest, who reads the character
and refers to his book for the interpretation
thereof. A small slip of paper is now given to
the devotee, which he carries home with him, and
places in his house or in his fields, in order to
bring him good luck. I observed that not unfrequently it was very difficult to satisfy these persons
with the paper given to them by the priest, and
that they often referred to those who were standing
around, and asked their opinion on the matter.

The scene altogether was a striking one, and was
well calculated to make a deep impression on the
mind of any one looking on as I was. Hundreds
of candles were burning on the altars, clouds of incense were rising and filling the atmosphere; from
time to time a large drum was struck which could
be heard at a distance outside the building; and
bells were tinkling and mingling their sounds with
those of the monster drum. The sounds of many
of these bells are finer than anything I ever heard
in England. Most of the fine ones are ancient,
and were made at a time when the arts ranked
higher in China than they do at the present day.

In the midst of all these religious services,
which candour compels me to say were outwardly
most devoutly performed, things were going on
amongst the worshippers which as foreigners and

Christians we cannot understand.   Many, who had either been engaged in these ceremonies or intended to take their part in them, were sitting, looking on, and laughing, chatting, or smoking, as if they had been looking on one of their plays. And it was not unusual to see a man fill his pipe with tobacco, and quietly walk up and light it at one of the candles which were burning on the altar.

After looking on this curious and noisy scene for a little while, I was glad to leave it for the quieter parts of the building.   I went in the first place to pay my respects to the high-priest, and found him occupying some small rooms built at one side of the large temple.   With Chinese politeness he received me cordially and made me sit down on the seat of honour in his little room.   A little boy who served him brought in a tray, on which a number of teacups were placed filled with delicious tea. Two* of these cups were put down before me, and I was pressed to "drink tea."   As the day was excessively warm, the pure beverage was most welcome and refreshing.   Reader, there was no sugar nor milk in this tea, nor was there any Prussian blue or gypsum ; but I found it most refreshing, for all that it lacked these *civilised* ingredients. The good old man was very chatty, and gave me a great deal of information about himself and the temple.   The revenues of the temple were derived partly from certain lands in the vicinity which

---

* The Chinese generally place *two* cups before a stranger.

belonged to it, and partly from the contributions
of devout Buddhists who came there to worship.
The high-priest himself also contributed largely to
its support. On inquiring how this happened, he
informed me that he was obliged to contribute a
large sum—I think he said 3000 dollars—before
he could be elected to the office he now held,
and that he held it for three years only, when
his successor would have to contribute a similar
sum. This sum was spent in keeping the temple
in repair. I understood him to say that the in-
ducement held out to men of his class is high
honours at the end of the three years when they
retire into private life.

When we had sipped our tea, I then told the
high-priest I had heard there was a *Shay-le* or
relic of Buddha in the monastery, and expressed a
desire to see it. He appeared pleased to find the
fame of the relic had reached my ears, and sent
immediately for the priest under whose charge
it was placed, and desired him to show it to me.
I now bade adieu to the old man, and followed my
guide to that part of the monastery where the
relic was kept. On our way he asked me whether
it was my intention to burn incense to Buddha
before the box which contained the relic was
opened. I replied that not being a Buddhist
I could not do that, but I would give him a small
present for opening the box—a way of settling
the question which seemed to please him quite
as well as buying candles and incense to burn at

the shrine. I found the precious relic locked up
in a bell-shaped dome. When this was opened
I observed a small pagoda carved in wood, and
evidently very ancient. It was about ten inches
or a foot in height, and four inches in width. In
the centre was a small bell, and near the bottom
of this the shay-le or relic was said to be placed.
" I can see nothing there," said I to my guide.
" Oh," said he, " you must get it between you and
the light, and then you may see it ; it is sometimes
very brilliant, but only to those who believe."
" I am afraid it will not shine for my gratification
then," said I ; but I stood in the position my
guide indicated. It might be imagination, I dare
say it was, but I really thought I saw something unusual in the thing, as if some brilliant
colours were playing about it. The Reverend
Dr. Medhurst, of the London Missionary Society,
who has since visited and examined the relic,
could see nothing " because he had no faith ;" and
if at any time there is anything to be seen, such
an appearance could no doubt be easily explained
from natural causes. The priest informed me the
precious relic had been obtained from the top of a
hill behind the temple by their forefathers, who
had handed it down with the traditions attending
it to the present generation, and that they wanted
no further proof of its being genuine.

Shay-le, or precious relics of Buddha, are found in
many of the Buddhist temples. In a former work *

* Journey to the Tea Countries of China and India.

I have described two in the celebrated monastery of Koo-shan, near Foo-chow-foo in Fokien. In a note published by the Reverend Dr. Medhurst the history of such relics is given by the Chinese in the following manner :—" The Buddhists say there are 84,000 pores in a man's body, and thus, by following corruption and passing through transmigration, he leaves behind him 84,000 particles of miserable dust. Buddha's body has also 84,000 pores, but by resisting evil and reverting to truth he has perfected 84,000 relics ; these are as hard and as bright as diamonds, affording benefit to men and devas wherein they are deposited. * * * * Eight kings contended for these relics, which were divided into three parts, one being assigned to the devas, one to the nagas, and the third to the eight kings. During Buddha's lifetime he was begging with O-nan in a lane, when they saw two boys playing with earth; one of them, being struck with the dignified appearance of Buddha, presented him with some pellets of earth, expressing a wish at the same time that he might in future become one of his most zealous worshippers. Buddha then addressed O-nan, saying, 'After my obtaining *nirvaan* (nothingness, *i.e.* death), this child will become a king, ruling over the southern kingdoms, and building pagodas for the preservation of my relics.' This was Ayuka, who afterwards built 84,000 pagodas ; nineteen of these were constructed in China, and one of them was fixed on the snow-hill in the prefecture of

Ningpo, commonly called Yuh-wong. About the time of the Three Kingdoms (A.D. 230) a priest named Hwuy came to Nanking, where he built a shed. The people thought him a strange being, and brought him to Sun-keuen, the ruler of the country, who asked him for the proofs of his religion. Hwuy replied that Buddha left a number of relics, over which Ayuka had built 84,000 pagodas. Sun-keuen thought it was all nonsense, and told him that if he could find a relic he might build a pagoda over it. Hwuy then filled a bottle with water, and offered up incense before it for twenty-one days; at the expiration of that period he heard a sound proceeding from the bottle resembling that of a bell. Hwuy then went to look at it, and perceived that the relic was formed. The next day he presented it to Sun-keuen; the whole of the courtiers examined it, and saw the bottle illuminated with all sorts of brilliant colours. Keuen took the bottle, and poured out its contents into a dish; when the relic came in contact with the dish it broke the vessel to pieces. Keuen was astonished and said, ' That is very curious.' Hwuy then addressed him, saying, ' This relic is not only capable of emitting light, but no fire will burn, nor diamond-headed hammer bruise it.' He then placed the relic on an anvil, and caused a strong man to strike it with all his might, when the hammer and anvil were both broken, and the relic remained uninjured. Keuen then assented to the construction of the pagoda. The Chinese say that they can sometimes discern the relic illumined with brilliant colours, and as big as a cart-wheel, while the unbelievers can see nothing at all."

Such are the Chinese traditions concerning these so-called precious relics of Buddha, which one meets with so frequently in Buddhist temples, not only in China, but also in India.

After inspecting this precious relic I returned through the various temples, which were still crowded with worshippers, to the open air. As the day was warm, I sought shelter from the scorching rays of the sun in a little wood of bamboos and pines which was close at hand. Here I mixed with groups of worshippers who were now picnicking under the shade which the trees afforded. Each little group had brought its own provisions, which appeared to be relished with great zest. In many instances I was asked to join with them and partake of their homely fare, an invitation which I declined, I trust, in as polite a manner as that in which it was given. Many of them seemed weary and footsore with their long journey, but all were apparently happy and contented, and during the day I did not observe a single instance of drunkenness or any disturbance whatsoever. The Chinese as a nation are a quiet and sober race : their disturbances when they have them are unusually noisy, but they rarely come to blows, and drunkenness is almost unknown in the country districts, and rare even in densely populated cities.

In these respects the lower orders in China contrast favourably with the same classes in Europe, or even in India.

When the sun had got a little to the westward, and his rays less powerful, I left the temple and took my way to the hills. In a few minutes that busy scene of idol-worship which I have endeavoured to describe was completely shut out from my view. As I went along I came sometimes unexpectedly on a quiet and lonely valley where the industrious labourers were busily at work in the fields, or on a hill-side where the natives were gathering their first crop of tea. Here is no apparent want, and certainly no oppression; the labourer is strong, healthy, and willing to work, but independent, and feels that he is " worthy of his hire." None of that idleness and cringing is here which one sees amongst the natives of India, for example, and other eastern nations.

Time passed swiftly by when wandering amongst such interesting scenery, and as evening was coming on I returned to the temple, in which I proposed taking up my quarters for the night. Now the scene had entirely changed : the busy crowds of worshippers were gone, the sounds of bell and drum had ceased, and the place which a short time before was teeming with life was now as silent as the grave. The huge idols—many of them full thirty feet high—looked more solemn in the twilight than they had done during the day.

The Mahârâdjas, or four great kings of Devas, looked quite fierce; Me-lie-Fuh, or the *merciful one*, a stout, jovial-looking personage, always laughing and in good-humour, seemed now to grin at me; while the three precious Buddhas, the past, present, and future, looked far more solemn and imposing than they usually do by day. The Queen of Heaven (Kwan-yin), with her child in her arms, and with rocks, clouds, and ocean scenery in the background, rudely carved in wood and gaudily painted, was the only one that did not seem to frown. What a strange representation this is, rude though it be! some have supposed that this image represents the Virgin Mary and infant Saviour, and argue from this that Buddhism and Christianity have been mixed up in the formation of the Buddhist religion, or that the earlier Buddhists in Tibet and India have had some slight glimmerings of the Christian faith. The traveller and missionary M. Huc is, I believe, of this opinion. At first sight this seems a very plausible theory, but in the opinion of some good Oriental scholars it is not borne out by facts. The goddess is prayed to by women who are desirous of having children, and she holds in her arms a child which she seems in the act of presenting to them in answer to their petitions. Chinese ladies have curious prejudices on this subject: they imagine that by leaving their shoes in the shrine of the goddess they are the more likely to receive an answer to their prayer. Hence it is not unusual to see a whole heap of tiny shoes in one of these shrines. In former days the custom of throwing an old shoe after a person for luck was not unusual in Scotland, and may have been introduced from that ancient country to China or *vice versâ*.

CHAPTER III.

Tea-gatherers and their wages — Food of Chinese labourers compared with the food of the same class in England — Old city of Tse-kee — Sheds and shops — Market — Mode of skinning frogs — Temple on hill and fine scenery — Lake near north gate — Temples and priests — My servant's mode of answering questions — Chesnut-trees discovered — Introduced to India — Chinese tombs and ceremonies — A widow comes to worship — Beggars and coffins — Different customs in different countries — Reflections.

I MADE Ayuka's temple my head-quarters for several days after the events took place which I have related in the previous chapter. My time was now fully occupied in visiting all the tea-farms in the neighbourhood, and in getting information concerning the cultivation and manufacture of tea. It was the harvest-time for the principal crop of the season, and the natives were observed on every hill-side busily engaged in gathering the leaves. These tea-gatherers were generally seen in small groups consisting of from eight to twelve persons. One old man was usually at the head of each group, the others being women and children. Each had a small stool formed like the letter T, but broad of course at the top, for sitting on while gathering the leaves on the lower sides of the bushes. The foot of the stool being pointed, it was easily forced into the ground in order to render it steady, and as easily drawn out and carried to a different spot. When these tea-gatherers are hired they are not paid by the day, but by the quantity of leaves they bring in to their employers. In making inquiries on the point I found they were paid at the rate of four and five cash a catty, and that they were able to gather from thirty to forty catty a-day.* In other words, each was able to gather from forty to fifty-three pounds of raw leaves per day, for which was received from 6d. to 9d., or thereabouts. But it is only very expert and well-trained hands that can make such a sum as this; children and very old people make, of course, something considerably less. Wages of labourers in the tea districts of China range from 2d. to 3d. per day with their food, which is almost always furnished by the farmers, and which may cost about 3d. or 4d. more, making the whole day's labour amount to 6d. or 7d. The food of these people is of the simplest kind — namely, rice, vegetables, and a small portion of animal food, such as fish or pork. But the poorest classes in China seem to understand the art of preparing their food much better than the same classes at home. With the simple substances I have named the Chinese labourer contrives to make a number of very savoury dishes, upon which he breakfasts or dines most sumptuously. In Scotland, in former days—and I suppose it is much the same now—the harvest

---

* 100 cash are about 4½d. of our money; a catty is equal to 1⅓ lb.

labourer's breakfast consisted of porridge and milk, his dinner of bread and beer, and porridge and milk again for supper. A Chinaman would starve upon such food. Again, if one looks at our sailors making their dinner upon dry salt beef and biscuit, the contrast is equally marked. The dinner of the Chinese sailor is not a whit more expensive, but much more agreeable, healthy, and civilised. Chinese tea-manufacturers whom I have been in the habit of taking to India always asserted they got sick when obliged to live on such food as is given to our sailors, and generally laid in a private stock of various little articles with which they were able to make up a dinner of a very different kind.

Having completed my investigations in this part of the country for the present, I bade adieu to my kind friends in Ayuka's temple, and returned to Ningpo on my way to the old city of Tse-kee. This is a very ancient place, about ten or twelve miles north-west from Ningpo, and near one of the branches of the river which flows past that town. Leaving Ningpo with the first of the flood-tide in the evening, and going on all night, I found myself close by the walls of Tse-kee at daylight next morning. As it was necessary for me to remain in this neighbourhood for some time, I looked out for a pleasant spot for head-quarters. Taking my boat into the canal or moat which has been made round a portion of the city, I found such a place as I wanted near the north gate ;

and as my boat was comfortable enough, though small, I determined to live in it, instead of going to a temple or an inn. Leaving my servants to prepare my breakfast and to get their own, I sauntered into the city. I found it a very ancient place, and famous as being the residence of many of the wealthiest persons in this part of China. Its walls seemed to be about three miles in circumference, but they enclosed numerous fields and gardens as well as houses. The dwellings of the rich were mostly surrounded with high walls, and were not visible from the streets. This is a common mode of building, as it secures the privacy of the female members of the family in a country like China, where it is the custom to keep them much secluded.

I had entered the city by the north gate, and in a few minutes had a crowd of people at my heels. " Where had I come from ?" " where was I going to ?" and " what was I wanting to buy ?" were questions which were put on all sides. The crowd appeared to be perfectly good-humoured, and treated me with the greatest deference and respect. Some ran on before me, and seemed to take a great deal of pleasure in spreading the information of my arrival. The consequence was, that every door and window was full of people anxious to get a look at the foreigner. It was perfectly useless to remonstrate or to get angry, so I was all smiles and took everything in good part. Near the centre of the city, and in one of the principal streets, I found a most excellent market. For fully half a mile this street was literally crowded with articles of food. Fish, pork, fowls, ducks, vegetables of many kinds, and the fruits of the season, lined its sides. Mushrooms were abundant, and excellent, as I afterwards proved by having some cooked. Frogs seemed much in demand. They are brought to market in tubs and baskets, and the vender employs himself in skinning them as he sits making sales. He is extremely expert at this part of his business. He takes up the frog in his left hand, and with a knife which he holds in his right chops off the fore part of its head. The skin is then drawn back over the body and down to the feet, which are chopped off and thrown away. The poor frog, still alive, but headless, skinless, and without feet, is then thrown into another tub, and the operation is repeated on the rest in the same way. Every now and then the artist lays down his knife, and takes up his scales to weigh these animals for his customers and make his sales. Everything in this civilised country, whether it be gold or silver, geese or frogs, is sold by weight.

Raw tea-leaves—that is, just as they had been plucked from the bushes, and unmanufactured— were also exposed for sale in this market. They were sold at from three farthings to five farthings a pound ; and as it takes about four pounds of raw leaves to make one pound of tea, it follows that the price paid was at the rate of threepence to fivepence a pound, but to this must be added the expense of manipulation. In this manner the inhabitants of large towns in China, who have no tea-farms of their own, can buy the raw leaves in the market, and manufacture the beverage for themselves and in their own way.

The streets in the city of Tse-kee are narrow, and the shops for the most part have a mean appearance. The wealthy inhabitants, with whom the city abounds, appear to get their supplies of everything except food from the large cities, such as Ningpo and Hangchow. But food must be supplied on the spot, and hence the necessity for such a fine market as I have noticed. It is here as in western countries—the market takes place in the morning. In the afternoon this busy street was almost deserted : the fishmonger had sold his fish, the butcher his pork ; and all that band of rosy-cheeked countrymen who in the morning had been vending their loads of vegetables and fruits had returned to their homes with strings of cash, the proceeds of their sales, in their baskets or slung over their shoulders.

The scenery round the ancient city of Tse-kee is of the most romantic and beautiful description. The city stands on a flat plain, and is surrounded by hills varying in height from two or three hundred to one thousand feet above the level of the plain. Some are crowned with temples having a most imposing appearance in the distance, and from

which the most charming views can be obtained.
One of these, and the finest, is near the east gate
of the city. It is approached by an avenue of
pine-trees, and a broad flight of stone steps leads
from the bottom of the hill to its summit, where
the temple stands. From the higher rooms of
this temple the visitor sees a wide extent of level
country, exceedingly fertile and well watered.
His eye follows the windings of the Ningpo river
for many miles in a westerly direction, until it is
lost amongst the distant hills. Canals, many of
which are broad and deep, intersect the country
in all directions, and afford not only a plentiful
supply of water for the irrigation of the rice-crops,
but bear on their surface thousands of boats of many
different sizes, all hurrying to and fro and carrying on the commerce of the country. It is a
pretty sight to see the numerous white or brown
sails over the land, bending to the breeze, or
flapping about in a calm sunny morning. Looking south and eastward, the eye rests upon the
wide plain of Ningpo, and in a clear day the high
mountains which bound its furthest sides are distinctly visible.

It is difficult, where all is so beautiful, to fix
upon the prettiest spot, but that near the north
gate, where my boat lay, appeared to me the most
lovely of all. Between the north gate and the
hills there is a pretty lake, which is crossed by a
causeway with arches and alcoves. This causeway led from the city to a range of temples

situated at the base of the hills. A side view of this causeway, with its round-arched bridge and alcove, the smooth water of the lake, the rich vegetation on its banks, and the temples at the foot of the hills, would form a lovely picture worthy of the pencil of our first European artists. I have looked on this scene in early morning when the mist was rising from the water, at noon on a summer's day when the water appeared to have been melted with the fierceness of the sun's rays, and again at " dewy eve " when all was still, —and a more fairy-like spot it would be most difficult to find.

I found the temple beyond the lake a large building, or rather a series of buildings, in tolerably good repair. Here were a number of priests and their attendants, and no lack of idols of great size. But these I have already noticed in Ayuka's temple, and shall not say anything further concerning them here. The high-priest received me with great kindness, and made me sit down in the seat of honour by his side. A little boy, who was destined one day to become a priest himself, but who was now attending on his superior, was ordered to set tea before us, which he did in the usual style. Our conversation turned, as it frequently did, upon the state of the country and the rebellion. The old man asked me very earnestly as to what I had heard of the Nanking rebels, and whether I thought they would come to Hang-chow and Ningpo. I told him he knew quite as much of their proceedings and intentions as I did, and that with my present knowledge it was impossible to form an opinion on the matter. He said, if they did come to either of the places named, they would not visit Tse-kee—an opinion which I ventured to dispute. I then asked him if he had heard of the massacre of the Buddhist priests on Silver Island, near Ching-keang-foo, the news of which had reached me a short time before. This massacre was reported by some to be the results of intense Christian feeling and hatred of idolatry. The old man had heard of this, but would not allow of the interpretation which was generally put upon the matter. He told me—and he was probably correct—that the priests had been trying to save the lives of some mandarins who had taken shelter in their temples, and that for this sin, and not for idolatry, they were put to death. The subject was evidently one of deep interest to all the Buddhist priesthood, a considerable number of whom now surrounded us as this conversation was going on.

While engaged in this manner with the high-priest the room had gradually become more and more crowded with the inferior priests, with worshippers who happened to be at the temple, and with the servants and labourers who were attached to it. It is a curious fact that, although the Chinese as a nation have a high respect for their superiors, they do not show it in the same manner as we do. Hence it is not unusual for strangers

E

and servants to crowd into a room where visitors are being received and entertained, and even to take part in the conversation. My own servant Tung-a was amongst the crowd, and was quite a lion for the time. Hundreds of questions were put to him as to my country, the time I had resided in China, and the objects I had in view in visiting the " central flowery land." He did not fail to answer the whole in a most satisfactory manner to himself and his audience, but whether his answers were to be depended upon or not was quite another matter, nor did he seem to care much so long as his interrogators were satisfied. Being engaged during my spare hours in making a collection of the insects of this part of China, Tung-a carried in his hand, in addition to a small cork-lined box and insect-net, a nice-looking bottle with a glass stopper. This was an object of much interest to the priests and their attendants, and was handed about from one to another all over the room. Before taking my leave I presented this bottle to the high-priest, who was quite charmed with my liberality, and almost went down on his knees to thank me. Oftentimes afterwards I renewed my visit to the old man, particularly during the heat of the day, when I was glad to seek shelter from the burning rays of the sun, and always found him kind and obliging. In the autumn of this year I received from him some valuable seeds which are now vegetating both in England and India.

The lower sides of all the hills round this old city are covered with trees, and have a very pretty appearance. The Chinese pine (*Pinus sinensis*), which is grouped about in all directions, attains to a great size ; several kinds of oak, both evergreen and deciduous, are also common ; but perhaps the most striking of all is the camphor-tree, which with its gnarled and angular branches is quite the monarch of the woods. Amongst these woods I met with the chesnut for the first time in China. This discovery was of great importance, as I was most anxious to introduce this to the Himalayan mountains in India. Many attempts had been made to introduce it from Europe, but they had not succeeded. The seeds of such trees as oaks, chesnuts, tea, &c., retain their vitality for a very short time after they are gathered if they are not sown and allowed to vegetate. It is therefore useless to attempt to send these seeds in dry paper parcels or in hermetically sealed bottles from Europe to the north of India. The chesnuts which I had met with in the markets of China, although excellent for the dessert, were generally too old for vegetating; but now, when I had discovered the locality where they grew, there was no longer any difficulty in procuring them quite fresh. There are two species cultivated on these hills. One is somewhat like the Spanish, and, although probably a different variety, it produces fruit quite equal in quality, if not superior, to the Spanish chesnut. The other is a delicious little kind, bearing fruit about the size and form of our common hazel-nut. Large quantities of both kinds were procured in the autumn of this year, sown in Ward's cases, and sent on to India. Part were sent to Government and part to the Agricultural and Horticultural Society. They vegetated freely during the voyage, and many hundreds of nice healthy young plants reached India in the most perfect condition. The chesnut may now be considered naturalized on the hills of India, and in a few years will no doubt make its appearance in the markets amongst other fruits.

The " Yang-mae," a species of *Myrica*, was also met with on these hill-sides, and some grafted plants secured for India. These are now luxuriating in the north-west provinces. This fine fruit will no doubt succeed admirably in the Himalaya, for already there is a variety—far inferior indeed to the Chinese kind, but yet a plant requiring the same soil and temperature—common on these hills. It is the *Kaiphul* of the hill-tribes of India.

The most beautiful spots on these hill-sides are chosen for the tombs of the dead, which are scattered about everywhere. The sombre pine, the juniper, the arbor-vitæ, and the cypress are generally planted round the graves. As common as these, and equally ornamental, is the *Photinia glabra*, a noble evergreen which in the winter becomes covered with bunches of red berries. The weeping-willow is also sometimes used, and has a very pretty effect, particularly when one is planted on each side of the tomb. These trees are planted in a half-circle round the grave, leaving the front open. Within this half-circle is the tomb itself, the most common kind being covered with a large mound of earth faced with stone in front, on which the name and age of the deceased are cut and painted. In front of this again is a stone pavement with smooth stone seats, whether destined for the visitor or for the spirit of the departed I cannot tell. Sometimes I met with tombs of the most elaborate workmanship, and constructed in many different ways. Each told its tale of wealth or poverty; some must have cost very large sums, while others consisted of the coffin laid upon the surface of the ground, and thatched with a little straw. It is a pretty sight, and yet a painful one too, to see the relations of the dead visiting the tombs of their ancestors, which they do at stated periods, for the purpose of burning sycee paper and incense, and chanting prayers to the gods or spirits of the departed. Sometimes a mother may be seen with her children, the youngest probably still an infant in her arms, assembled in front of the grave of the husband and father. The widow is wailing and lamenting her bereavement, and the poor little ones look on so seriously, while every now and then they prostrate themselves before the grave. Or, it may be, it is the aged who are paying the same respect to the last resting-place

of those who had been taken away in early life,
and to whom they had looked forward as the stay
and prop of their declining years. Or again, a
solitary individual might be seen performing the
same rites — young, middle-aged, or old, as the
case might be—which suggested the idea that he
was poor and friendless, the last of his race. It
has been asserted that there is little genuine feeling in all this, that it is a custom which must be
observed, and that it would be just as well if such
a custom did not exist. I believe, however, there
is as much genuine sorrow amongst the Chinese
for the loss of relatives as there is amongst ourselves; and if we consider the way they dote upon
their children, and the reverence and love they
have for aged parents, we can come to no other
conclusion. That in many instances all is mere
show and required by custom, I have no doubt.
On one occasion, as I was wandering amongst these
hills, a chair passed me containing a very beautiful
lady dressed in the gayest satin. I caught a slight
glimpse of her countenance as she passed, and was
so much struck with her beauty that I instantly
stood still and looked after the chair. It immediately turned off the little hill-road in the direction of a tomb that had been lately made, where it
was set down by the bearers. Following this chair
were two female servants and a coolie with a box
of clothes, a basket of provisions, and some sycee
paper and incense. The lady, on stepping out
of the chair, commenced robing herself in deep

mourning by putting on a gown of sackcloth over her gay dress, but on seeing I was looking on she stopped immediately and threw the gown to her attendants, with whom she was laughing and chatting away, as if grief and she were perfect strangers to each other. Anxious as I was to witness her proceedings, I felt it was wrong and indelicate in me to remain in my present position, so I walked onwards until a small hedge and clump of bamboos hid the party from my view. I then turned into the plantation, and selected a spot where through an opening in the foliage I could see all without being seen myself. The handsome widow, for such she apparently was, had again put on her sackcloth robe, her women were standing by her side, and the wailing commenced in the most business-like manner. This continued for nearly half an hour, while at the same time incense was burned, and various tawdry-looking strips of paper were hung about the grave. At last the ceremony was finished, the coarse sackcloth was consigned to the coolie, and the lady, all gay as before, and with but little traces of grief, stepped into her chair and was carried away.

For many weeks after these visits to the tombs numerous long strips of gay-coloured paper are seen hanging about the graves. In my researches amongst these hills I was much struck with one thing, which I must mention here, and from which all may learn a useful lesson. Here and there, amongst those tombs which had been cleaned and repaired, and which bore all the marks of having been recently visited by relatives, were some from which no friendly hand had cleared away the weeds. Ages ago they had been built without regard to expense, and for many years they had been, no doubt, visited by loving friends, who had burned incense upon them, and strewed them with wild flowers and paper streamers. But now they were going fast to decay; they were not visited or repaired at the usual and stated times; and their tenants had been long since forgotten. And as it had been with these, so it would be with the others which were now so carefully attended to. A few years more, and their tenants too would be forgotten, however rich or however much loved.

When a wealthy Chinese dies at a distance from his home, his body is brought back to his native place by his relations in order that he may sleep with his fathers. In front of an old temple near Tse-kee I observed a number of coffins lying under the verandah, and on inquiry found that they had all been brought from some distance, and had been laid down there until a lucky spot could be found out for their final resting-place. Some had apparently lain here for a long period of time. Under the same verandah, and amongst these coffins, a colony of gipsy beggars had taken up their quarters, which to me had a curious appearance. However, these people seemed to have no supernatural fears of any kind, and were on such friendly terms with their dead companions, that

the tops of the huge coffins were used as supports
for their mosquito curtains. " What a traveller's
story ! Beggars with mosquito curtains,—the living
sleeping with the dead ! " Even so, gentle reader ;
we are now in China.

In a country like England we pride ourselves
upon our civilization and good taste. But let us
fancy a Chinese traveller paying us a visit and
writing a description of our grave-yards. How
different would his pictures be from those which
I have now given, and how horrified would he
be with our barbarism and want of taste ! " The
English," he would say, " do not respect their
dead ; they crowd them into churchyards in
densely populated towns, and plant no pine-trees
or wild flowers about their graves. In many instances they even dig them up before they are
fully decomposed, in order to make room for
others ! Their children look upon such places
with dread, and will not pass them willingly after
nightfall." Such would be his reflections, or at
least would have been a few years ago. Let us
hope that in a very short period the good sense
of the people and the energy of Government will
do away with such relics of barbarism.

But what does it matter, says some stern moral-
ist, where one is buried—whether in the deep sea,
the crowded city, or amid the beauties of nature
on the hill-side ? I do not argue the point, but my
taste leads me to prefer the customs of the Chinese,
where one can sleep in peace after being buried,

where one's grave is looked upon with love and affection, and not with fear; nor would I object to the spot being visited by loving children, who come to shed a few heartfelt tears, and plant a few wild flowers on the tomb of him they loved so fondly.

CHAPTER IV.

Entomology — Chinese ideas respecting my collections — My sanity doubtful — Mode of employing natives to assist me — A scene on returning to my boat — Curious tree — Visit from a mandarin — An endeavour to explain my objects in making collections of natural history — Crowds of natives — Their quietness and civility — Return mandarin's visit — My reception — Example of Chinese politeness — Our conversation — Inquisitiveness of his ladies and its consequences — Beauty of ladies at Tse-kee — Our luncheon and adieu.

THE hilly districts amongst which I was now sojourning were particularly rich in beautiful and rare insects. A small bottle, an insect-box, and a net were continually carried both by myself and men, and many were the fine things we captured, as the cabinets of most of the entomologists in Europe can now testify. This proceeding seemed to astonish the northern Chinese beyond measure, and, from the mixture of awe and pity depicted in many a countenance, they evidently thought me a little cracked in the head. The more intelligent amongst them believed I was collecting for medical purposes, and that all my specimens were destined to be chopped up in a mortar and made into pills to be swallowed by the sick. The Chinese have not the slightest idea of the study of entomology, and laughed at me when I attempted to explain to them that insects are collected for such a purpose. Their medicinal value seemed to them a much better reason for the trouble of collecting. Amongst themselves an idea is prevalent that the larvæ of coleopterous and other insects form excellent food to give occasionally to young children, and hence in my rambles I met not unfrequently persons employed in collecting larvæ for this purpose. A species of toad, found in the rotten hollow trunks of trees during the hot months, is eagerly sought after by the young men in the army who are being trained to the use of the bow, and to whose bones and sinews it is supposed to give additional strength. This strange-looking animal sells in the market at from fourpence to eightpence each, but it is extremely rare.

The children in the different villages were found of the greatest use in assisting me to form these collections, and the common copper coin of the country is well adapted for such purposes. One hundred of this coin is only worth about fourpence-halfpenny of our money, and goes a long way with the little urchins. A circumstance connected with transactions of this kind occurred one day, which appears so laughable that I must relate it. As I went out on my daily rambles I told all the little fellows I met that I would return in the evening to the place where my boat was moored, and, if they brought me any rare insects there, I would pay them for them. In the evening, when I returned and caught a glimpse of my boat, I was surprised to see the banks of the stream

crowded with a multitude of people of all ages and
sizes—old women and young ones, men and boys,
and infants in arms were huddled together upon
the bank, and apparently waiting for my return.
At first I was afraid something of a serious nature
had happened, but as I came nearer I observed
them laughing and talking good-humouredly, and
guessed from this that nothing had gone wrong.
Some had baskets, others wooden basins, others,
again, hollow bamboo tubes, and the vessels they
carried were as various in appearance as the motley
group which now stood before me. " Mâ jung !
mâ jung ! " (buy insects ! buy insects !) was now
shouted out to me by a hundred voices, and I saw
the whole matter clearly explained. It was the
old story, " I was collecting insects for medicine,"
and they had come to sell them by the ounce or
pound. I had unintentionally raised the population of the adjoining villages about my ears ; but
having done so, I determined to take matters as
coolly as possible, and endeavour either to amuse
or pacify the mob. On examining the various
baskets and other vessels which were eagerly
opened for my inspection, what a sight was presented to my view ! Butterflies, beetles, dragon-
flies, bees — legs, wings, scales, antennæ — all
broken and mixed up in wild confusion. I endeavoured to explain to the good people that my
objects were quite misunderstood, and that such
masses of broken insects were utterly useless to
me. " What did it signify—they were only for

medicine, and would have to be broken up at any
rate." What with joking and reasoning with
them, I got out of the business pretty well. As in
all cases I found the women most clamorous and
most difficult to deal with, but by showing some
liberality in my donations of cash to the old women
and very young children I gradually rose in their
estimation, and at last, it being nearly dark, we
parted the best of friends. I have been placed in
circumstances somewhat similar on various occasions since, but I have hitherto managed to come
safely out of the scrape. Sometimes amongst all
this chaff there were grains of wheat, and not the
least striking was a beautiful species of Carabus
(*C. cœlestis*), which was brought to me at this
time, and for which I gave the lucky finder the
large sum of thirty cash, with which he scampered
off home, delighted with his good luck. Paying
away sums like this for insects seemed to confirm
the natives in the views they had originally formed
respecting my character. The Chinese, however,
are as a people eminently practical in all their
views, and it mattered not to them whether I was
sane or not so long as they got the cash. They
now set to collecting in all directions, and brought
me many fine things. On returning home to my
boat in the evenings I was called to from every
hill-side, " Mâ jung! mâ jung!" (buy insects!
buy insects!) and then the little fellows were seen
bounding down towards the road on which I was
walking. This distribution of cash amongst the

children soon made me quite a favourite with their
parents, and in my walks in the country I was
invited into their houses, where I received much
kindness and hospitality. The poorest cottager
had always a cup of tea for me, which he insisted
on my sittting down and drinking before I left his
house. Before leaving this part of the province I
distributed a number of bottles, each being about
half filled with the strong spirit of the country
(samshoo). These were given to those who promised to make collections for me during my absence ; they were told to throw the insects into the
spirit when caught, and let them remain until I
came to claim and pay for them. By this means I
was able to add many novelties to my collection
when I again visited Tse-kee in the autumn, to
form my other collections of plants and seeds.

On one of my excursions amongst these hills
I met with a curiously-formed tree, which at first
sight seemed to confirm the old Virgilian tale of
apples growing upon plane-trees. It was one of
those junipers (*J. sphærica*) which grow to a considerable size in the north of China, and which the
Chinese are fond of planting round their graves.
But although a juniper at the top and bottom, an
evergreen tree with large glossy leaves (*Photinia
serrulata*) formed the centre. On reaching the
spot where it grew, the appearance presented was,
if possible, more curious and interesting. The
photinia came out from the trunk of the juniper
about 12 feet from the ground, and appeared as

if it had been grafted upon it; indeed, some Chinese in a neighbouring village, to whom the tree was well known, did not hesitate to express their belief that such had been the case, but I need scarcely say this was out of the question. Upon a close examination of the point of apparent union, I found that, although the part between stock and graft, if I may use the expression, was completely filled up, yet there was no union such as we see in grafted trees. There could then be only one way of accounting for the appearance which these two trees presented, and which is pretty well shown in a drawing taken by a Chinese artist. The photinia was no doubt rooted in the ground, and had 12 feet of its stem cased in the decayed trunk of the juniper. The apparent union of the trees was so complete, that nothing could be seen of this arrangement; but upon tapping the lower part of the trunk it sounded hollow, and was no doubt decayed in the centre, although healthy enough outside.

Upon showing the accompanying sketch to a learned Chinese, the teacher of Mr. Meadows, at Ningpo, he, like the villagers, fully believed the photinia had been grafted upon the juniper; and further, he informed me it was a common thing in the country to graft the Yang-mae (*Myrica sp.*, a fine Chinese fruit-tree) upon *Pinus sinensis*, and that by so doing the fruit of the Yang-mae became much larger and finer in flavour. Having been engaged in procuring some

Yang-mae trees, which the Government of India
was anxious to introduce to the Himalaya, I was
somewhat better informed upon this subject than
the *learned* Chinaman.   I told him the fine variety
of Yang-mae was grafted upon the wild kind, which

Remarkable Tree.

the Chinese call the *San* or hill variety (*Myrica sa-
pida*); and further, I showed him some plants which
I had just purchased : but all was of no use ; he was
"convinced against his will," and still firmly believes
the Yang-mae is usually grafted on the pine.

F

Travelling as I was all alone, and engaged in making collections of natural history, the objects of which the natives could not comprehend, it was not to be wondered at if my fame was spread far and wide over the country. I had visits from several mandarins and other wealthy inhabitants of the district, and the way in which some of the more timid of these gentry presented themselves was to me highly amusing. One day, when I was busy in arranging my collections, I heard a stranger's voice calling my servant, and on looking out at the window I observed a respectable-looking man with several attendants within a few yards of my boat. From his manner he was evidently most anxious to see me and what I was after, but at the same time he seemed doubtful of the reception I might give him. My servant having assured him that I was perfectly harmless, he mustered courage at last to come alongside. In the mean time I opened the boat, and invited him to come inside. I suppose my appearance and manners must have been more favourable than he had been led to expect by the report which had reached his ears, for he immediately made me a most polite bow, and accepted my invitation. When I spread out my entomological collections for his inspection, he seemed perfectly astonished. " Did you really get all these in this district? " said he. " Strange, that, although I am a native, yet there are hundreds of them I have never seen before." I ventured to hint that perhaps he had not looked for them,

which he said was very true, and no doubt accounted for his not having seen them. As my boat
was made fast to the bank of the canal, we were
surrounded by crowds of the natives, who, hearing
that I was showing my collections to the mandarin,
were all anxious to have a peep. Hundreds of
questions were put to each other on all sides as
to what I could possibly be going to do with the
numerous strange things which I had got in my
boxes. The more wise amongst the crowd informed the others that all the insects were collected to be made into medicine, but as to the diseases which they were destined to cure, the wisest
amongst them were obliged to plead ignorance.
My servants and boatmen were often appealed to
for light upon the subject, but they only laughed
and confessed their entire ignorance ; nor did
they take the slightest trouble to convince their
countrymen that they were wrong in their con-
jectures.

When I had shown my collections to my visitor,
he put the question which the crowd had been discussing outside, and which discussion he had heard
as much of as I had done. Had I entered into the
merits of the study of entomology, he most certainly would not have been able to bring his mind
to believe I was telling him the truth. If, on the
other hand, I had told him I intended to make medicine of my collections, although he would have
believed me, yet this would have been untrue. So
I thought I might give him another idea which he

would comprehend and appreciate. " In my own land," said I, " many thousand le from this, we have a great and good Queen who delights in the welfare and happiness of her people. For their instruction and amusement a large house* has been constructed—far larger than any of your temples or public buildings which have come under my observation — and into this house have been brought many thousands of plants and animals collected in every country under heaven. Here each species is classified and named by scientific men appointed for the purpose, and on certain days in every week the doors are thrown open for the admission of the public. Many thousands avail themselves of these opportunities, and thus have the means of studying at home the numerous forms of animals and plants which are scattered over the surface of the globe. Many of the insects and shells which you see before you are destined to form a part of that great collection, and thus persons in England who are interested in such things will have the means of knowing what forms of such animals exist in the hills and valleys about Tse-kee." My visitor seemed much interested with the information I gave him, and, although he did not express any surprise, I trust he received a higher idea of our civilisation than he had entertained before. What surprised him more than anything else was my statement that a Queen was the sovereign of England. I have often been

* The British Museum.

questioned as to the truth of this by the Chinese, who think it passing strange, if it be really true.

Before taking his leave he gave me a pressing invitation to pay him a visit at his house in the city on the following day, or on any day it might be convenient for me. I promised to do so, and got my servant to take down his address, in order that we might not have any difficulty in finding his house. The door of the boat was now thrown open, and I handed him out to the banks of the canal. Here we made most polite adieus in the most approved Chinese style, in the midst of a dense crowd, who had been attracted by the rank of my visitor, and partly perhaps by the reports which had been spread about myself.

The crowd which had now collected was of a mixed character; but owing, I suppose, to the number of wealthy and respectable people in the city, the individuals were generally well-dressed and clean, and perfectly respectful and civil in their demeanour. Applications were made to me on all sides for permission to enter the boat and inspect my collections. This being entirely out of the question, I had a portion of the cover removed in order that their curiosity might be satisfied from the banks of the canal. Entering the boat myself, I opened box after box, and spread out my collections before them. My table, bed, the floor of the boat, and every inch of space was completely covered with examples of the natural history of the place. " Can all these things have been collected here?" was on every lip; "for many of them we have never seen, although we are natives of the place and this is our home." And when I pointed out some of the more remarkable amongst the insects, and gave them the names by which they are known to the natives, I was complimented and applauded on all sides. "Here," said I, for example, "is a beautiful *Ka-je-long* (carabus), which I am anxious to get more specimens of; if you will bring some to me I shall pay you for them. That Kin-jung (golden beetle) you need not collect, for it is common in every hedge." "*Oo-de-yeou?*"—Do you want butterflies? "No," I replied, "for you cannot catch them without breaking them." And so the conversation went on, every one being in the best possible humour. When I had shown them the greater portion of my collections, the cover of the boat was let down, and everything put away into its proper place. I was now anxious to disperse the crowd, and for that purpose informed them that, as the afternoon was getting cool, I was now going out to make further additions to my collections. "Thank you, thank you," said many of them, making at the same time many most polite bows after the manner of the country, which I did not fail to return. And so we parted the best of friends. When I returned from my excursion it was nearly dark; the crowd had all gone to their homes, and quietness now reigned where all had been noise and bustle a few hours before. One or two little boys

were sitting on the banks of the canal waiting my
arrival, in order to dispose of some insects which
they had been lucky enough to capture during the
day.   And so I went on from day to day, gradually increasing my collections, with the help of
hundreds of little boys, who were delighted to
earn a few " cash" so easily.   The effect produced
upon the villagers was also most marked, and I
was welcomed wherever I went, and everywhere
invited to "come in, sit down, and drink tea."
This picture is not very like many which have
been given of China and the Chinese, but it is true
to nature nevertheless.   I trust it may give a
higher idea of the civilisation of this people than
we are accustomed to form from the writings of
those whose principal knowledge was derived from
views at the great southern seaports of the
empire.

The day after that on which I had been honoured with a call from the mandarin, I dressed
with more than ordinary care, sent for a sedan-
chair, and set out to return his visit.   When I
arrived at his house I found that he was expecting
me.   He was dressed in a long gown, bound
round the waist with a belt which had a fine clasp
made of gold and jade-stone, and on his head was
a round hat and blue button.   He received me
with many low bows in the Chinese manner,
which I returned in the same way.   He then led
me into a large hall, and invited me to take the
seat of honour.   In all the houses of the wealthy

there are two raised seats at the end of the reception-room, with a table between them. The seat on the left side is considered the seat of honour, and the visitor is invariably pressed into it. Scenes which seem most amusing to the stranger are always acted on an occasion of this kind. The host begs his visitor to take the most honourable post, while the latter protests that he is unworthy of such distinction, and in his turn presses it upon the owner of the mansion. And so they may be seen standing in this way for several minutes before the matter is settled. It is the same way when a man gives a dinner; and if the guests are numerous, it is quite a serious affair to get them all seated. In this case it is not only the host and his household who are begging the guests to occupy the most honourable seats, but the guests themselves are also pressing these favoured places upon each other. Hence the bowing, talking, sitting down, and getting up again, before the party can be finally seated, is quite unlike anything one sees in other parts of the world, and to the stranger is exceedingly amusing, particularly if he does not happen to be hungry.

After duly expressing my unfitness to occupy the left-hand seat, and attempting to take the other, I was at last forced into the seat of honour, the mandarin himself taking the right-hand one. As soon as we were seated a servant came in with several cups of tea upon a round wooden tray, which cups he placed upon the table between us.

Another servant presented himself, bringing a handsome brass pipe with a long bamboo stem, which he presented to his master. My host handed it immediately over to me, and begged I would use it, assuring me at the same time that the tobacco was the best which could be had in Ningpo. I declined the invitation, but took a cigar out of my pocket, and returned the compliment which he had just paid me. He informed me he had once tried a cigar, but that it was too strong for him; so we compromised matters by each smoking what he had been accustomed to— he his long bamboo pipe, and I my cigar. As we sat and sipped our tea—a delicious kind of Hyson Pekoe—he asked me many questions concerning my country and its productions. Our steamers and ships of war he had seen at Ningpo, and he owned they had pleased him greatly. "To be able to go against wind and tide was certainly very wonderful." But when I told him that by means of balloons we could rise from the earth, and sail through the air, he looked rather incredulous, and with a smile on his countenance asked me whether any of us had been to the moon.

While this conversation was going on, a large crowd had assembled in the court, and many of them were pressing into the reception-hall, in which we were seated. The numerous servants and retainers of the mandarin were also inside, and even sometimes took a share in the conversation which was going on; nor did this seem to give any offence to their superior.

On one side of the room there was a glass window having a gauze or crape curtain behind it, and apparently constructed to give light to a passage leading to some of the other parts of the mansion. While sitting with my host I had more than once observed the curtain move and expose a group of fair faces having a sly peep at me through the window. These were his wives and daughters, whom etiquette did not permit to appear in public or in the presence of a stranger. I did not appear to notice them—although I saw them distinctly enough all the time—for had I done so they would have disappeared immediately; and as one rarely has an opportunity of seeing the ladies of the higher classes in China, I was willing to look upon their pretty faces as long as possible. A circumstance occurred, however, which put a speedy end to their peep-show, and for which they had no one but themselves to blame. Whether they had fallen out amongst themselves about places at the window, or whether it was only a harmless giggle, I cannot tell— it sounded very like the latter; but the noise, whatever it was, caught the ear of their lord and master, who turned his head quickly to the window in question, and darted a look of anger and annoyance at the unfortunates, who instantly took to their heels, and I saw them again no more.

The ladies in this part of China are famed for

their beauty. It is a curious and striking fact that in this old city and its vicinity one rarely sees an unpleasing countenance. And this holds good with the lower classes as well as it does with the higher. In many other parts of China women get excessively ugly when they get old, but even this is not the case at Tse-kee. With features of more European cast than Asiatic, and very pleasing, with a smooth fair skin, and with a slight colour in their cheeks, just sufficient to indicate good health, they are almost perfect, were it not for that barbarous custom of compressing the feet. Perhaps I ought to add, that, from the want of education—and this applies to females generally in China—there is a want of an intellectual expression in the countenance which renders it, in my opinion, less beautiful than it would otherwise be.

I had now been chatting with my acquaintance for more than half an hour, and thought it time to take my leave. But when I rose for this purpose he informed me he had prepared luncheon for me in another room, and begged I would honour him by partaking of it before I went away. I tried to excuse myself, but he almost used force in order to induce me to remain. He now led me into a nicely furnished room, according to Chinese ideas, that is, its walls were hung with pictures of flowers, birds, and scenes of Chinese life. It would not do to criticise these works of art according to our ideas, but nevertheless some of them were very interesting. I observed a series of pictures which told a long tale as distinctly as if it had been written in Roman characters. The actors were all on the boards, and one followed them readily from the commencement of the piece until the fall of the curtain. Numbers of solid straight-backed chairs were placed round the room, and a large massive table occupied its centre. This table was completely covered with numerous small dishes, containing the fruits of the season and all sorts of cakes and sweetmeats, for which the large towns in this province are famed. In addition to these there were walnuts from the northern province of Shantung, and dried Leechees, Longans, &c., from Fokien and Canton. Then there were many kinds of preserves, such as ginger, citron, bamboo, and others, all of which were most excellent. A number of small wine-cups, made of the purest china, were placed at intervals round the table.

Several of the old gentleman's friends had now joined us, and we took our places round the table with the usual ceremony, each one pressing the most honourable place upon his neighbour. The day was excessively warm, and I felt very little inclination to eat, but I was pressed to do so on all sides. " Eat cakes," said one ; " Eat walnuts," said another; " Drink wine," said a third ; and so on they went, asking me to partake of every dish upon the table. It was useless to refuse, for they seized hold of the different viands and heaped them on my plate and on the table at its side. Various kinds of Chinese wines, hot and cold, were also pressed upon me, some of which were palatable, but scarcely suited to the English taste. I took a little of each in order to please my entertainer, and then confined myself to tea, which was also set before us.

I had now prolonged my visit much beyond the time I had set apart for it, and quite as long as politeness demanded. But time spent in this manner was not altogether unprofitable, inasmuch as one gets an insight into Chinese life and manners which we cannot acquire in the streets or on the hill-side. My kind host and his friends accompanied me to the outer door of the mansion, and, with the palms of our hands laid flat together and held up before us, we bowed low several times, muttered our thanks, and bade each other farewell.

CHAPTER V.

Visit a collector of ancient works of art — His house and garden —
    Inspect his collections of old crackle china and other vases, &c. —
    Fondness of Chinese for their own ancient works of art — Description
    of ancient porcelain most prized by them — Ancient enamels —
    Foo-chow enamels — Jade-stone — Rock crystal — Magnetic iron
    and other minerals — Gold-stone — Red lacquer and gold japan —
    Porcelain bottles found in Egyptian tombs — Found also in China
    at the present day — Age of these — Mr. Medhurst's remarks.

A SHORT time after the events took place which
I have related in the last chapter, and before
leaving this part of the country, I paid a visit to
another Chinese gentleman, whose acquaintance I
had formerly made in an old curiosity shop in
Ningpo. Like myself he was an ardent admirer
and collector of ancient works of art, such as
specimens of china, bronzes, enamels, and articles
of that description. Neither of us collected what
are commonly known as *curios*, such as ivory balls,
grotesque and ugly carvings in bamboo or sandal-
wood or soapstone, and such things as take the
fancy of captains of ships and their crews of jolly
tars when they visit the Celestial Empire. Above
all things, our greatest horror was modern china-
ware, an article which proves more than anything
else in the country how much China has degenerated in the arts. The venders of such things

as we were in the habit of collecting knew us both well, and not unfrequently made us pay for the similarity of our tastes.   Oftentimes I was informed, on asking the price of an article, that my Tse-kee friend was anxious to get it, and had offered such and such a price, and I have no doubt the same game was played with him.   That what they told me was sometimes true I have no doubt, for in more than one instance I have known specimens purchased by him the moment he heard of my arrival.   But for all this rivalry we were excellent friends, and he frequently invited me to visit him and see his collections when I came to Tse-kee.

I found him the owner and occupant of a large house in the centre of the city, and apparently a man of considerable wealth.   He received me with the greatest cordiality, and led me in the usual way to the seat of honour at the end of the reception-hall.   His house was fur-

Curious Pilgrim-shaped Bottle, enamelled with Butterflies, &c.

nished and ornamented with great taste.   In front of the room in which I had been received was a little garden containing a number of choice plants in pots, such as azaleas, camellias, and dwarfed trees of various kinds. The ground was paved with sandstone and granite, and, while some of the pots were placed on the floor, others were standing on stone tables. Small borders fenced with the same kinds of stone were filled with soil, in which were growing creepers of various kinds which covered the walls. Here were the favoured *Glycine sinensis*, roses, jasmines, &c., which not only scrambled over the walls, but were led inward and formed arbours to afford shade from the rays of the noon-day sun. In front of these were such things as Moutans, *Nandina* (sacred bamboo of the Chinese), *Weigela rosea*, *Forsythia viridissima*, and *Spiræa Reevesiana*. In opposite corners stood two noble trees of *Olea fragrans*, the celebrated " Kwei-hwa," whose flowers are often used in scenting tea ; while many parts of the little border were carpeted with the pretty little *Lycopodium cœsium*, which I introduced to England some years ago. This pretty fairy-like scene was exposed to our view as we sat sipping our tea, and with all my English prejudice I could not but acknowledge that it was exceedingly enjoyable.

The reception-room was hung with numerous square glass lanterns gaily painted with " flowers of all hues ;" several massive varnished tables stood in its centre, while a row of chairs was arranged down each side. Between the chairs stood small square tables or tepoys, on some of which were placed beautiful specimens of ancient china vases. Everything which met the eye told in language not to be mistaken that its owner was not only a man of wealth, but of the most refined taste.

After a few commonplace civilities passing between us I expressed a wish to inspect his collections. He led me from room to room and pointed out a collection which was enough to make one's "mouth water." In some instances his specimens stood on tables or on the floor, while in others they were tastefully arranged in cabinets made expressly for the purpose of holding them. He showed me many exquisite bits of crackle of various colours —grey, red, turquoise, cream, pale yellow, and indeed of almost every shade. One vase I admired much was about two feet high, of a deep blue colour, and covered with figures and ornaments in gold; another of the same height had a

Porcelain Vase enamelled with figures of Animals and Plants.

white ground with figures and trees in black,
yellow, and green—rare and bright colours lost
now to Chinese art, and never known in any
other part of the world.

In one of the rooms I observed some handsome
specimens of red lacquer most elaborately and
deeply carved, and also fine pieces of gold japan.
There were also numerous bronzes and enamels on
copper, which my friend informed me were from
800 to 1000 years of age. His collections of jades
and agates was also extensive and valuable.

Taking the collection as a whole, it was the
finest I had ever seen, and was a real treat to me.
On going round the different rooms I observed
more than one specimen I had been in treaty
for myself, and I thought I could detect a good-
humoured smile upon my friend's countenance, as
the same idea was passing through his mind which
was passing through my own.

On returning to the reception-room I found one
of the tables covered with all sorts of good things
for luncheon, which I was now asked to partake of.
It was, however, getting late in the afternoon, and
near my own dinner-hour, so I begged myself off
with the best grace possible, and with many low
bows and thanks took my leave much gratified
with what I had seen.

It is well known that the Chinese value ancient
works of art, but they differ from western nations
in this, that the appreciation of such articles is
confined to those of their own country. As a

general rule they do not appreciate articles of
foreign art, unless such articles are useful in daily
life.   A fine picture, a bronze, or even a porcelain
vase of "*barbarian*" origin, might be accepted as
a present, but would rarely be bought by a Chinese
collector.

But while they are indifferent about the ancient
works of art of foreign countries, they are pas-
sionately fond of their own.   And well they may,
for not only are many of their ancient vases
exquisite specimens of art, but they are also samples
of an art which appears to have long since passed
from amongst them.   Take, for example, their
modern porcelain, examples of which may be seen
in almost every tea-shop in London.   The grotesque figuring is there it is true, but nowhere
do we find that marvellous colouring which is
observed on their ancient vases.   I often tried to
find out whether as a nation they had lost the art
of fixing the most beautiful colours, or whether in
these days of cheapness they would not go to the
expense.   All my inquiries tended to show that
the art had been lost, and indeed it must be so,
otherwise the high prices which these beautiful
things command would be sure, in a country like
China, to produce them.

Without coloured drawings it is difficult to give
the general reader a correct idea of what these
specimens are which are so much prized by the
Chinese ; and although there are some valuable
private collections in England, yet our museums,

to which the public have access, are but meagrely
supplied.   My descriptions, however, will probably
be understood by collectors of such articles in
this country.

To begin with what is called old crackle porcelain by collectors.—The Chinese have many kinds
of this manufacture,
some of which are
extremely rare and
beautiful.   In the
whites and greys
the crackle is larger,
and the older speci-
mens are often bound
by a metallic-look-
ing band, which sets
off the specimens to
great   advantage.
White and grey are
the common colours
amongst   modern
crackle — a manu-
facture not appre-
ciated either by the
Chinese or ourselves

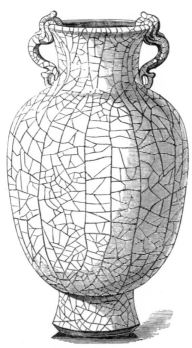

Vase of Sea-green Crackle.

—but the latter is easily known from its inferiority
to the more ancient.   The yellow and cream-
coloured specimens are rare and much prized—
these are seldom seen in Europe.   The greens,
light and dark, turquoise, and reds are generally
finely glazed, and have the crackle-lines small

and minute.   In colouring these examples are
exquisite, and in this respect they throw our
finest specimens of European porcelain quite into
the shade.   The green and turquoise crackle
made in China at the present day are very
inferior to the old kinds.   Perhaps the rarest and
most expensive of all ancient crackles is a yellowish
stone-colour ; in my researches I have seen only

Oviform Bottle of rare turquoise colour.   Gourd-shaped Bottle of yellowish
stone-colour Crackle.

one small vase of this kind, and it is now in my
collection.

Of other ancient porcelain (not crackle) prized
by the Chinese, I may mention the specimens
(generally vases) with a white ground, enamelled
with figures of various colours, as green, black,
and yellow.   It is a curious fact that the attempts
made at the present day by porcelain manufacturers to fix such colours invariably fail.

The self-coloured specimens, such as pure whites, creams, crimsons, reds, blues, greens, and violets, are very fine, and much prized by Chinese collectors. Some exquisite bits of colouring amongst this class may be met with sometimes in their cabinets, and also in old curiosity shops. I purchased a vase in Canton about fourteen inches high, coloured with the richest red I had ever seen. I doubt much if all the art of Europe could produce such a specimen in the present day, and, strange though it may appear, it could certainly not be produced in China.

But the most ancient examples of porcelain, according to the testimony of Chinese collectors, are in the form of circular dishes with upright sides, very thick, strong, and heavy, and invariably have the marks of one, two, or three, on the bottom, written in this form, II, III. The colours of some of these rare specimens, which have come under my observation, vary; but the kinds most highly prized have a brownish-yellow ground, over which is thrown a light shot sky-blue, with here and there a dash of blood-red. The Chinese tell us there are but a few of these specimens in the country, and that they are more than a thousand years old. A specimen shown me by a Chinese merchant in Canton was valued at three hundred dollars! In endeavouring to make a dealer lower his price for one in Shanghae, he quietly put it away, telling me at the same time that I evidently did not understand the value of the article I wished to purchase. It was with some difficulty I got him to produce it again, and eventually I procured it for a much less sum than I could have done in Canton.

Ancient Porcelain Vessel.

Within the last few years the attention of collectors in this country has been drawn to the ancient enamels of China. Many fine specimens were seen in the Great Exhibition of the Works of Art of all Nations in Hyde Park, and since that time a number of specimens have found their way into Europe. The specimens to which I allude have the enamel on copper, beautifully coloured and enlivened with figures of flowers, birds, and other animals. The colouring is certainly most chaste and effective, and well worth the attention of artists in this country. According to the testimony of the Chinese, this manufacture is of a very early period; no good specimens have been made for the last six or eight hundred years.

In the province of Fokien I met with some ancient bronzes, beautifully inlaid with white metal or silver. These were rarely seen in any other part of China. The lines of metal are small and delicate, and are made to represent flowers, trees, animals of various kinds, and sometimes Chinese characters. Some fine bronzes, inlaid with gold,

Ancient Vase enamelled on Metal.

are met with in this province. As a general rule, Chinese bronzes are more remarkable for their peculiar, and certainly not very handsome, form than for anything else. There are, however, many exceptions to this rule.

The curiosity - shops, which are met with in all rich cities, as well as the cabinets of collectors, are generally rich in fine specimens of the jade-stone cut into many different forms. The clear white and green specimens are most prized by collectors.

Considering the hardness of this stone, it is quite surprising how it is cut and carved by Chinese workmen, whose tools are generally of the rudest description. Fine specimens of rock - crystal, carved into figures, cups, and vases, are met with in the curiosity-shops of Foo-chow-foo. Some of these specimens are white, others golden-yellow, and others again blue and black. One kind looks as if human hair was thrown in and crystallized. Imitations of this stone are common in Canton made into snuff-bottles, such as are commonly used by the Chinese.

Amongst other stones and minerals which are found amongst the Chinese are lapis-lazuli, malachites, magnetic iron, and numerous other samples of the rarer productions of the country. But the most curious and most expensive of all is what is called gold-stone. This is an article of great beauty, and very different from the imitation kinds which are made in France, and largely exported to India. Samples of the imitation frequently find their way to Canton, but are little valued by the natives. Most of the Chinese, learned in such matters, with whom I came in contact, affirmed the true gold-stone to be a natural production, and said it came from the islands of Japan. It is very rare in China; I have not met with it in India; and whether it be a natural production or a work of art, it is certainly extremely beautiful. My friend Mr. Beale, of Shanghae, who has some fine specimens, presented one to me for the purpose of having it examined in London, but I have not yet had time.

Specimens of red lacquer, deeply carved with figures of birds, flowers, &c., and generally made in the form of trays, boxes, and sometimes vases, are met with in the more northern Chinese towns, and are much and justly prized. What is called " old gold japan " lacquer is also esteemed by Chinese connoisseurs, and the specimens of this are comparatively rare in the country at the present day.

These are a few of the principal ancient works of art met with in the cabinets of the Chinese and in the old curiosity-shops which we find in all large towns.

According to the united testimony of my Chinese friends, most of the porcelain I have noticed is of a date much more ancient than those bottles which have been found from time to time in Egyptian tombs. I have in my possession examples of these bottles found in China—generally in doctors' shops —identical in form, no doubt of the same age, and having the same inscriptions on them as those found in Egypt, and from all that I can learn they are not older than the Ming dynasty. An article on the proceedings of the " China branch of the Royal Asiatic Society," by W. H. Medhurst, Esq., her Majesty's Consul at Foo-chow-foo, proves this most satisfactorily, by showing that the in-scriptions are portions of poetical stanzas by stand-ard and celebrated Chinese authors who flourished about that time. As the concluding part of Mr. Medhurst's paper bears somewhat upon the matters I have been discussing, I shall take the liberty of introducing it in this place.

" I have not been able to ascertain anything equally satisfactory regarding the discovery of porcelain. The earliest notice of its existence, as a ware, that I can find, occurs in a poem by one Tsow-yang, a worthy who lived in the reign of Wăn-te, of the Han dynasty, 175-151 B.C.; but it is only casually mentioned as ' green porcelain.'

Pan-yŏ, a writer of the reign of Tae-che, of the
Tsin dynasty, A.D. 260-268, speaks of 'pouring
wine into many-coloured porcelain cups;' and the
biography of Ho-chow, an eminent character of
the Suy dynasty, A.D. 608-622, tells us that its
hero restored the art, then long lost in China, of
making *Lew-le*, a sort of vitreous glaze, by constructing it of porcelain. Writers of the Tang and
Sung dynasties mention it oftener, its use having
perhaps become more general in their time. I
should, therefore, infer that the manufacture was
not known previously to the first-mentioned date,
as it is not probable that so useful and valuable
a ware would have escaped historical or casual
notice, had it existed in sufficient quantity to
allow of its being applied to the manufacture of
common bottles.

" I need only add that I have trusted in no
instance to hearsay evidence in bringing forward
the information I have herein collected, but have
carefully examined each authority myself previously to recording it upon paper; and perhaps it
may not be out of place for me to remark in conclusion, that my teacher scouts the idea of associ-
ating these bottles with the Pharaonic epoch as
utterly visionary and absurd, it being impossible,
he says, that vessels composed of a ware universally acknowledged to be no older than the Han
dynasty, and inscribed with quotations from verses
that cannot, if the history of Chinese poetry
be true, have been written before the Tang dy-

nasty, could have found their way into tombs which were contemporary with the earliest recorded events of Chinese chronology. He is, on the contrary, decidedly of opinion that the bottles in question were manufactured during the Ming dynasty."

Bottle, same as found in Egyptian Tombs.

CHAPTER VI.

Boat-travelling — Unsettled state of the country — A midnight alarm — Old quarters at Tein-tung — A good Buddhist priest — Chinese farmers — Their wives and families — Chinese women's passion, and its effects — Women's curse — The author is seized with fever — A native doctor and his mode of treatment — Method of taking honey from bees — Mosquito tobacco — Its composition and manufacture.

THE scenes and adventures which I have endeavoured to describe in the previous chapters, such as making collections of insects and other objects of natural history, paying and receiving visits from Chinese friends, and examining collections of ancient works of art, although noted down in order to give an idea of the manners and customs of the most wonderful people on the surface of the globe, were merely my amusements in the midst of other and far more important labours. The country was examined for many miles in all directions, and arrangements made with the small farmers for large supplies of seeds of the tea-plant and other fruit and forest trees which were likely to be valued in India. My mode of travelling by boat, in a country where the canals and rivers are the highways, was well adapted to the ends I had in view. I was, as it were, always at home ; my bed, my clothes, and my servants were always

with me. I could go from valley to valley and
from hill to hill; I could " bring up " when it was
necessary; and when my labours were finished in
one place, I could go on, bag and baggage, to
another. Whenever the country was known to
me, or supposed to contain objects of little interest,
I used to travel by night and work during the
day. Thus my boatmen and myself worked alter-
nately; they slept by day and sailed by night,
while I slept by night and worked by day.
At this time the country was in a very unsettled state, owing to the rebellion which was
raging in many of the districts in the adjacent
provinces, and hundreds of loose characters, honest
enough when the Government was strong, were
now committing acts of robbery upon the quiet
and inoffensive natives. Very few Chinese travelled by night, unless in large bands, whose
numbers were considered a sufficient protection.
My boatmen often remonstrated when they got
the order to move on, telling me it was not the
labour they were afraid of,—they were willing to
work,—but that we should be attacked and robbed,
or perhaps murdered. These little scenes were to
me oftentimes exceedingly amusing. I would first
hear the boatman come to the bows where my
headman Tung-a was, and in a low whisper communicate his fears to him, and ask him at the
same time to use his influence with me in order
that we might remain where we were until daylight. Then after a conference of this kind Mr.

Tung-a would present himself with a very grave face, and inform me that the Lou-da (head boatman) was afraid to go onwards on account of robbers whom we were likely to meet during our night-journey. We then held a little council of war, consisting of the boatmen—including the boy I have already noticed, who, by the by, gave his opinion like a man — my servants, and myself. After a careful examination into the matter, if I saw their fears arose from natural timidity more than from any real danger, I used to point to my gun-case, and tell them not to be afraid; and so in nine cases out of ten our little council broke up with a determination to go on. But it would have been the height of folly for a solitary traveller in a little-known country to despise warnings of this kind, more particularly when the unsettled state of the empire was taken into consideration. The boatmen had the strictest orders to awake me should any suspicious vessel make her appearance, and my rest was frequently disturbed during the night, often, no doubt, without the slightest reason. They were also to let the strangers know they had a " Hong-mow-jin " (the name by which foreigners are known in this part of China) in the boat who had fire-arms with him which he was prepared to use in case it was necessary. From an intimate knowledge of the natives in Chekiang, I considered these two pieces of information of great value in preventing an attack, for most of the natives here, unless they

are very hardened indeed, have a kind of superstitious dread of foreigners and foreign fire-arms.

Amongst many false alarms I had at this time,
there was one which I thought would have proved
rather serious. It was about midnight, and the
night was excessively dark. We were all sound
asleep, except one boatman, who was sculling the
boat—if indeed he was not as sound as any of us,
for these fellows go asleep at the scull like an
Indian at the punka — when we experienced a
sharp shock from our boat coming in contact with
another. I was up in an instant, thinking the
long-threatened night attack had come at last.
Throwing the moveable portion of the roof of my
boat on one side, I saw our antagonist lying alongside of us. My men were out on the bows, and
my boatmen at the stern, ready to repel the in-
vaders. Through the darkness I could discern a
number of people crowding the other boat, but
not attempting to board us. I immediately hailed
them, and asked them who they were, and why
they had run against us. They replied they
were Ningpo men, that they were not robbers,
and that the accident had occurred owing to the
darkness of the night. We now set to work and
got the boats clear, and each proceeded on his
journey. I believe those who gave us the alarm
were more frightened than we were, and that each
took the other for the pirate. My servants and
boatmen were, however, of a different opinion;
they believed them to be thieves, and said that had

a Chinese been in our boat instead of a foreigner
he would have gone away rather the poorer for
the encounter. The true state of the case must,
I am afraid, remain for ever a mystery; but it
does not signify much.

As the summer advanced — it was now the
month of July—the weather became too hot to
live in boats. The thermometer frequently stood
at 100°, and once or twice rose to 110°, in the
shade. It was time, therefore, to look out for
other quarters, and, as I had a good deal to do
in the districts to the south of Ningpo, I determined on taking up my quarters in the old
Buddhist temple of Tein-tung. I have already
described this ancient place in my 'Wanderings
in China;' to which the reader who wishes to know
more about it is referred. It is situate amongst
the mountains some twenty miles south-east from
Ningpo, and in the midst of an extensive tea-
country, which is becoming of more importance
every day on account of the large demand for
this article which has sprung up in Shanghae
since that port was opened to foreign trade. When
I arrived at Tein-tung I took up my quarters
with the priest with whom I had lived formerly—
a man with one eye, who is now well known to
foreigners who visit the temple. He is a very
superior specimen of the Buddhist priesthood,
intelligent and strictly honest and honourable.
I have often left things in his care for long
periods of time, and felt as certain of having

H

them returned to me as if they had been in the Bank of England. A man of this kind was invaluable, as I was thus enabled to make his house a sort of head-quarters for my collections in the province until they could be conveyed to Shanghae for shipment to India or to Europe.

On the present occasion he seemed delighted to see me again, and gave me a hearty welcome. Having established myself in my old quarters, I took the mornings and evenings for my outdoor excursions, and generally stopped in the house during the heat of the day. In this way, with the help of my good friend the priest, I entered into engagements with many of the small farmers for supplies of tea-seeds to be gathered in the following autumn as soon as they were ripe. In a short time all the little boys and girls in the country were making collections of insects, land-shells, and other objects of natural history for me, and were delighted with the few cash they were able to earn in this manner. I was thus fully employed even during the heat of the day, when it would have been imprudent to stir abroad.

The farmers in China, as a class, are highly respectable, but, as their farms are all small, they are probably less wealthy than our farmers in England. Each farm-house is a little colony, consisting of some three generations, namely, the grandfather, his children, and his children's children. There they live in peace and harmony together; all who are able work on the farm, and if more labour is required, the stranger is hired to assist them.   They live well, dress plainly, and are industrious, without being in any way oppressed.   I doubt if there is a happier race anywhere than the Chinese farmer and peasantry. Being well known in this part of the country, and having always made it a point to treat the people well, I was welcomed wherever I went.   I began to feel quite at home in the farmers' houses. Here the female members of the family have much more liberty than those of a higher rank. They have small feet as usual, but they are not so confined to the house, or prevented from looking on and speaking to strangers, as the higher classes are.   If a stranger enters the court of the house unexpectedly, he will see a number of ladies, both old and young, sitting in the verandah, all industriously employed on some work—some spinning, some sewing or embroidering, and one probably engaged in culinary operations; and if the stranger be an unknown foreigner, the whole will rise hurriedly, and disappear like a covey of partridges, overturning wheels, stools, and anything else that may be in their way.   This was a frequent scene in my earlier visits, but it gradually wore off when it was found I was a civilised being like themselves.   These same ladies afterwards would often ask me to sit down, and even set a chair for me, and bring me a cup of tea with their own fair hands; and while I drank my tea, they would go on with their work, laughing and chatting as

I

freely as if I had been a thousand miles away. But many of these Chinese ladies with all their coyness are regular termagants, as the following curious anecdote will show.

Happening one day at this time to be in a bamboo forest, I came upon two men engaged in cutting down some fine bamboo-trees. Just as I came up with them, a farmer's wife made her appearance from an opposite quarter, and was apparently in a state of great excitement. The men, it appeared, had bought a certain number of the trees, which at the time of sale had been duly marked. But in cutting, instead of taking those they had bargained for, they had just cut down a very fine one which was not for sale. The old lady was so excited that she either did not see me, or her anger made her disregard the presence of a stranger. She commenced first in low short sentences to lament the loss of the bamboo, then louder and louder sentence after sentence rolled from her tongue, in which she abused without mercy the unfortunate men for their conduct. At last she seemed to have worked herself up to a frantic state of excitement; she threw off her head-dress, tore her hair, and screamed so loud that she might have been heard for more than a mile. Her passion reached the climax at last, and human nature could stand it no longer. With an unearthly yell and a sort of hysteric gulp she tumbled backward on the ground, threw her little feet in the air, gave two or three kicks, and all was still. Up to this point I had been rather amused than otherwise, but, as she lay perfectly still and foamed at the mouth, I became alarmed. The poor men had been standing all this time, hanging their heads, and looking as sheepish as possible. I now looked round to see what effect this state of things had on them. They both shrugged their shoulders, laughed, and went on with their work. About a quarter of an hour afterwards I came back to the spot to see how matters stood—she was still lying on the ground, but apparently recovering. I raised her, and begged her to sit up, which she did with a melancholy shake of the head; but she either could not or would not speak. In a little while afterwards I saw her rise up and walk slowly and quietly home.

Such scenes as that which I have just noticed are very common in the country. A short time after this took place I was passing a peasant's cottage, when I heard another woman just commencing—when one's ear gets accustomed, he can always tell the commencement, middle, or near the end. I stood with several persons outside the cottage listening to this one, and soon ascertained that her husband had been unfaithful to her—a circumstance which she had just found out. It was the same scene over again; she got gradually more and more excited, and then fell back senseless on the ground, and threw her feet in the air. I now ventured round to the door, which was

standing wide open. Her eldest child, a boy
about ten years of age, was trying to raise her
from the floor; his sister, some two years younger,
was crying as if her little heart would break;
while an infant was playing with its toy on the
floor quite unconscious of the sin and misery going
on around it.

These Chinese termagants work themselves up
into such passions sometimes for very slight
things, and their imprecations or curses are quite
fearful. One night an old woman in Ningpo had
a couple of fowls stolen. Next morning, when
she discovered her loss, she came outside her door,
and began in the following strain :—" I have lost
two fowls ; some one has stolen my two fowls.
May he never thrive who has stolen my fowls!"
—and then a dead dog caught her eye as it was
floating down the river—" May he die like that
dog! May his body never be buried! May his
children never visit his tomb!" and so on. I
forget if this old lady went quite off; many of
them stop short and get pacified before they reach
the climax.

In the month of August I had a somewhat sudden and violent attack of fever. Whether this
was the result of exposure to the sun, or from
causes over which I had no control, it is impossible for me to say. Unfortunately I had no medicine with me at the time, and as I was far from
foreign medical advice I was glad to put myself
into the hands of a Chinese practitioner. I con-

fess I did so with considerable reluctance; but "a drowning man will catch at a straw." There were several medical men in the little tea-village of Tein-tung-ka, within two miles of the temple. My good friend the priest, with whom I was staying, offered his services to go and fetch one of the best of these, an offer which was gratefully accepted. When the doctor arrived I was in bed with a burning fever upon me. After putting several questions as to the time the fever came on, whether I had daily attacks, and the time each attack continued, he then felt my skin and pulse, and looked as if he understood the nature of the disease, and could cure me. " I understand from the priests and your servants you are in the habit of bathing every morning in the cold stream which flows past the temple; this must be discontinued. You are also in the habit of having considerable quantities of Ke-me* put in your soup; this you must give up for the present, and you will live on conge for a few days." I told him his directions should be attended to. He then despatched a messenger to his house for certain medicines, and at the same time ordered a basin of strong hot tea to be brought into the room. When this was set before him he bent his two forefingers and dipped his knuckles into the hot tea. The said knuckles were now used like a pair of pincers on my skin, under the ribs, round the back, and on several other parts of the body. Every now and then the ope-

---

* A kind of vermicelli, very good about Ningpo.

ration of wetting them with the hot tea was repeated. He pinched and drew my skin so hard
that I could scarcely refrain from crying out with
pain ; and when the operation was completed to
his satisfaction, he had left marks which I did not
get rid of for several weeks after.

When the messenger arrived with the medicine,
the first thing I was asked to swallow was a large
paper of small pills, containing, I suppose, about a
hundred, or perhaps more. " Am I to take the
whole of these ? " I asked, in amazement. " Yes ;
and here is a cup of hot tea to wash them down."
I hesitated ; then tasted one, which had a hot, pep-
pery kind of flavour, and, making up my mind,
gulped the whole. In the mean time a teapot had
been procured capable of holding about three large
breakfast-cups of tea. Into this pot were put six
different vegetable productions — about half an
ounce of each. These consisted of dried orange
or citron peel, pomegranate, charred fruit of Gar-
denia radicans, the bark and wood of Rosa Banksi-
ana, and two other things unknown to me. The
teapot was then filled to the brim with boiling
water, and allowed to stand for a few minutes,
when the decoction was ready for the patient. I
was now desired to drink it cup after cup as fast
as possible, and then cover myself over with all
the blankets which could be laid hold of. The
directions of my physician were obeyed to the
letter, but nevertheless I lay for an hour longer
ere perspiration broke, when of course I got

instant relief. Before taking his leave the doctor
informed me he would repeat his visit on the third
day following about ten in the morning, this being
about an hour before the fever was likely to return.   He told me not to be at all afraid, and
gave me the welcome news that the next attack,
if indeed I had any more, would be slight, and
that then I would get rid of it altogether.

True to his promise, the old man was with me
on the third day, about ten o'clock in the morning.
" Has the fever come on ? "   " No," I replied ; " it
is scarcely the time yet. I suppose I shall have
it in another hour." He now desired me to lie
down in bed, and the pinching process was repeated in the same way as it had been done before,
but if anything it was more painful. I had then
to swallow another large dose of pills, and lastly
the hot decoction from the teapot.   Ere I had
drunk the last cupful my skin became moist, and
I was soon covered with profuse perspiration.
The fever had left me, and I was cured. I was
probably the first *Hong-mou-jin* the doctor had
treated, and he was evidently much pleased with
the results of his treatment.

Medical men at home will probably smile as
they read these statements, but there was no mis-
taking the results. Indeed, from an intimate
knowledge of the Chinese, I am inclined to think
more highly of their skill than people generally
give them credit for. I remember well, when I
came first to China in 1843, a celebrated prac-

titioner in Hongkong, now no more, gravely informed me the Chinese doctors gathered all sorts of herbs indiscriminately, and used them *en masse*, upon the principle that if one thing did not answer the purpose another would. Nothing can be further from the truth. That they are not surgeons I am fully prepared to admit; that they are ignorant of many of our most valued vegetable and mineral medicines is also true; but, being a very ancient nation and comparatively civilised for many ages, many discoveries have been made and carefully handed down from father to son which are not to be despised, and which one ought not to laugh at without understanding. Dr. Kirk, of Shanghae, whose opinion is entitled to the highest respect, informed me he had discovered a most valuable tonic in common use [probably a species of gentian], equal, if not superior, to any of the kind in our pharmacopœias, and there are, no doubt, many other things of equal value unknown to Europeans and well worth investigation.

During my sojourn in this place I had an opportunity of witnessing a novel mode of taking honey from beehives. The Chinese hive is a very rude affair, and a very different looking thing from that we are accustomed to use in England, and yet I suspect, were the bees consulted in the matter, they would prefer the Chinese one to ours. It consists of a rough box, sometimes square and sometimes cylindrical, with

a moveable top and bottom. When the bees are
put into a hive of this description, it is rarely
placed on or near the ground, as with us, but is
raised eight or ten feet, and generally fixed under
the projecting roof of a house or outbuilding. No
doubt the Chinese have remarked the partiality
which the insects have for places of this kind
when they choose quarters for themselves, and
have taken a lesson from this circumstance. My
landlord, who had a number of hives, having
determined one day to take some honey from two
of them, a half-witted priest who was famous for
his prowess in such matters was sent for to perform the operation. This man, in addition to his
priestly duties, had the charge of the buffaloes
which were kept on the farm attached to the
temple. He came round in high glee, evidently
considering his qualifications of no ordinary kind
for the operation he was about to perform. Curious
to witness his method of proceeding with the
business, I left some work with which I was busy,
and followed him and the other priests and servants of the establishment to the place where the
hives were fixed. The form of the hives, in this
instance, was cylindrical; each was about three
feet in height and rather wider at the bottom than
the top. When we reached the spot where the
hives were placed, our operator jumped upon a
table placed there for the purpose, and gently
lifted down one of the hives and placed it on its
side on the table. He then took the moveable

top off, and the honeycomb, with which the hive was quite full, was exposed to our view. In the meantime an old priest having brought a large basin, and everything being ready, our friend commenced to cut out the honeycomb with a knife made apparently for the purpose, and having the handle almost at right angles with the blade. Having taken out about one-third of the contents of the hive, the top was put on again, and the hive elevated to its former position. The same operation was repeated with the second hive, and in a manner quite as satisfactory.

But it may be asked, " Where were the bees all this time ? "—and this is the most curious part of my story. They had not been killed by the fumes of brimstone, for it is contrary to the doctrines of the Buddhist creed to take away animal life—nor had they been stupified with a fungus, which is sometimes done at home ; but they were flying about above our heads in great numbers, and yet, although we were not protected in the slightest degree, not one of us was stung ; and this was the more remarkable as the bodies of the operator and servants were completely naked from the middle upwards.

The charm was a simple one ; it lay in a few dry stems and leaves of a species of Artemisia which grows wild on these hills, and which is largely used to drive that pest the mosquito out of the dwellings of the people. This plant is cut early in summer, sun-dried, then twisted into

bands, and it is ready for use. At the commencement of the operation which I am describing, one
end of the substance was ignited and kept burning
slowly as the work went on. The poor bees did
not seem to know what to make of it. They were
perfectly good-tempered and kept hovering about
our heads, but apparently quite incapable of doing
us the slightest injury. When the hives were
properly fixed in their places the charm was put
out, and my host and his servants carried off the
honey in triumph. " Come," said he to the operator and us who were lookers on, " come and
drink wine." " Ay," said the half-witted priest,
" drink wine, drink wine." So we all adjourned to
the refectory, where wine in small cups was set
before us.

In a former work on China—' A Journey to the
Tea Countries'—I noticed a curious substance
called " mosquito tobacco," or " mosquito physic,"
for it is known by both of these names, which I
had met with for the first time when travelling in
the western parts of the province of Chekiang on
my way to the Bohea mountains and the great
black-tea country of Woo-e-shan. The day before
the discovery was made had been very hot, and
during the night such swarms of mosquitoes came
that neither my servant nor myself had been
allowed to close our eyes. I had no curtains with
me, and looked forward with dread to many such
sleepless nights during the journey. " Why don't
you procure some mun-jung-ean ? " said the boat-

men to my servant. Delighted to find there was some simple remedy, I sent on shore to the first village we passed, and procured some sticks of this invaluable substance. I found it answer the purpose admirably, and used it every night during the remainder of that journey wherever I happened to sleep, whether in boats, in temples, or in the common inns of the country.

When I reached England the account which I gave of this substance attracted a good deal of notice from entomologists and others, and I was frequently asked if I had brought any of it home, or if I knew what the ingredients were of which it was composed. I was obliged to plead negligence in not having done the former and ignorance as regards the latter. However much the substance delighted me at first, its constant use, its cheapness, and being an article extremely common, led me, I suppose, to neglect it, as we often do common things. This is the only explanation I can give for my neglect, which, when I came to consider the matter at home, surprised me probably more than those who had made inquiries regarding it. My ignorance of the ingredients which composed it will not excite so much surprise in the minds of those acquainted with the character of the Chinese.

Having occasion to visit the island of Chusan in the end of August, in order to make some arrangements about grafted Yang-mae trees, I found a quantity of this mosquito tobacco in a joss-stick

maker's shop in the city of Ting-hae. On taking
it home with me to the house in which I was
located, I lost no time in trying its effect upon
the mosquitoes, which were numerous at this hot
season of the year. On its being lighted the
fumes rose slowly upwards, and the air was soon
filled with odours which were not at all disagreeable, not more so than the joss-stick or incense
which is burned in every Chinaman's house who
can afford the luxury, and in all the temples. It
appeared, however, to be no luxury to the mosquito, for, in two or three minutes after it was
ignited, not a buzz was heard nor a mosquito to be
seen.

My next object was to endeavour to find out
the ingredients which were used in the manufacture of this curious substance. For this purpose I paid another visit to the shop in which
I had bought it. In one part of the premises
the people were employed in beating up the
various articles used in the manufacture of incense, and in another part others were busy
making the joss-stick. The head of the establishment paid his respects to me very politely, and
asked me whether I had found the mosquito
tobacco answer the purpose. I replied that nothing could have done better, and then commenced
to ask him some questions regarding the ingredients used, their proportions, and the mode of
manufacture. At first he was very communicative.
He informed me the following articles were used :

namely, the sawings of juniper or pine trees (pih heang fun, or sung shoo), artemisia-leaves reduced to powder (nai-hai), tobacco-leaves (ean fun), a small portion of arsenic (pe-za), and a mineral called *nu wang*.

With regard to the proportions of each, it appeared that, to thirty pounds of the pine or juniper sawings, about twenty of artemisia, five of tobacco, and a small quantity of arsenic were added. But ere we had come to this point my informant's jealousy had been aroused, and his statements were evidently not much to be depended upon. He now began to question me in return for the answers he had given—" What did I want this information for? if I wanted to buy the article, he had it for sale, and it was cheap enough." To make matters worse, he then coolly told me he was not quite certain that the information he had given me was correct, as he did not understand the process himself, but engaged men to make it for him, which individuals came from the interior.

Nothing further could be gained from my jealous acquaintance at this time, but I was determined not to let the matter rest here, but rather endeavour to gain the end I had in view by other means. At this time I had a very sharp and intelligent artist—a native of Chusan—employed in making drawings of coniferous trees for Miss Boulton, of Hasely Court, Oxfordshire. He had been travelling with me all over the country, and had now come over to Chusan in order to make some drawings on the island, and also to pay a visit to his father, who combined the professions of artist and doctor in his own person.   Both father and son were now set to work in order to get the information required.   They were told not to hurry themselves or appear very anxious about it, but to take care as to the correctness of anything they might learn on the subject.   In two months I received the result of their investigations, which coincided very closely with my own.   Pine and juniper sawings, wormwood-leaves, and tobacco-leaves, reduced to powder, a small portion of nu-wang and arsenic.   Each article was well beaten up with water, then the whole mixed together, and in the form of a thick paste rolled on a slip of bamboo.   On exposure to the air the substance dried quickly, and was then put away for sale. When finished the sticks are somewhat like the common joss-stick of the country, or about the thickness and length of a light walking-cane.

Another substance, much cheaper than the last, is found in every town and village in the central and eastern provinces of the empire where I have been, and no doubt it is in use over the greater part of China.   Long, narrow bags of paper—say half an inch in diameter and two feet long—are filled with the following substances, namely, the sawings of pine or juniper, mixed with a small portion of nu-wang and arsenic.   The proportions are thirty pounds of sawings, two ounces of nu-wang, and one ounce of arsenic.   This mixture is not

made up in the form of a paste like the latter, but
simply well mixed, and then run into the bags in
a dry state.   Each bag being filled is closed at the
mouth, and then coiled up like a rope and fastened
in this position with a bit of thread.   Many hundreds of these coils, neatly done up and placed one
above another, may be seen exposed for sale in the
shops during the hot season, when mosquitoes are
numerous.   When about to be used, the thread
which keeps the coil together is cut, then the coil
is slightly loosened, so that its sides do not touch
each other, for if this happened it would ignite at
various parts and soon be consumed.   The outer
end is then lighted, and the whole is laid carefully
down upon a bit of board, when it goes on burning
for the greater part of the night.   One hundred of
these little coils may be bought for a sum equivalent
to threepence of our money, and two of them will
suffice for a night in an ordinary-sized room.

A third substance, cheaper than either of the
above, is made of a species of artemisia or worm-
wood (*A. indica*) which grows wild on every hill
in this part of China.   It is the same kind I have
already noticed as forming one of the ingredients
in the genuine mosquito tobacco, and is that which
was used in taking the honey from the bees in the
temple of Tein-tung.   It is gathered and thoroughly
dried, then twisted or plaited into ropes, in which
condition it is fit for use.   Although cheaper, and
consequently more in use amongst the poorer
classes, than the other kinds, it is not so efficient,

and it gives out more smoke than is agreeable to a European.

I may be questioned whether the small quantity of arsenic used in making the mosquito tobacco is entirely harmless. I am not sufficiently acquainted with the chemical action which goes on during combustion to answer this in the negative. But it must be borne in mind that the quantity of this poisonous mineral is exceedingly small; and the fact that mosquito tobacco is used by probably one hundred millions of human beings would seem to prove that it could not have any bad effect upon their health.

K

CHAPTER VII.

Difficulty in procuring black-tea manufacturers — Return to Shanghae
— City taken by a band of rebels — Chief magistrate murdered —
Strange prejudices of foreign residents — Their professions of
neutrality — Chinese warfare — Dr. Lockhart's hospital and patients
— Value of medical missions — Public opinion changes — Shanghae
evacuated by the rebels — Entered by the Imperialists — Cruelty
of soldiers — Effects of the rebellion on the face of the country.

THE arrangements I had been making during the
summer months with farmers and tea-cultivators
for supplies of plants and seeds in the autumn,
were brought to a successful termination in the
end of August. But as tea-seed does not ripen in
China until October or November, I had two
months before me to attend to another and equally
important part of my duties. This was to procure
and forward to India some first-rate black-tea
manufacturers—a task which I found much more
difficult than that of selecting and exporting seeds
and plants. The Chinese are supposed to be an
erratic race, and are found almost populating such
places as the straits of Malacca, Java, and Manilla.
Of late years shiploads of coolies have been sent
to the West Indies, while thousands have emigrated
to the gold-fields of California and Australia.
But nearly all these are natives of the province of
Canton, and the southern part of Fokien, and

moreover are men who have either been brought up in seaport towns, or only a short distance inland. Had such men suited my purpose, I could easily have procured them in any number. But unfortunately the best black-tea districts of China are far inland; the natives of such districts are simple countrymen who have never seen the sea in the course of their lives, and who have a very indistinct idea of countries which lie beyond it. And besides, such men as I wanted were able to earn good wages at home, and consequently less inclined to push their fortunes abroad. Although it would, therefore, have been the simplest thing possible to procure *Chinamen*, it was a very different matter to get hold of good tea-manufacturers.

There were two ways of accomplishing the object in view, either by going to the homes of such men myself, or by getting them through respectable Chinese at one of the northern ports. The first of these methods was not very likely to succeed; it is not probable that a stranger and a foreigner could induce such men to leave their homes, however liberal the offers he might make them might be. They could, or at least they would, have had no confidence in the fulfilment of such promises. I had, therefore, adopted the second mode of gaining the desired end, and now determined to return to Shanghae for a few days in order to see what progress had been made in the matter by the Chinese who had promised me their assistance.

On returning to Shanghae I found no progress whatever had been made, and indeed men's minds were so full of the rebellion raging in the country at the time that little else could have been expected. In the end of August and beginning of September rumours were current that the Fokien and Canton men, who are rather numerous at this port, were about to rise and hoist the standard of the new Emperor, T'hae-ping-wang, in this ancient city. The authorities, who had long felt their weakness, issued proclamations denouncing a man named Le, who, with some forty others, was taken up and detained for some hours at the office of the magistrate. The official, however, did not dare to punish these persons : indeed, he was coolly informed that if he did so his own head would pay the penalty. This threat had the desired effect : Le and his companions were set at liberty, and it is needless to say grew bolder and more unruly than ever they had been before. As a further step to preserve the peace of the city, a body of lawless men belonging to a secret society, who could not be controlled, were taken into the pay of the Government. This was a last resource, and placed the Government upon a mine which could be sprung at any moment for its destruction.

The morning of the 7th of September, being the day on which the mandarins usually pay their visit to sacrifice in the temple of Confucius, was chosen by the rebels for the attack upon the city. Without knowing anything about their plans, I happened to pay a visit to the city soon after daybreak. On entering at the north gate I observed a number of men looking earnestly at some object in the guard-house, and saw at a glance that something of an unusual nature had taken place. Ascending the steps of the guard-room with the Chinese, I was horrorstruck at finding the mats and pillows belonging to the guard saturated with human blood. Upon inquiry, I found that a band of men, believed to be composed chiefly of the members of the secret society already noticed, and called the " Small Sword Society," had entered the city and were then on their way to the houses of the chief mandarins, namely, the Taoutae and Che-heen. They had met with some feeble resistance from the guard, whom they soon overpowered and made themselves masters of the gate.

When the rebels reached the centre of the city, they divided themselves into two divisions,—one of which marched to the Che-heen's office, and the other to the Taoutae's. The guard at the Che-heen's, consisting of about forty men, fled without making the slightest resistance, and are supposed to have been in league with the rebels. Some one ran to inform the magistrate that his house was attacked, and the old man came out and endeavoured to pacify the rebel mob with a few fair words and promises for the future. He was told, however, that such promises were now too late, upbraided for his former conduct, and barbarously murdered on the spot.

The division which marched to the Taoutae's was equally successful, and met with no resistance. Report says this officer—who was the highest in Shanghae—behaved very bravely on this trying occasion. Having been informed of the intended attack a minute or two before it took place, he dressed himself in his official robes and came out to meet the rebels. Most of his attendants had fled, and, seeing that the few men who remained true were a very unequal match for the rebels, he prevented them from offering any resistance. " If you want my life," said he, " you have the power to take it,—see, I am unarmed and defenceless." The rebel chief replied that they did not want his life, but that he must forthwith hand over the official seals, and take an oath not to molest those who were now the masters of the city. He immediately gave up the seals, and retired to his own apartment, where he was allowed to remain unmolested while the other parts of the buildings were plundered and gutted.

In the afternoon I paid another visit to the city with the Rev. Mr. Edkins, of the London Missionary Society. On arriving at the north gate we found a strong guard stationed there, who, after some little persuasion, allowed us to pass in. From the appearances which presented themselves at every turning, it was evident the rebels had made a good use of their time. Not only were all the gates strongly guarded, but patrols of two men each were marching through the city in all directions and preserving order. These guards had strict orders to preserve the property of the inhabitants from thieves of all kinds, and to punish in a summary manner all who might be caught stealing. Two men who were taken in the act were immediately put to death without judge or jury or trial of any kind. The, order which prevailed in all quarters, considering the lawless bands who were in possession of the city, was very remarkable.

Threading our way through the narrow streets, in the direction of the public offices, which had been the scene of such disturbances in the morning, we were everywhere treated with marked respect both by the inhabitants and by the various patrols. When we reached the house of the Cheheen a strange scene was presented to our view. Hundreds of people were busily engaged in ransacking the premises and carrying off everything which could be taken away. The furniture of the various rooms and all moveable articles had gone first, and the crowd were now busily employed in taking down the windows, doors, all kinds of framework, wooden pillars, and indeed everything which could be converted into use. This crowd was not what in England we would call a mob, but a set of respectable, orderly plunderers,—or perhaps *luters* would be a better word,—whose proceedings were sanctioned by the victorious rebels now in possession of the city. However particular the latter seemed with reference to the preservation of private property, that of the mandarins and Government seemed to be given over to the people for plunder as a matter of course. When we reached the upper end of the collection of buildings which formed the official residence of the Che-heen, we observed a crowd of people, who seemed to be lookers-on like ourselves, moving to some apartments on one side of the central hall. Following in their steps, we came to a court, or small Chinese garden, containing a few ornamental plants in pots and a pretty arbour covered with the *Glycine sinensis*. In a small room, now in ruins, at the upper end of the court, a crowd of people were observed gazing intently at some object on the floor, and from the expression on every countenance we readily conjectured that this must be the body of the Che-heen, who had been murdered in the morning, and which we were now desirous of seeing. As we approached the spot, the crowd readily made way, when a melancholy and shocking sight was presented to our view. On a mat, in the middle of the room, lay the body of the murdered magistrate, covered with the wounds which had been inflicted by his ruthless countrymen. It was a sickening sight, so we turned away and made our way out through the busy crowd, who were still employed in what appeared to be considered a kind of legal plunder.

Leaving the offices of the magistrate, we now proceeded to the residence of the Taoutae, or

highest civil officer in the city. Here a scene of
a different kind, but scarcely less curious, was
presented to us. This place had been made the
head-quarters of the rebels, and we found the
doors strictly guarded by their men. The guards
allowed us to pass without question; and, walking
up a straight path to the furthest end of the
buildings, we found a large hall filled with armed
men, engaged in arranging some matters connected with their food and wages. A more black-
guard or unruly looking collection of human
beings I had never before seen. Some were
armed with short swords, others with muskets or
pistols, and a number with rusty-looking spears of
all forms and sizes. Here and there we observed
some busily engagd in grinding their swords, and
every now and then feeling their edges like a
butcher about to slay an animal for his stall.
The greater number were taking part in a hot
discussion which was then going on with their
leaders, all talking at the same time, and, apparently, in the greatest disorder; but, as this is
Chinese custom, it gave us but little surprise or
concern. The uniform worn by this motley band
was most varied in its character; but each man
wore a distinguishing badge of some kind, either
round his head, or as a sash round his body, or
on his breast. The Fokien bands had generally
a red band tied round the head; while the Canton
men had a white one, said to be a badge of mourning for the Ming dynasty—their ancient kings.

Having seen quite enough of these unruly spirits, we left their halls, and walked quietly homewards through the streets of the city. Every place was perfectly quiet :—some of the shops were open, and the people generally seemed to be looking on with Chinese indifference.

In the new foreign town measures were taken by the English and American residents for their own protection. On the morning after the occurrences had taken place which I have just been narrating, the pretty Chinese Custom-house, which is so great an ornament to the foreign town, and which had been evacuated by the authorities, was completely gutted by the Chinese, and no one interfered to prevent them. It was attacked by no mob of lawless vagabonds, but by the sober and industrious people in the neighbourhood, who seemed to consider its contents a kind of *lute* to which they were justly entitled. Every one agreed, when too late, that it was a pity to allow such a proceeding within our own boundary,—more particularly when a single consulate official, or a single sailor from one of the men-of-war in port, could have prevented it, without any force being necessary further than to stand at the door and warn the people off.

The description which I have thus attempted to give of the taking of Shanghae by this rebel band will throw some light upon the character of the Chinese,—but it is difficult to give to civilised nations in the West a correct idea of this extra-

ordinary people. Will it be credited that a city
containing upwards of 200,000 inhabitants —
walled and fortified, and, to a certain extent,
prepared for an attack—allowed itself to be taken
by a band of marauders scarcely numbering 500
men, badly armed, undisciplined, and bent on
plunder ? And yet such is the fact, for, however
strict the rebels appeared to be in their endea-
vours to preserve private property, they were
robbing the Government and "squeezing" some
of the more wealthy among the inhabitants. It
seemed to be generally acknowledged that they
had, as yet, no connexion with the Kwang-si
rebels, although they expected to have shortly.
It was, no doubt, the intention of many of them
to "feather their own nests" pretty well in the
first place, and then hand over the conquered
city to any one who chose to take it off their
hands. In the mean time the poor people suffered,—trade, both foreign and native, was para-
lyzed,—and one trembled for the fearful calamities
which now hung over this unhappy country.

For this state of things in Shanghae the foreign
residents have been greatly to blame, inasmuch as
they not only did not endeavour to prevent them,
but actually encouraged the attack. I do not
mean that they ought to have taken to arms and
fought on the side of the Imperialists, but the
moral force in their hands was very great; and
had it been generally known that foreigners were
opposed to any attack upon Shanghae, it is more

than probable such an attack would never have
been attempted. But a course very different from
this was pursued. The sympathies of foreigners
generally were all enlisted on the side of the
rebels and against the government of the country.
It was no secret that we as a body, instead of
opposing an attack upon the city, would hail it
with pleasure, and wish it success, although we
would otherwise remain neutral. Civil and naval
officers, missionaries, merchants, and shopkeepers,
all—with a few honourable exceptions—were in
favour of the debauched band of robbers who took
the city of Shanghae on the 7th of September.
The unprejudiced observer of these events had
now to witness a most extraordinary and anoma-
lous proceeding, namely, that of our men-of-war
gallantly putting down the ·hordes of pirates
which were infesting the coast, while the land
pirates, such as those who took the city of Shanghae, were encouraged and applauded. And why?
Because the latter spent their days and nights in
smoking opium, in drunkenness, and in all kinds
of debauchery, and gave out they were followers
of Tai-ping-wang, or, as he was called, the Christian King !

It would be too sweeping an assertion to place
the whole of these men in the same class. Some
perhaps were patriots anxious for the good of their
country, but I am afraid these characters were
comparatively rare. And yet the good ones were
probably amongst those who held out to the last,

and who suffered the greatest obloquy when " public opinion " changed.

Public opinion, when by this is understood the intelligence of a people, is generally correct ; and it is difficult to account for the errors of the Shanghae community, more particularly when it is considered that it consists of men of education and sound common sense. The supposed Christian character of the Kwang-si rebels had no doubt a tendency to interest and captivate, and perhaps the corrupt nature of the present government of the empire might make many wish for a change. But whatever the main body of the rebels at Nanking might be — and the visits of foreigners to that camp had been too few and brief in duration to enable them to form a correct estimate of their politics and religion — there surely could be no doubt as to the character of those who claimed connexion with them in Shanghae. And add to this, that there was but one opinion regarding them shared by all respectable Chinese in this part of the country—and that was that they were nothing more than thieves and robbers—and one wonders still the more.

For more than a year this band held possession of the ancient city of Shanghae. A large force was sent against them by the government, and encamped at various points round the city-walls, and at a safe distance from the ramparts. The object of the Imperialists appeared to be not so much to drive them out by hard fighting as by

gradually cutting off their supplies to starve them
into capitulation.   Here again their plans were to
a certain extent frustrated by *neutral* foreigners.
The foreign settlement, as it is called, occupies a
large tract of ground situated on the north-east side
of the city just outside the walls, and is bounded on
the east by the Shanghae river.   Notwithstanding
the complaints and remonstrances of the government of the country, many persons were unscrupu-
lous enough to keep supplying the insurgents with
arms and ammunition of all kinds in large quantities, for which they were liberally paid with the
spoils stolen from the public treasury or wrung
from the inhabitants.   Some were in the habit of
making large sums of money by running cargoes
of gunpowder, carrying it into the city, advising
and counselling the rebels, and then when danger
approached sneaking back to the foreign settlement for the protection which the flags of England
or America afforded them.   Nor was this conduct
effectually checked by either of these governments
for a considerable length of time, although they
had full power to have done so.   And this is what
we call being neutral !

The battles or skirmishes which took place
every few days betwixt the besiegers and besieged
during the time the city was in the hands of the
rebels were most amusing performances.

During the time of the siege Dr. Lockhart's
Chinese hospital was crowded with patients. Some
came to have limbs amputated, others to have balls

extracted, and others again to have their wounds dressed. All were attended to in the kindest manner " without money and without price." It did not signify to the Christian missionary whether the person carried to his door for medical aid was an imperialist or a rebel ; it was enough that he was a human being suffering pain and desiring to be relieved. And hence the wounded of both parties met in the same hospital, and each had his wounds attended to by the same friendly hand.

In his report for 1854 Dr. Lockhart relates the following circumstance :—" One Sunday afternoon two wounded persons were brought in ; one was a Canton man, an artilleryman at the battery on the eastern side of the river, or Poo-tung ; he had fired his gun once, and was reloading it when the charge exploded and so severely injured his arm that it had to be amputated below the elbow, and he did well. The first shot that he fired had crossed the river, and struck a woman near the city-wall on the leg, destroying all the soft part from one side of the limb. These two patients met at the hospital about an hour afterwards." He then tells us :—" A man was brought in one morning whom a rebel had caught, supposing him to be an imperial soldier, and tried to behead (!), but owing to the man's struggles he was unable to effect this, though he inflicted most severe injuries upon him." Then a beggar is brought in who had been struck on the leg by a cannon-ball ; his wound is dressed, he is lodged and fed and sent away cured. An old fisherman was dropping his anchor at the mouth of the river on a windy day, when his hand got entangled in the cable, so that it was almost twisted off. The thumb was found to be much mangled, the back of the hand was almost destroyed, and the metacarpal bones fractured, so that the fingers and palm were all that were left. The result of skilful treatment is that the hand " is now almost well, though the man will not have much motion in his fingers."

Such are the labours of the medical missionaries; skilful, unwearied, and free to all as their native air, or their refreshing streams. The soldier, the sailor, merchant, mechanic, farmer, and labourer, high and low, rich and poor, have the benefits of the hospital freely offered to them. In 1853 no fewer than 11,028 patients had been operated upon, or treated in some way, while in 1854 the number amounted to 12,181.

But the Medical Missionary Society have objects which are even of a higher nature than " healing the sick and curing all manner of diseases." When the patients assemble for medical treatment in the hall of the hospital they have the Gospel preached to them by one of the members of the London Mission. Private religious instruction is also given to patients in the different wards. And thus, while the heart of the cold and unfeeling Chinese is softened and opened up by kindness—which he feels to be disinterested, and which acts like spring showers upon plants—the seeds of the Gospel of

Christ are sown upon it, and, it is hoped, in many, very many instances, they may vegetate and produce their fruits in after years when the patients have returned to their homes.

The charitable labours of the medical missionary are not confined to the hospital within the bounds of the foreign settlement. He has also a dispensary in the midst of the crowded city, which he visits on stated days and attends to outdoor patients, many of whom may not be able to come as far as the hospital. Indeed, wherever his labours are required he is to be found ministering to the wants of the sick, and doing all he can to alleviate pain. The following extract from one of Dr. Lockhart's reports will show that the jails are also visited, and give a good illustration of the cold-blooded cruelty of the Chinese government :—

" In the beginning of the summer, attention was called by some of the natives in the city to the fact that there were a number of men who had been severely wounded in the Che-hëen's (or magistrate's) jail; a visit was immediately paid to the place, when it was ascertained that, in a yard which was one of the departments of the inner prison, about fifty pirates, all Canton and Fokien men, had been confined; but that on the morning of the day when it was visited they had tried to break out of prison and were very riotous, on account of some additional hardship that the officers intended to inflict on them, and also because some of the party were to be separated from

L

the rest. The soldiers of the garrison had been called out, who fired several rounds of musketry into the yard and the prisoners' cells, till the rioters were rendered quiet, or at least disabled; when the soldiers rushed in and beat them with wooden poles for some time. After this the whole of the prisoners were loaded with extra manacles, and those who had not been severely wounded were forthwith submitted to the bastinado till they could hardly walk.

" The scene presented in the yard, and the cells around it, was one of perhaps common occurrence in Chinese prisons, but, it is to be hoped, not often seen elsewhere. Four men were killed, and lay at the door in a heap, just as they had been thrown down; one man had compound fracture of the thigh; three had compound fracture of the tibia, the result of gun-shot; others had fractures of the leg and arm. On inquiring from these what had caused their injuries, they said they were occasioned by blows from the poles with which they were attacked by the soldiers after the firing had ceased; several had received severe sword-cuts, and others had bullet-wounds in various parts of the body and limbs. About twenty were wounded in the affray; the remainder had the skin of their backs, thighs, and legs beaten off by the bastinado; and the moans and cries that proceeded from all parts of the yard were heartrending. The men that had the compound fractures had not only chains on their hands, and bars of wood chained to their feet, but also on one knee a band or oval hoop of iron, placed over the knee, while the leg was flexed on the thigh, and to confine this in its place a rod of iron was thrust through the middle of the hoop at the ham and locked, so that it could not be removed; the knee was thus kept forcibly bent, causing much agony to the wretched prisoners.

" It was then late in the afternoon, and almost dark; all that could be done, however, was effected as speedily as possible; bullets cut out, wounds dressed, fractured limbs bound up and put in position, as far as time and circumstances would allow; and the next day, bandages, splints, ointment, and whatever else was wanted, were taken and applied to the sufferers. Attempts were made, by application to the officers, to induce them to take off the hoops and chains from the fractured limbs, but the application was refused; and at a later period, when the request was more urgently pressed, the officers said that they would not do it, and that they hoped the men would all die, and the sooner the better; also that they wished no help or relief to be afforded to them.

" However, the pirates themselves were very thankful for the relief they experienced, and they assisted and nursed one another very kindly. The way in which orders were given, and relief administered, in the cells, was a curious process; one of the occupants was an intelligent young man, and spoke English very well; he had been beaten on the thighs, and had logs of wood chained to his legs, so that he could not walk ; this man was put on the back of another, who had chains only on his hands, and was thus carried about from cell to cell to receive instructions, and give directions as to what was to be done in the intervals of the visits.   The bodies of the four dead men remained in an outer cell for more than a week, but a mass of ice was thrown upon them to keep them from putrefaction to some extent, until the affair had been examined into, and reported to the superior officers.   One or two more died, and in process of time the rest recovered of their wounds, after rather a large consumption of plasters and bandages. When the city was afterwards taken by the Triads, the young man above alluded to was found to be in command of a detachment of men, and in charge of the Little East gate ; and being dressed up in velvet and satin, presented a very different appearance from what he had done when loaded with chains and covered with rags in the prison."

The Chinese as a people are cold and indifferent to religion of any kind : humanly speaking, nothing less than a miracle will convert them to Christianity.   Missionaries have been in China for many years ; larger numbers have been sent out from England and America since the last war, when the country was partially opened up to foreigners.   These men have been labouring there, I believe, in most instances, most conscientiously, and with an ardour and single-mindedness of pur-

pose which is worthy of all praise, and yet what
is the result? How few have "believed their
report"! The Chinese as a nation are jealous,
selfish, and eminently conceited; it is therefore
difficult to convince such minds that nations many
thousand miles distant will subscribe large sums
of money merely for their religious benefit, or that
men are to be found who will leave friends and
home with no other views than to convert them
from heathenism to Christianity. And hence it
would seem that the labours of the medical missionary societies would prove a powerful auxiliary
in aiding the spread of the Gospel amongst such
a people. All nations, even the most cold and
selfish, have some kindly feelings in their nature
capable of being aroused and acted upon. If anything will warm such feelings in the minds of the
Chinese, the labour of the medical missionary is
well calculated to do so. The blind receive their
sight, the lame are enabled to walk, and the
wounded are cured. And when the better feelings
of the man are thus expanded into something like
gratitude, his prejudices are more likely to give
way, and thus his mind may become softened and
more apt to receive religious impressions.

Having been led to make these remarks upon
the value of medical missions, I will now return
to the Shanghae rebellion. For many months the
army of the Imperialists seemed to make no impression upon the rebel bands who held the city.
Battles, such as has been described, were fought

every few days, the success, such as it was, being
sometimes on the one side and sometimes on the
other. Mines were dug and sprung, breaches were
made in the walls and as quickly repaired, and it
seemed as if the siege was likely to last for an indefinite period of time. But public opinion began to
waver, and then changed altogether ; it was found
out at last that the bands who had taken and held
possession of the city were not patriots fighting
for their country's good, but merely a set of land-
pirates, whose brethren we had been taking means
to destroy on the high seas. The commanders of
the French ships of war in the port, who had
never viewed them with a friendly eye, and who
had had some disputes with them on various occasions, now took a decided part against them and
in favour of the Imperialists. A breach was made
in the city wall and the rebels attacked in their
stronghold, which they defended with much skill,
and eventually forced the French to retreat after
having lost some of the best and bravest of their
officers.

But this trifling success was unavailing. The
imperial government, having frequently remonstrated with the foreign consuls against their settlement being used as a communication with the city,
was at length listened to, and *allowed* to build a
high wall in order that this connexion might be
cut off. The insurgents thus hemmed in on all
sides and likely to be eventually starved, bom-
barded by the French ships, having to repulse the

attacks of the Imperialists, and deserted by nearly all their friends, at length came to the determination to evacuate.

When the rebels evacuated the city, the *brave* Imperialists entered it and immediately set it on fire in various places.   The evening on which this took place was perfectly calm, and the scene must have been one of the grandest and at the same time one of the most painful ever beheld.   The fire was first seen running along the ramparts and destroying tent after tent—these having been occupied only a few hours before by the insurgents. Then the city was observed to have been set fire to in several places, and, owing to the construction of the houses (they are built chiefly with pine and bricks), the fire spread with fearful rapidity.   The whole city, about three miles in circumference, appeared to be in flames—guilty and innocent were perishing together, thousands were rendered houseless and driven from their homes, and where to go they knew not.   In the midst of all this terror and confusion the imperial soldiers were plundering what had been left by the rebels, which I believe was not very much, and hunting down the unfortunate, in order to cut their heads off and claim the promised reward.   Some of the latter, as a last resource, hid themselves in coffins, hoping thus to escape their ruthless pursuers. Many of them were discovered and slain, and then the soldiers used this as a pretence for breaking open the coffins of the dead, in order to get the money or gold and silver ornaments which are often deposited with the bodies after death. Of all that band of marauders who fled from Shanghae that night, but few remained either to fight or to steal. The numerous heads which were afterwards seen on poles, and trees, and walls, the fearful stench which poisoned the air for many weeks during the hot weather which followed, told a sickening tale of crime and blood. The bravery displayed by them on many occasions showed plainly of what stuff the Chinese are made, and what as a nation China may yet become, and made one regret it had not been shown in a better cause.

When I arrived at Shanghae, a few days after the evacuation, I found fully one-third of this ancient city in ruins. The poor inhabitants were wandering about looking out for the spots where their dwellings formerly stood, and in many instances marking their boundaries with a few stones or bricks. Most of them seemed completely heartbroken and paralysed, and were taking no steps to rebuild their former homes. The gardens and nurseries in the city and suburbs have necessarily suffered severely. It was quite melancholy to look into many of them. One just outside the north gate, which furnished me with some of my finest plants when I was collecting for the Horticultural Society of London, was completely destroyed. A fine *Glycine sinensis*, which formerly covered a large trellis, was now half-buried in ruins, but still putting forth its long racemes of blue flowers half-covered with the broken tiles and bricks, and told in mournful accents its tale of peaceful times. A noble tree of the carnation-flowered peach, which in former years used to be loaded with rose, white, and striped blossoms, and admired by all who saw it, had been cut down for firewood, and the stump alone remained to tell where it grew. Hundreds of pot-plants were huddled together, broken, and destroyed. The little house where the gardeners used to live was levelled with the ground; and the old lady, the proprietor whom I had known for some years, and who managed the concern after her husband's death, was gone—no one knew where. In the city many places were in the same condition. A great portion of the celebrated tea-gardens was destroyed. Here there was one little garden situated in front of a gentleman's house and surrounded with high walls. In addition to numerous plants in pots, it contained two pretty specimens of *Sophora japonica pendula*, grafted high, as we see the weeping-ash in England, and presenting an appearance not unlike it in the distance. The house and high walls were in ruins, and the trees, which had somehow escaped, could now be seen a long way off, budding and becoming green amidst this scene of desolation. The face of the country for some miles from the city walls was also entirely changed. Formerly it had a rich appearance, and was studded all over with clumps of trees. All had been cut down for firewood for the imperial army. Clumps of *Cryptomeria japonica, Juniperus sphærica*, and bamboos had entirely disappeared. The celebrated peach-gardens near the south and west gates of the city, which at this time of year (April) used to be one sheet of bloom, had now nothing remaining except the stumps of the trees. What I regretted as much as anything was some noble specimens of *Salisburia adiantifolia*—the "Ging-ko" of the Japanese. This is apparently indigenous to this part of China, and attains to a very large size; indeed, it is by far the largest tree in the district. Its fruit, which at first sight has somewhat the appearance of the almond, is much esteemed by the Chinese, and consequently abundant in the markets.

Such are some of the effects of rebellion in a half-civilised country like China. The picture which I have endeavoured to paint applies, unfortunately, to many other parts of the country besides Shanghae. Hundreds of towns and villages were in the same state; their inhabitants had been driven from their homes by fire and sword, the innocent in many instances perished with the guilty, and even women and children were not spared. One party was just as bad as the other, and the "tender mercies" of both "were cruel." Amongst foreigners residing in this country enthusiasm had generally given way to common sense, and they had now no hopes of the Christian character of the Canton or Shanghae rebellion ; indeed there has ever been strong proof that thieves or pirates would be a much more appropriate name to apply to the rebels in these towns than the sacred one of Christian.   Let us hope for better things as regards the Nanking insurgents and their leader Tai-ping-wang, when we know them as intimately as we have known their countryman at Shanghae and Canton.

Although the picture which I have given of some parts of China is a melancholy one, it must not be supposed to represent the general condition of the empire. China is a large country, and those parts disturbed by rebellion bear but a small proportion to the remainder, which is perfectly undisturbed.   Indeed, even a mile or two away from a place in the hands of the rebels we find the country quiet and the husbandman engaged in cultivating his land. Thus it is that notwithstanding all these disturbances we have no lack of tea, silk, and the other articles which form the bulk of our exports.

CHAPTER VIII.

Return to the tea-districts of Chekiang — Mode of making collections of seeds amongst Chinese peasantry — Messengers sent to Moo-yuen and Ping-shuy — Ping-shuy teas — Agricultural and Horticultural Society of India — Varnish-tree — Wax-insect tree — Soap-tree — Death and funeral of a Buddhist priest — New blue dye — Its cultivation and manufacture — " Green indigo " — Its introduction to India and Europe.

THE events recorded in the last chapter spread themselves over more than a year of time, namely, from the autumn of 1853 to the spring of 1855, and their relation, in order to present them in a connected form, has carried me somewhat in advance of my narrative. It is now necessary to go back to the beginning of October, 1853. Having finished my work in Shanghae, I took my departure for the tea-districts in Chekiang in order to make collections of seeds and plants for the government plantations in the Himalaya.

When I arrived amongst the tea-hills in that province, I found the seeds of the tea-plant just ripe, and all my old friends busily employed in collecting them in anticipation of my arrival. In my earlier experience with the Chinese things were much more difficult than they were now. Then the country-people used to fly from me whenever I appeared amongst them, and I was often obliged to gather the seeds myself, and with my own people. Now we were better acquainted, and my only difficulty was to prevent them from bringing me too many.

Having established myself in my old quarters in the temple of Tein-tung, I went to work in Chinese style. It was given out by my people and the priests that I had arrived for the purpose of making purchases of tea-seeds, that I wanted five or six hundred catty, and would continue to purchase all that were brought to me, providing they were of good quality, until that quantity was made up. On the day following this announcement, and for many days afterwards, the people began to flock to the temple in great numbers, for the purpose of selling their tea-seeds. The venders were chiefly old men, women, and children—a class who could do light work, such as gathering tea-seeds, although not heavy field-labour. My time was fully occupied from daylight until dark in examining, settling the price according to quality, and weighing the seeds. In this labour I was greatly assisted by my good friend the priest to whom I have already alluded, and who, having a small tea-plantation himself, was an excellent judge of the seed. Many were the little disputes we had as to quality and price, which were always carried on with the most perfect good-humour, and generally referred to the priest for arbitration. He was much respected by the natives themselves, and his word was considered as satisfactory and final. It was a pleasing

sight to observe those happy smiles on their countenances when they had sold their little stock and
put the strings of cash into their baskets. In a
few days I had completed the quantity which
I intended to export from this part of the country.

While making collections in this district I had
despatched two of my own people on whom I could
depend to the districts of Moo-yuen and Ping-shuy,
in order to bring me seeds from those places. Moo-
yuen is in the Hwuy-chow country, and is well
known for producing the finest green teas exported
to Europe and America. Ping-shuy is in the province of Chekiang, not very far from the old city
of Shao-shing-foo, which will be found noticed in
my 'Journey to the Tea Countries.' The Ping-
shuy district is becoming a place of considerable
importance—the teas are beautifully made there;
and as it is much nearer to Shanghae than Hwuy-
chow, the land-carriage is considerably less in
amount. Indeed, the whole of these Chekiang tea-
districts have received great advantages from the
opening of Shanghae to foreign trade; their teas
have advanced in price, and large quantities of
them are made up annually to suit the foreign
taste, and sent to that port for sale.

Both my messengers returned in due time, and
had most fully accomplished the objects for which
they were sent. But our collections did not consist of tea-seeds only. Large quantities of the
chesnuts I have alluded to in Chapter III. were
procured at this time in the vicinity of Tse-kee;

seeds of the hemp-palm, valuable on account of the fibre which it yields, and *Cryptomeria japonica,*

Rain Cloak.   Hemp Palm.

a fine timber-tree, were obtained in large quantities on the hills near Tein-tung; and one of my messengers succeeded in bringing me a good supply of the seeds of the funereal cypress from Hwuy-chow.   All these and many other useful and ornamental trees and shrubs are now flourishing on the slopes of the Himalaya, in the north-west provinces of India.

Shortly after my arrival in China the council of the Agricultural and Horticultural Society of India applied to the government of Bengal for any assistance I could render them in the way of sending the society seeds and plants of useful and

ornamental trees and shrubs which were likely
to be of value in India. The request of the
society was immediately complied with, and I was
directed to afford any assistance which might be in
my power. My attention was directed by the
society to the Chinese varnish-tree,* the wax-insect
tree,† the soap-bean tree,‡ the various trees valuable
for their fruit or timber, and ornamental plants;
but above all to the green-indigo (so called),§
which yielded a dye which was at that time
attracting much attention in France.

The tree which yields the Chinese varnish is a
species of Rhus, which, although producing an
article of great value, is extremely dangerous.
The varnish is largely used in the country for
giving a fine polish to tables and chairs used in
the houses of the wealthy. The beautiful lacquer-
ware so extensively exported from Canton to
foreign countries, and which is so well known and
justly admired, is produced by this tree. It has
the valuable property of being less liable than
French-polish to be injured by a heated vessel
which may be placed upon it; but it is very
poisonous, and requires to be handled with
great care by the workmen who use it. Indeed, after furniture is dry, it is very unsafe
for certain constitutions until it has been in use
for some time, and the smell entirely gone. A
friend of mine, Mr. Jones, American consul at

---

* Rhus sp.　　　† Fraxinus sp.　　　‡ Cæsalpinia sp.
§ Rhamnus sp.

Foo-chow-foo, used some furniture which had been
lacquered some time and was apparently quite dry,
and yet was very ill for a long time from its
effects ; so ill that he thought he should be obliged
to leave the country and go home.   And this is no
solitary instance, for I have known several persons
suffer most severely from the same cause.

The wax-insect tree is no doubt a species of ash
(fraxinus).   It grows abundantly on the banks of

Wax Tree.

ponds and canals in the province of Chekiang ; and
a small quantity of wax is also produced in this

M

province. I was indebted to Dr. McCartee, of Ningpo, for some beautiful specimens of the fresh insect upon the branches of this tree. This insect has been named *coccus pela* by Mr. Westwood. When fully developed on the trees it has a most remarkable appearance; they seem as if covered with flakes of snow. The wax is an article of great value in Chinese commerce, and a small portion is exported.

The fleshy pods of the *cæsalpinia* are largely used as soap in all parts of China, and may be bought in every market-town.

All these trees and many others have been introduced to India through the Agricultural and Horticultural Society, and some of them distributed largely amongst its members. The green-indigo (so called) has also been discovered and introduced both to England and to India.

During my sojourn in the old temple of Tein-tung, which I have already said was my head-quarters whilst at work amongst these hills, I witnessed some ceremonies connected with the death and funeral of a Buddhist priest who lived next door to where I was located, which appeared so curious and full of interest at the time that I was induced to give a description of it in my journal.

There are two orders of the priesthood in a large Buddhist monastery. The first and most numerous is that whose members assemble daily in the largest hall or temple, and perform a sort of cathedral service, which I have given a description of in my

'Journey to the Tea Countries.' In a retired spot amongst some lofty trees on the hill-side near Tein-tung the traveller may see an unmeaning-looking brick building some ten feet high and hollow inside. The dome of this building is blacked with smoke, as if it was not unusual to light fires inside. On inquiry he will find that in this place the bodies of the priests just mentioned are burned after death. A little further on, on the same hill-side, there is a neat-looking temple, not different in external appearance from the numerous structures of this description seen all over these hills, but on going inside several closed white-washed urns are met with, and these contain the ashes of the priests. I never had an opportunity of witnessing the ceremony of burning these bodies; but my old friend the priest with whom I was staying confessed that the sight was any-thing but pleasing.

The second order of the priesthood—my landlord was one of them—occupy neat little houses ad-joining the large halls, where they generally seem to lead a lazy kind of life, and have only the private devotions of their little temple to attend to; that is, they are not required to attend the service in the large hall. Their bodies are not burned after death like the former, but are conveyed to the most lovely spots on the sides of the hills— spots on their own little farms which they had selected for themselves during their lifetime. One of this order died during this autumn when I was located in the monastery, and the ceremonies connected with his wake and funeral I shall now endeavour to describe :—

A young priest—a mere boy—came running breathless one morning into the house where I was staying, and called out to my host, " Come with me, make haste, for Tang-a is dying." We hastened to the adjoining house, which was the abode of the sick man, but found that the king of terrors had been before us, and the priest was dead. By this time about a dozen persons were collected, who were all gazing intently on the countenance of the dead man. After allowing a few minutes to elapse, orders were given to have the body washed and dressed, and removed from the bed to a small room with an open front, which was situated on the opposite side of the little court. Mosquito curtains were then hung round the bed on which the body was placed, a lamp and some candles were lighted, as well as some sticks of incense, and these were kept burning day and night. For three days the body lay in state, during which time, at stated intervals, four or five priests decked in yellow robes chanted their peculiar service. On the third day I was told that the coffin was ready, and, on expressing a wish to see it, was led into an adjoining temple. " Are there two priests dead ?" said I, on observing another coffin in the same place. " No," said one, " but that second coffin belongs to the priest who lived with deceased, and it will remain here until it is needed."

On the evening of this day, when I returned from my labours amongst the hills, I called in again to see what was going on, and now a very different scene presented itself. And here I must endeavour to describe the form of the premises in order that this scene may be better understood. The little house or temple consisted of a centre and two wings, the wings being built at right angles with the centre and forming with it three sides of a square : a high wall connected the two wings, and so a little court or Chinese garden was formed, very small in extent. A square table was placed inside the central hall or temple, one in front of it, and one in front of each of the two wings. Each of these tables was covered with good things—such as rice, vegetables, fruits, cakes, and other delicacies, all the produce of the vegetable kingdom, and intended as a feast for Buddha, whom these people worship. This offering differed from others which I had often seen in the public streets and in private houses, in having no animal food in any of the dishes. The Buddhist priesthood profess an abhorrence of taking away animal life or of eating animal food, and hence no food of the kind was observed on any of the tables now before me. On two strings which were hung diagonally across the court, from the central temple to each end of the front wall, were suspended numerous small paper dresses cut in Chinese fashion, and on the ground were large quantities of paper made up in the form and painted the colour of the

ingots of Sycee silver common in circulation. The
clothes and silver were intended as an offering to
Buddha—certainly a cheap way of giving away
valuable presents. A rude painting of Buddha
was hung up in the centre of the court, in front of
which incense was burning,—and these with many
other objects of minor note completed the picture
which was presented to my view. "Is not this
very fine?" said the priest to me; "have you any
exhibitions of this kind in your country? You
must pay a visit in the evening, when all will be
lighted up with candles, and when the scene will
be more grand and imposing." I promised to
return in the evening, and took my leave.

About eight o'clock at night an old priest came
to inform me that all was lighted up, that the
ceremonies were about to begin, and kindly asked
me to accompany him. On our entrance the
whole court was blazing with the light of many
candles, the air was filled with incense, and the
scene altogether had an extraordinary and imposing
effect. A priest dressed in a rich scarlet robe, and
having a sort of star-shaped crown on his head,
with four others of an inferior order, were marching up and down the court, and bowing lowly
before the images of the gods. At last they
entered the central hall, and took their seats at
two tables. The high-priest, if I may call him so,
occupied the head of the room, and had his chair
and table placed on a higher level than the others,
who were exactly in front of him. A servant now

placed a cup of tea before each of them, and the service began. The high-priest uttered a few sentences in a half-singing tone, making at the same time a great many motions with his fingers as he placed and replaced a number of grains of rice on the table before him. Two little boys, dressed in deep mourning (white), were engaged in prostrating themselves many times before the table at which the high-priest sat; and, as a singular contrast to all this seeming devotion, a number of Chinese were sitting smoking on each side, and looking on as if this was a play or some other kind of like amusement. The other priests had now joined in the chant, which was sometimes slow, and at other times quick and loud, but generally in a melancholy tone, like all Chinese music.

A priest who was sitting at my elbow now whispered in my ear that Buddha himself was about to appear. "You will not see him, nor shall I, nor any one in the place except the high-priest, who is clothed in the scarlet robe, and has a star-shaped crown on his head — he will see him." Some one outside now fired three rockets, and at once every sound was hushed; one might have heard a pin drop on the ground; and the priest at my elbow whispered — "Buddha comes." — "Prostrate yourselves: ah! pull your caps off," said one to the young priests in white, already 'noticed. The boys immediately took off their little white caps, and bent lowly on the straw cushions placed in front of the various altars, and

knocked their heads many times on the ground.
At this particular moment the whole scene was
one of the strangest it had ever been my lot to
witness, and, although I knew it was nothing else
than delusion and idolatry, I must confess it produced an almost superstitious effect on my feelings.
" And is Buddha now here in the midst of us ? "
I asked the gentleman at my elbow. " Yes, he
is," he said ; " the high-priest sees him, although
he is not visible to any one besides." Things
remained in this state for a minute or two, and
then the leader of the ceremonies commenced once
more to chant in that drawling tone I have already noticed, to make various gyrations with his
hands, placing and replacing the rice-grains, and
the others joined in as before.   My old friend the
priest, who had brought me in to see these ceremonies, now presented himself and told me I had
seen all that was worth seeing, that the services
were nearly over, and that it was very late and
time to go home.   On our way to our quarters he
informed me the funeral would take place early
next morning, just before sunrise, and that if
I wished to attend he would call me at the proper
time.

Early in the twilight of next morning, and just
before the sun's rays had tinged the peaks of the
highest mountains, I was awakened by the loud
report of fireworks.   Dressing hastily, I hurried
down to the house where the scene of the preceding evening had been acted, and found myself

among the last of the sorrowful procession. Looking into the court and hall, I found that the
sacrifices had been entirely removed, the tables
were bare, not a morsel of any kind remained, and
it seemed as if the gods had been satisfied with
their repast. The silver ingots, too, and the numerous gaudily-painted dresses which had been presented as an offering, were smouldering in a corner
of the court, having been consumed by holy fire.

As the funeral procession proceeded slowly down,
inside the covered pathway adjoining the temple,
the large bell tolled in slow and measured tones,
rockets were fired now and then, and numerous
priests joined in as we went along. Having
reached the last temple of the range, the body was
deposited on two stools in front of one of the huge
images, and, China-like, before proceeding further,
all went home to breakfast. This important business finished, the assembly met again in the temple,
and performed a short service, while the coolies
were busily employed in adjusting the ropes by
which they carried the coffin. All being ready,
two men went outside the temple and fired three
rockets, and then the procession started. First
went two boys, carrying small flags on bamboo
poles, then came two men beating brass gongs,
and then came the chief mourner, dressed in white,
and carrying on a small table two candles which
were burning, some incense, and the monumental
tablet. After the chief mourner came the coffin,
followed by the young priests of the house to which

the deceased belonged, also clad in white, then the
servants and undertaker, and last of all a long
train of priests.

I stood on one side of the lake, in front of the
temple, in order to get a good view of the procession as it winded round the other. It was a
beautiful October morning; the sun was now
peeping over the eastern mountains behind the
monastery and shedding a flood of light on water,
shrubs, and trees, while every leaf sparkled with
drops of dew. In such a scene this long and striking procession had a most imposing effect. The
boys with their flags, the chief mourner moving
slowly along with his candles burning in the clear
daylight, the long line of priests with their shaven
heads and flowing garments, the lake in front, and
the hills covered with trees and brushwood behind, were at once presented to my view. As we
passed a bridge, a little way from the temple, a
man belonging to the family of the deceased, and
who carried a basket containing *cash*—a Chinese
coin—presented a number of the followers with
a small sum, which they received with apparent
reluctance. Most of the priests followed the bier
but a short distance from the temple; but the
chief mourner, the intimate friends, and servants,
with a band of music, followed the body to its last
resting-place. The spot selected was a retired and
beautiful one, on the lower side of a richly-wooded
hill. Here, without further ceremonies than the
firing of some rockets, we left the coffin on the

surface of the ground, to be covered with thatch or brickwork at a future opportunity.

The procession, or rather what remained of it, for it was now very small, returned to the temple. As we passed the small villages and cottages on our way the inmates crowded the doors, not to look at the procession, for such things were not unfrequent, but to express their wonder that a foreigner should have taken a part in it. When we arrived at the temple I looked in to see what was going on in the house from which the body had been taken, and in which such a strange scene had been acted the night before. It had been swept out, the tables had been put back into their proper places, two priests were quietly smoking their pipes in the verandah, the cook was preparing the forenoon meal in the back part of the house, and, except that that meal seemed more sumptuous than usual, there was nothing to indicate that a short time previous it had been the house of death. Such is life and death in China—not very unlike in some particulars what it is in other parts of the world.

In this part of the Chekiang province, and also amongst the Fung-hwa mountains to the westward of Ningpo, there are large quantities of a blue dye produced, which is in fact the indigo of this part of the country. Those who have read my 'Wanderings in China,' published in 1846, may remember the account given there of a valuable kind of indigo, made from a species of woad (*Isatis indigotica*) which is cultivated extensively in the level country a few miles to the westward of Shanghae. The kind which attracted my attention in Chekiang is equally valuable, if not more so. It is made from a species of *ruellia*, which, until it gets a better name, may be called *Ruellia indigotica.* It is a curious circumstance that the same plant, apparently, has lately been discovered in the Assam country in India, where it is also cultivated for the blue dye it affords. I had an opportunity of examining it in the garden of the Agricultural and Horticultural Society at Calcutta, by whom it had been introduced, and where it was standing alongside of the Chinese kind, to which it certainly bears a most striking resemblance : the point of identity will easily be determined when the plants come into flower. Strange it will be if it is ultimately found that this species, which produces a dye unknown to commerce, is in cultivation all the way across from the eastern shores of China to the borders of Bengal, and this is far from being improbable.

This ruellia seems to be easily cultivated; it grows most luxuriantly, and is no doubt very productive. Having evidently been found indigenous a little farther to the south, in a warmer latitude, it is not hardy in the province of Chekiang any more than cotton is about Shanghae ; but nevertheless it succeeds admirably as a summer crop. It is planted in the end of April or beginning of May, after the spring frosts are over, and is cleared from the ground in October before those of autumn make their appearance. During this period it attains a height of a foot or a foot and a half, becomes very bushy, and is densely covered with large green leaves. It is cut down before any flowers are formed.

The Chinese method of preserving plants for next year's crop is most ingenious and well worth notice. Being somewhat tender, as I have already remarked, the roots which are left in the ground after the gathering season are all destroyed by the first frosts of winter. But the Chinese cultivator does not depend upon these for the crop of the following year, nor does he take them up or cover them in any way. They have done their duty for one year, and are now left to their fate.

Cuttings are found to be much more vigorous and productive than the old roots, and to the formation and preservation of these cuttings the Chinese cultivator directs his attention. When the stems are cut down for the manufacture of indigo, a sufficient quantity have their leaves stripped off, and are afterwards taken into a house or shed to be properly prepared. The leaves thus stripped from the cuttings are thrown into the tanks with the other stems and leaves, so that nothing is lost except what is actually required for the purposes of propagation. The stems are now tied up firmly in large bundles, each containing upwards of 1000, and the ends of each bundle are cut across, so as to leave them perfectly neat and even both at top and bottom. These bundles are each about a foot long, and, of course, nearly round. Having been thus prepared, they are carried to a dry shed or outhouse, where, in some snug corner, they are packed closely and firmly together, and banked round with very dry loam. A portion of the dry soil is also shaken in between the bundles; and this being done, the operation is complete. Should the winter prove unusually severe, a little dry straw or litter is thrown over the surface of the cuttings, but nothing else is required. During the winter months the cuttings remain green and plump ; and, although no leaves are produced, a few roots are generally found formed, or in the act of forming, when the winter has passed, and the season for planting has come round. In this state they are taken to the fields and planted. The weather during the planting season is generally showery, as this happens about the change of the monsoon, when the air is charged with moisture. A few days of this warm showery weather is sufficient to establish the new crop, which now goes on growing with luxuriance, and requires little attention during the summer—indeed none, except keeping the land free from weeds.

In the country where this dye is grown there are numerous pits or tanks on the edges of the fields. They are usually circular in form ; and one which I measured was eleven feet in diameter, and two feet in depth. About 400 catties* of

* A Chinese catty is equal to 1⅓ lb.

stems and leaves are thrown into a tank of this size, which is then filled to the brim with clear water. In five days the plant is partially decomposed, and the water has become lightish-green in colour. At this period the whole of the stems and leaves are removed from the tank with a flat-headed broom made of bamboo twigs, an admirable instrument for the purpose. When every particle has been removed, the workmen employed give the water a circular and rapid motion with the brooms just noticed, which is continued for some time. During this part of the operation another man has employed himself in mixing about thirty catties of lime with water, which water has been taken out of the tank for the purpose. This is now thrown into the tank, and the rapid circular motion of the water is kept up for a few minutes longer. When the lime and water have been well mixed in this way the circular motion is allowed to cease. Four men now station themselves round the tank and commence beating the water with bamboo rakes made for this purpose. The beating process is a very gentle one; as it goes on the water gradually changes from a greenish hue to a dingy yellow, while the froth becomes of a beautiful bright blue. During the process the head workman takes a pailful of the liquid out of the tank and beats it rapidly with his hand. Under this operation it changes colour at once, and its value is judged of by the hue it presents. The beating process generally lasts for about half an

hour. At the end of this time the whole of the
surface of the tank is covered with a thick coating
of froth of the most brilliant colours, in which blue
predominates, particularly near the edges.

At this stage, it being desirable to incorporate
the froth with the liquid below it, I witnessed a
most beautiful chemical operation which took me
completely by surprise, and showed how universally
must be the knowledge of the effect of throwing
" oil upon the waters." A very small portion of
cabbage-oil—only a few drops—was thrown on the
surface of the froth, the workmen then stirred and
beat it gently with their flat brooms for a second
or two, and the whole disappeared as if by some
enchanter's wand. And so small a quantity of oil
was necessary for this purpose that even when the
cup had been emptied, and had only the oil that
was necessarily adhering to its edges, it was thrown
into another tank, and produced the desired effect.

The liquid, which is now darker in colour, is
allowed to stand quiet for some hours, until the
colouring matter has sunk to the lower stratum,
when about two-thirds of the surface is drawn off
and thrown away. The remaining third part
is then drawn into a small square tank on a
lower level, which is thatched over with straw,
and here it remains for three or four days. By
this time the colouring matter has separated itself
from the water, which is now entirely drained
off—the dye occupying three or four inches of the
bottom in the form of a thick paste, and of a beau-

tiful blue colour. In this state it is packed in
baskets, and exposed for sale in all the country
towns in this part of China. What its intrinsic
value may be when compared with the indigo
of commerce, I have no means of ascertaining, but
it is largely used in this part of the world, where
blue is the most fashionable colour, judging from
the dresses of the people. And it is possible that
with our knowledge of chemistry a colour of this
kind might be greatly improved. After being
grown and manufactured as I have described,
it is sold at rates varying from 50 to 100 cash
a catty, say from 2*d*. to 4*d*. per lb. Some is sold
as low as 30 cash, but this is very inferior ; the
greater part produced is sold at from 60 to
80 cash a catty, and it must be of a very superior
quality if 100 cash is paid. Like the Shanghae
indigo made from *Isatis indigotica*, it is called
" Tien-ching" by the Chinese. While upon the
subject of Chinese dyes, I shall now give some
account of the " green indigo," which has been
attracting much notice lately both in India and in
Europe.

A portion of cotton cloth obtained in China by
the French manufacturers, being greatly admired
on account of the peculiar green of its dye, was
submitted to the celebrated chemist M. Persoz.
with a request that he would endeavour to ascertain the composition of the green colour. The
following is a translation of his report upon this
subject to the Academy of Sciences :—

N

ON A GREEN COLOURING MATERIAL PRODUCED IN CHINA.

BY MONS. J. PERSOZ.

I HAVE the honour to place before the Academy a specimen of a colouring material used in China as a green dye for textile fibres. With the permission of the Academy I will briefly state how I was led to a knowledge of the existence of this dye.

Mons. Daniel Koechlin-Schouc forwarded to me last autumn a specimen of calico dyed in China, of a rich and very permanent green, with a request that I should endeavour to ascertain the composition of the green colour. Every attempt that I made upon the specimen to detect evidence of the presence of a blue or yellow failed, and I was led to the conviction, by isolating the colouring principle, that the green was produced by a dyeing material of a peculiar nature and *sui generis*. It further was evident,—

1st. That the colouring matter was an organic product of vegetable origin;

2nd. That the fabric on which it was fixed was charged with a strong dose of alum and a little oxide of iron and lime, bodies the presence of which necessarily implied that mordants had been used in dyeing the calico.

These results were so positive, and at the same time so opposed, not only to everything known in Europe regarding the composition of green colour, but also to all that is recorded by writers regarding the dyeing processes employed in China for the production of green, that I was induced to go into a more detailed investigation of the subject; and about the end of last November I applied to Mr. Forbes, the American consul at Canton, for some of this valuable material. I am indebted to his kindness for a specimen weighing about one gramme (15½ grains).

The substance is met with in thin plates, of a blue

colour, having a strong analogy with that of Java indigo, but of a finer cake, and differing besides from indigo both in its composition and in all its chemical properties. On infusing a small fragment of the substance in water, the liquid speedily became coloured of a deep blue, with a shade of green. After the temperature had been raised to the boiling point, a piece of calico, prepared for printing with mordants of alum and oxide of iron, was dipped in it, and a true dye was the result. The following appearances were observed :—

The portions of the fabric to which alum had been applied showed a deep green, of more or less intensity, according to the strength of the mordant.

The portions charged with both alum and oxide of iron yielded a deep green, with a shade of olive.

The portions charged with oxide of iron alone yielded a deep olive.

The parts of the cloth where no mordant had been applied remained sensibly paler.

The colours thus obtained were treated with all the reagents to which the Chinese calico had in the first instance been subjected, and they behaved in precisely the same manner. From these experiments it may be inferred,—

1st. That the Chinese possess a dye-stuff presenting the physical aspect of indigo, which dies green with mordants of alum and iron.

2nd. That this dye-stuff contains neither indigo nor anything derived from that dyeing principle.

Mons. Legentil, President of the Chamber of Commerce of Paris, having perceived the importance of France being speedily put in possession of this valuable material, with a view to the interests of science and of industry, took the necessary steps several months ago for procuring a suitable quantity with the least possible delay, and, at the same time, to have inquiries made as to its origin and mode of preparation.

N 2

I purpose submitting to the Academy a full account of this new dye as soon as I am enabled to make a more detailed and satisfactory examination of it.*

This matter attracted a good deal of notice both in France and in England, and the officials of both countries stationed in China were written to by their respective governments and desired to get what information they could upon it. But in China it is a difficult matter to obtain correct information upon anything which does not come directly under one's eye; and if the correspondence upon this subject was published, it would, no doubt, exhibit as many amusing blunders as used to be made about the Chinese rice-paper plant in former days. By some the flowers of the Whi-mei (*Sophora japonica*) were sent home as the "green indigo;" but this plant yields a yellow dye, and, even when mixed with blue to make a green, the green is not that kind noticed by the French manufacturers.

From an extensive knowledge of the productions of China, gained during several years of travel, I was not so easily imposed upon as others, but notwithstanding this advantage it was some time before I could be sure that I was "upon the right scent." At last I remembered having seen a peculiar kind of dye cultivated largely some miles to the westward of Hang-chow-foo, and I determined to visit that part of the country again,

---

* Translated from the 'Comptes Rendus de l'Académie des Sciences.' Séance de Lundi, 18 October, 1852.

and examine the dye more minutely. Here I found fields under cultivation with a kind of *Rhamnus* apparently. The Chinese farmer called it " Loh-zah," or " Soh-loh-shoo," and showed me samples of the cloth which had been dyed with it. To my delight these samples corresponded exactly with those sent back from France, one of which was in my possession. But he told me that two kinds were necessary — namely, the variety they cultivated in their fields, and one which grew wild on the hills—in order to produce the dye in question. The former they called the *yellow* kind, and the latter the *white* kind. The dye itself was not extracted by them, they were merely the growers, and therefore I could get no information as to its manufacture. I however secured a good supply of plants and seeds of both kinds, which were afterwards sent to India and England.

My further inquiries on the subject of the manufacture of the " green indigo " were conducted in connexion with Dr. Lockhart and the Rev. J. Edkins, of Shanghae. We found that a considerable portion of this dye was made near a city called Kia-hing-foo, situated a few miles west from Shanghae, and Mr. Edkins procured a bundle of chips there which exhibited the state in which the article is sold in the market. Since I left China I have received the following interesting letter from Dr. Lockhart, which throws much light on the subject. The information was procured by Mr. Edkins, and may therefore be fully relied upon.

"The bark of two kinds of the tree known as the 'green shrub' (Lŭk-chae), one wild, which is called the *white*, and another cultivated, which is called the *yellow*, are used to obtain the dye. The white bark tree grows abundantly in the neighbourhoods of Kea-hing and Ningpo; the yellow is produced at Tsăh-kou-pang, where the dye is manufactured. This place is two or three miles west from Wang-tseen, a market-town situated a little to the south of Kea-hing.

"The two kinds are placed together in iron pans and thoroughly boiled. The residuum is left undisturbed for three days, after which it is placed in large earthenware vessels, and cotton cloth, prepared with lime, is dyed with it several times. After five or six immersions the colouring matter is washed from the cloth with water, and placed in iron pans to be again boiled. It is then taken up on cotton yarn several times in succession, and when absorbed in this way it is next washed off and sprinkled on thin paper. When half dry the paper is pasted on light screens and strongly exposed to the sun. The product is called Lŭk-kaou. In dyeing cotton cloth with it ten parts are mixed with three parts of subcarbonate of potash in boiling water.

"The dye made at Tsăh-kou-pang is not used to dye silk fabrics, because it is only a rough surface which takes it readily. To colour silk with it so much of the material must be used that it will not pay. All cotton fabrics, also grass-cloths, take the colour readily. *The dye does not fade with washing, which gives it a superiority over other greens.*

"It is sent from Kea-hing as far as Shantung. It is also made in the province of Hoonan and at Ningpo, but the dye at these places is said to be of an inferior quality. It has long been used by painters in water-colours, but the application of it to dye cloth was first made only about twenty years ago. If some method could be discovered of applying it to silk fabrics it would become still more useful."

The information obtained by Mr. Edkins on this subject is, no doubt, perfectly correct. It agrees in the most important particulars with what I had gleaned from time to time amongst the Chinese in various parts of the country. The chips he brought with him from Kea-hing were identical with the " Soh-loh," or " Loh-zah " (Rhamnus sp.), which I have already mentioned, and his statement that two varieties of the plant are used to produce the dye agrees with my own observations.

The mode of extracting the dye from the bark or wood (for both seem to be used), as practised by the Chinese, appears to be slow and tedious, but with our superior knowledge of chemistry this might possibly be improved.

From these investigations it would appear that

two colouring principles are necessary to the production of this dye. This, however, will not affect the value of it as a rich and *permanent* green, a quality which has been appreciated by the French manufacturers, and which is also well known to the Chinese.

CHAPTER IX.

Journey to the Snowy Valley and waterfalls — Kong-k'how pagoda —
Adventure with a blind man — Elaborate carving — A new acquaintance, Mr. A-chang — Iron-ore — Mountain stream — Its rafts and
cormorants — The temple of the Snowy Valley — Description of the ،
falls — Our dinner and guests — How Mr. A-chang enjoys it — His
lecture on medical botany and lucky spots for graves — A Buddhist
recluse — Continue our journey across the mountains — Natural
productions — Fine variety of bamboo — Its introduction to India
— Romantic glen — Arrive at our boats and bid adieu to Mr.
A-chang.

DURING my travels in the province of Chekiang
I had frequently heard of some celebrated waterfalls near a place named Seue-tow-sze, or the
" Snowy Valley Temple," which is situated amongst
the mountains some forty or fifty miles to the
south-west of the city of Ningpo. Having not
been in this direction, and being anxious to examine the natural productions of these hills, I
determined on paying a visit to the falls.

Leaving Ningpo about mid-day, with the first
of the flood-tide, a party of English gentlemen and
myself sailed rapidly up the river in some small
country boats which we had hired for the journey.
The country through which we passed, and which
may be called the plain of Ningpo, is perfectly
level, and is not remarkable for any striking feature ; but it is exceedingly fertile and produces

large crops of rice, which is the staple food of
the inhabitants. It is thickly covered with small
towns, villages, and farm-houses; and, like all the
fertile plains in China which have come under my
observation, it teems with population. As our
boatmen went on during the night, we found ourselves next morning at the base of the hills which
bound the plain on the south-west, and in the
district of Fung-hwa. On one of these hills stands
a pagoda named *Kong-k'how-tâ*, which is visible
for many miles, and from which an excellent view
of the low country is obtained. Making our boats
fast to the river-bank, we stepped on shore and
took the first turning which led to the hill on
which the pagoda stands. When we reached the
summit of this hill, which appeared to be about
1000 feet above the level of the sea, we were
rewarded with one of those splendid views which
are, perhaps, more striking in the fertile districts
of China than in any other country. Beneath us,
and stretching to the north and eastward, was the
level plain through which we had passed during
the night. The city of Ningpo occupied its centre,
and it seemed bounded on all sides, except the
north and east, by hills and mountains varying in
height from 1000 to 3000 féet—while far away to
the eastward lay the islands of the Chusan archipelago, studded about in the China Sea. From
this pagoda one can count six or seven others,
each of which marks the position of some ancient
city in the plain, or Buddhist monastery on the

hills.   Towns and villages were visible in whichever direction our eyes were turned, and every
part of the extensive plain appeared to be under
cultivation.   Indeed industry and perseverance
seem to be absolutely necessary in order to make
the ground yield food for such a mass of human
beings.   If the population of the country really
amounts to more than three hundred millions—
and there seems to be no reason to doubt this—
and taking into consideration that a vast extent
of its surface is covered with mountains so barren
that they must ever defy all attempts at cultivation, the valleys and other portions of cultivated
land would require to be fertile indeed, and to
have a nation as industrious and persevering as
the Chinese to make the ground productive.

On ascending the hill, and examining its natural
productions as I went along, I somehow or other
got off the little pathway, and found myself all at
once brought up by a fence which seemed to enclose a small monastic building.   Inside of this
fence there were a number of trees and bushes
which seemed worth looking at, and I was also
desirous of seeing the little temple itself.   Following the fence some way round in the hope of
finding an entrance, the ground began to get very
rugged, and my progress was greatly impeded.
At last I thought there would be no great harm
in jumping over the fence, which I could easily
do, as it was only four or five feet in height.   No
sooner did the idea enter my mind than it was put

into execution, and I was inside the enclosure in
a moment.   A number of watch-dogs, which I
had disturbed, came running towards me, looking
very fierce and making a loud noise.   Chinese
dogs are generally harmless enough and great
cowards, so that in this instance, with a good
stout stick in my hand, I felt no alarm whatever,
but went quietly on with my botanical researches.
In a few seconds an old man, who had been disturbed by the barking of the dogs, came rushing
towards me with a stout bamboo in his hand, and
looking as if he intended to use it.   He was evidently in a towering passion.   " Where had I
come from ? "   " What did I want ? "   " Why had
I come over the fence ? " were questions which he
put loudly and rapidly, interspersing them from
time to time with remarks which were not at all
flattering to my character or intentions.   I knew
that I had done wrong, but the offence seemed
slight comparatively, and one which a stranger
and a foreigner in China might commit without
being called to account for it in this boisterous
manner.   I remonstrated with the old man, commencing in the most polite and approved manner
by asking him " if he had had his breakfast ? "*   I
then told him, when I could get a word in, that I
was no thief, that I had merely come to pay him

* This is a polite mode of salutation amongst the Chinese, not
unlike our own way of making remarks upon the weather.   It is related
of a loving couple who had been separated for many years, that the
first words the wife said to her husband were—" Have you had your
dinner ? "

a visit, and that if he treated me so rudely I would go away again. Matters were in this state, when a young man came running up to the old one, smiling and making a low bow to me at the same time. This new actor on the scene whispered a word or two into the old man's ear, one of which sounded very like *Hong-mou-jin* (foreigner). In the twinkling of an eye his countenance changed, the storm had passed into sunshine, his bamboo was thrown from him, and, clasping the palms of his hands together, he made me a low bow and asked me to forgive him, *for he was blind.* It was indeed so, and hence the whole cause of the strange, and, to me, unaccountable scene in which I had been one of the actors. I was now surprised at my own blindness in not detecting this before; but the whole thing occurred so suddenly that I had little time for observation.

The old man, now all smiles and good-humour, led me round his garden — blind, stone-blind, though he was — and told me the names of his various trees and shrubs, and the uses to which each was applied when it happened that it had any virtues in medicine, or if it " was good for food." I was then led into his house, where I was invited to partake of the usual beverage — tea. Remaining for a few minutes to accept his hospitality, I bade him adieu, and joined my companions on the top of the hill.

After inspecting the pagoda we proceeded onwards in our boats to a place called Too-poo-dow,

which is a few miles further up the river and as
far as it is navigable for boats. We remained here
for the night, and made preparations for a land-
journey to the Snowy Valley, which we determined
to take on the following day. Early next morning,
while breakfast was getting ready, we went to see
a pretty, small temple called the Sieu-Wang-Meou,
which the people told us was well worth visiting.
This temple is finely situated on a small hill,
having rich woods behind and the river winding
past in front,—but as a building it is chiefly remarkable for a most elaborately carved stone altar
—the finest specimen of the kind which I have
met with in China. While engaged in examining
this curious work of Chinese art, a respectable-
looking old man came running breathless into the
temple and introduced himself as Mr. A-chang,
and told us he was a mandarin or small government officer connected with the temple. A slight
glance at his features told us he was no common
man. He was most loquacious and particularly
civil and obliging ; he went all over the edifice
with us, explaining, or endeavouring to explain,
the elaborate carving of the altar and the various
rude pictures which covered the walls. Having a
long journey before us, we had little time to spare,
and were, therefore, obliged to take a hurried
leave of our obliging friend, who told us he would
pay us a visit at our boats before we started for
the Falls. We had just finished breakfast, when
to our surprise the old gentleman presented him-

self, dressed, and evidently prepared for a journey.
"Ah!" said he, "I told you I would see you
before you started, and I have made up my mind
to go with you and show you the road." As he
seemed a most amusing character, and, moreover,
was most useful in enabling us to make arrangements with coolies and chair-bearers, we made no
objection to his joining our party. And we had
no reason to regret the circumstance, for he was
invaluable as a guide and afforded a rich fund of
amusement. Our coolies being at last engaged
and loaded with some few necessaries, and our
mountain-chairs all ready, we despatched our boats
to another part of the country—a place called
Ning-kang-jou, some miles further west and on
another branch of the river.

About twenty or twenty-five miles south-west
from Too-poo-dow there is a beautiful mountain-
pass called by the natives Yang-ling. Here, in
addition to the common trees of these mountains, the
funereal cypress grows in great abundance, and
forms a striking feature in the landscape. This
part of the country is said by the Rev. Dr. Medhurst
to be rich in iron-ore. At a place called Sha-k'he
there is an iron-foundry. "The furnace for melting
the iron was about five feet high and three feet in
diameter, filled to the brim with charcoal and iron-
ore. The blast was formed by a rude box-bellows,
and at the time we arrived the whole was in a
state of operation. We asked them from whence
they obtained their iron-ore, and they pointed to

the adjoining stream, from the bottom of which
they obtained large quantities of black sand, which
was for the most part iron. Having melted it in
this furnace, and formed cakes of raw iron, about
a foot square and an inch thick, they then brought
it to the forge, and reduced it to the state of
wrought iron, in blocks four inches long by two
wide and one thick. This they carried to the
market and sold." *

From Too-poo-dow to the Snowy Valley the distance is about nine or ten miles. Headed by our
mandarin friend, and surrounded by hundreds of
the natives of both sexes, old and young, we
started on our journey. The road, which was a
narrow footpath, led us up the valley and every
now and then we approached the banks of the
stream, which was now quite narrow, shallow, and
in some places very rapid. Although no longer
navigated by boats, it was still made to serve the
purpose of the industrious inhabitants in a number
of other ways. Small rafts, made by lashing a
few bamboo poles together, were plying about in
all directions, bringing the productions of the hills
down to Too-poo-dow, where they could be put
into boats and so conveyed onwards to the lowland
towns for sale. Large quantities of basket-tea,
liquid indigo, paper, mats, wood, and such-like
hill productions were observed coming down the
river in this way. Fish seemed most abundant in
the little stream ; and as it was now far beyond the

* Rev. Dr. Medhurst, in N. China Herald.

influence of tides and clear as crystal, my old
friends, the fishing cormorants, were employed in
catching large fish for their masters and small
ones for themselves.

The valley through which we passed, although
in many places very sandy from the effects of the
swelling of mountain-streams, was yet generally
rich and fertile. On the road, at stated distances
apart, were covered resting-places for travellers,
where shelter from a storm or shade from the
noonday sun might be had by rich or by poor.
Little villages and farm - houses were observed
clustered about in various directions, and the labourers who were at work in the fields seemed
happy and unoppressed. Looking upon a quiet
scene like this, one could scarcely believe that a
civil war was raging in the country, not a greater
distance off than 100 miles, where acts of savage
cruelty were daily perpetrated which made one's
blood run cold. Yet such was the fact.

After winding up the valley for about six miles
we came to the foot of a mountain-pass, and began
gradually to ascend. As we reached a higher
elevation, the scenery became more varied in appearance than it had been in the plain, and very
beautiful. We were surrounded by hills and
mountains of every conceivable form,—some were
peaked, precipitous, and barren, while others
sloped gently upwards, and were covered densely
with pines and brushwood. Far away down in the
valley below us, the little stream, at whose source

we had now arrived, was seen winding its way
amongst the hills, and hastening onwards to swell
the noble river which flows past the city of
Ningpo.

When we arrived at the top of the pass we found
ourselves at the entrance of the Snowy Valley,
which lay a little beyond, and nearly at the same
elevation, estimated at about 2000 feet above the
level of the sea. This valley is surrounded on all
sides by mountains. At one point is the pass
which I have just noticed, and at another is an
opening for a small mountain-stream, which, as it
leaves the valley, falls over a precipice of rocks
into a glen some three or four hundred feet below,
and forms the noble falls we had come to see. The
temple of the Snowy Valley, an old and dilapidated
Buddhist building, occupies the centre or upper
end of the valley, and to that we proceeded in
order to procure quarters for the night for ourselves and our coolies. Here we found our old
Chinese friend ready to receive us, and, with the
priests of the monastery, gave us a cordial and
hearty welcome. It was now late in the afternoon,
within an hour of sunset; but as our baggage had
not arrived, we determined to go out and visit the
upper part of the falls, reserving the lower or
glen view until the following morning. To our
surprise, Mr. A-chang—who had walked all the
way, and who we supposed must be very tired—
intimated his intention of accompanying us. We
therefore set out with him as our guide, and in a

few minutes we reached the edge of the valley and heard the noise of the falls. As we followed our guide along a small path, through trees and brushwood, we were scarcely prepared for the view which was about to be presented to our eyes. All at once we arrived at the edge of a precipice, which made us quite giddy as we looked over it. The water rolled out of the valley over the precipice, and long before it reached the bottom it was converted into showers of spray. Far below us was a deep and narrow glen, through which the little stream was quietly meandering after leaving the falls. As we skirted the mountains on the west side of the Snowy Valley we found our progress every now and then arrested by perpendicular rocks such as I have just noticed; and during the rainy season there are several other falls, which, our guide informed us, were not much inferior in beauty to that which we had just visited.

As it was now nearly dark, and rather dangerous work travelling amongst such scenery, we retraced our steps to the old monastery. Here we found our coolies had arrived with our beds and other necessaries, and the cook was busy preparing dinner. When our meal was ready we requested Mr. A-chang to honour us with his company, and all sat down with a full determination to do justice to the viands before us, and for which the long journey and fresh air of the mountains had made us fully prepared. A-chang seemed to relish the dinner—English though it

was—as much as any of us. He ate with knife
and fork, tossed off his glass of beer, and took
wine with us all round, in the most approved
manner. When dinner was over he asked for a
cigar and a glass of brandy and water, and evidently intended to enjoy himself for this evening
at least. In order to amuse and humour him we
proposed his health with "three times three,"
and made the old temple ring again as we
gave him a specimen of our national airs, 'Rule
Britannia' and 'God save the Queen.' But the
old man was not to be outdone : he returned
thanks to us for drinking his health : he recited
poetry of his own ; sang Chinese songs ; and every
now and then burst out into a hearty laugh,
which we could not help joining in without knowing very well why we did so. The court outside
was full of Chinamen, who were evidently enjoying with great zest Mr. A-chang's songs and
recitations. Inside, perched upon a chair, sat a
young priest, with his eyes fixed upon the bottles
on the table. An empty beer-bottle had been
given to him at the commencement of dinner,
and his whole soul seemed to be bent on getting
another. He neither moved, smiled, nor spoke,
but looked on in a dreamy manner, and never
took his eyes off the bottles. Our attention was
drawn to the boy by this singular proceeding,
and we desired one of the servants to find another
bottle and give it to him, which having been
done, the little fellow disappeared for the night.

As we were all rather tired with the day's exertions, we felt an inclination to retire early to rest. We had some difficulty in inducing our mandarin friend to leave us, as he was evidently prepared to "make a night of it;" but as Englishmen have degenerated very much, and cannot imitate now the noisy drunken squires of the olden time, we gave him sundry hints, which he took at last, and left us to our own meditations. We were now shown into a wretched room in which were placed some five or six bedsteads, on each of which was a dirty straw mat, with some straw below it. The mats and straw were removed by our servants, the rude bedsteads were dusted down, and our own clean things then put in order. Retiring immediately our friend left, we were soon sound asleep.

We rose early next morning, and as we were dressing by candle-light we heard the clear, loud laugh of Mr. A-chang, who was already dressed and prepared to conduct us to the glen below the falls. After passing the compliments of the morning, he begged a cigar to smoke as we went along. Leaving the falls on our right hand, we crossed the ridge of hills at the end of the glen and descended on the opposite side. When we neared the bottom we obtained a fine view of the falls in all their grandeur. The rocks over which the water came seemed so precipitous that it scarcely touched them until it nearly reached the bottom, some three or four hundred feet below. As we wandered down the glen, by a little mountain road which ran parallel with the stream, we obtained an excellent view of the rugged and perpendicular cliffs above us. I thought I could discern points of connexion between the two sides of the glen, which proved it to have been formed by some earthquake, or other convulsion of nature, out of a mountain which had been thus rent asunder.

Our guide now astonished us by coming out in a new character. Seeing me pay some attention to the botany of the district, he immediately began to give me a lecture upon the uses of the various trees and herbs we met with. "This," said he, " is the *Tung-oil* tree, which yields a valuable oil, much used by carpenters ; this is the *Lew-san* tree (*Cryptomeria Japonica*), valued for its ornamental appearance and fine timber." Seeing a fine species of gentian in full bloom, I asked him whether it was of any value. " Oh, yes," he replied, " it is a valuable medical plant, and is used by the doctors—it is an excellent stomachic." And so on he went, explaining to us the uses of almost every plant we met with on the roadside as we went along. "You are a very wise man, you seem to know everything," said I to him,— and I was quite in earnest, and intended this for no unmeaning compliment. The old man smiled ; he was evidently much pleased, and replied, " I also understand *Fung-shwuy* (soothsaying) ; I can tell the proper positions for graves—see, here is the compass I employ to find the proper direction." As he said this, he took out of his pocket a mariner's compass, and put it into my hand. He then offered to give me a lesson on his art, for which I expressed my gratitude,—and he began in the following way. " This spot," said he, " which you see formed out of the hill-side, and on which some Indian corn has been growing during the past summer, has been selected for a grave." " And why has this particular spot been selected," I asked ; " what are its peculiar merits ? " " Look around you," said he ; " look at the beautiful hills on your right hand and on your left ; see the falls in the distance, and the little stream winding quietly down the glen below ; change the scene, and carry your eyes to the far-off hills in front of you, where another stream is flowing towards us and joining that which has left the falls ; look at the green fields on its banks and the richly-wooded, undulating hills behind ; look at all these, and then you will answer your own question." It was, indeed, a lovely spot, and one which did not require the eloquence of Mr. A-chang to make me feel that it was so. On our way up the hill we came to another place, which at first sight appeared equally beautiful ; I called his attention to this, and asked him whether it was not quite equal to the last. " Oh, no," he said : " look behind you ; don't you see that furrow in the hill which would bring the water down upon the grave ? No, no ; this place is very well for a rice-field, but it will not answer for a tomb."

Much pleased with our descent into the glen below the falls, we now returned to the temple to make preparations for resuming our journey. While breakfast was getting ready, I paid a visit to the Superior, or High Priest, who had been discovered in a small room or kind of cell by one of our party the evening before. He was in voluntary confinement, and had been in this place for nearly three years. The door of the cell was padlocked on the outside, and he received his food and was communicated with through a hole in the wall. He seemed a respectable-looking, middle-aged man, rather corpulent for a Buddhist priest, and his confinement did not seem to disagree with him. He informed me the time of his voluntary penance would expire in the third month of the following year, and then he would leave his cell and return again to the world. I believe such examples of voluntary penance are not unusual amongst the Buddhist priesthood. I saw another in the old temple of Tein-tung; he was a native of Hang-chow-foo, the capital city of the province. He told me he had already spent nine years of his life in voluntary seclusion,—that is, he had been shut up three times, and for three years each time. When I made his acquaintance he was undergoing his fourth three years. This man was a very superior specimen of the Buddhist priesthood, open and frank in his manners, and was much more intelligent than these persons generally are. However much deluded I considered him, I was inclined to believe him sincere.

These recluses are supposed to spend their whole time in prayer, in reading Buddhist books, and in repeating the name of Buddha over and over again continually. A small lamp burns day and night in their cells, and the listener hears the low and monotonous sound of Ameda Buddha, or Nae-mo-o-me-to-fa; and if he looks in upon them through the little aperture in the wall which is used for passing in their food, he will see them either counting their beads as an accompaniment to their devotions, or prostrating themselves before a little altar in the cell.

When a number of these priests are shut up in one cell, it is said that prayer to Buddha, or the repetition of his name, never ceases day nor night. When some become weary and feel the want of sleep, others take their places, and so the work goes continually on and on, until the three years have expired, when the holy men come out again to mix with the world.

Before leaving the temple our party went in a body to the window of the high-priest's cell to thank him for the shelter we had received during the night, and to leave him a small present for the kindness. He seemed much gratified with our attention, and we parted the best of friends, and with a kind invitation to renew our visit in the following year.

Our beds and the few necessaries we had brought
with us being packed up, we loaded our coolies
and bade adieu to the temple of the Snowy Valley.
I have already stated that the valley is estimated
at about 2000 feet above the level of the sea.
Leaving it by a narrow road on its northern side,
we began to ascend another pass, which led us
nearly up to the top of the highest mountain-range,
and which cannot be less than 3000 feet in height.
For several miles our view was entirely bounded
on all sides by hills varying in height and form.
Every now and then our road led us down into a
narrow valley, out of which we had to climb again
to the top of another hill of the same elevation as
the preceding.

These mountains were but thinly populated;
but wherever the soil was at all fertile we found
little clusters of farm-houses, whose inhabitants
seemed much surprised at our appearance as we
passed along. With their wonted politeness and
hospitality, they pressed us to enter their houses
and partake of the only beverage they had to offer
us, which was tea. The tea-bushes were noticed
growing plentifully on many of the hill-sides ; but
the produce in this part of the country is entirely
used by the natives themselves, and not made up
for the foreign market. Wheat and barley, with
various other green crops, are cultivated in winter
and reaped in spring or during the early summer
months. The summer crops consist of sweet potatoes, two kinds of millet, one of buckwheat, and

an excellent variety of Indian corn. A small quantity of rice is also grown in the valleys; but the land capable of producing the crop is not very extensive. Many of these hills are well wooded. I re-marked as we went along good forests of Chinese pine (*Pinus sinensis*), the Japan cedar (*Cryptomeria Japonica*), and the lance-leaved fir (*Cunninghamia lanceolata*). The forests of the Japan cedar and the lance-leaved pine were extremely picturesque and beautiful. The trees generally were young and not remarkable for size, but were growing vigorously, and likely, if allowed to stand for a few years, to make valuable timber. In addition to this consideration, there were a symmetry and grace in the general appearance of these forests which one rarely sees in temperate climates, if we except perhaps the Himalaya mountains. The hemp-palm (*Chamærops sp.*) — a tree of great importance to the Chinese in a commercial point of view, on account of the sheets of fibre which it produces yearly on its stem — also occupied a prominent place on the sides of these mountains; and the graceful *mow-chok* — the most beautiful bamboo in the world—was grouped about in wild profusion.

This bamboo I have never met in any other part of the world. In the central and eastern provinces of China it is largely cultivated, par-ticularly on the sides of mountains where the soil is rich, and in the vicinity of temples and other monastic buildings. Its stems are straight, smooth, and clean, the joints are small, it grows to the height of from sixty to eighty feet. Twenty or thirty feet of the lower part of its stem are generally free from branches. These are produced on the upper portion of the tree, and then they are so light and feathery that they do not affect the cleanness of the main stem. In addition, therefore, to the highly picturesque effect it produces upon the landscape, it is of great value in the arts, owing to the smoothness and fineness of its structure. It is used in the making of sieves for the manipulation of tea, rolling-tables for the same purpose, baskets of all kinds, ornamental inlaid works, and for hundreds of other purposes, for which the bamboo found in India is wholly unsuitable.

Like all other species of the same tribe, it grows with great rapidity and perfects its growth in a few months. To use a common expression, " one could almost see it growing." I was in the habit of measuring the daily growth in the Chinese woods, and found that a healthy plant generally grew about two feet or two feet and a half in the twenty-four hours, and the greatest rate of growth was during the night.

The young shoots just as they peep out of the ground are highly esteemed as food, and are taken to the markets in large quantities. I was in the habit of using them as a vegetable every day during the season, and latterly was as fond of them as the Chinese are themselves. Sometimes I had them split up, boiled, and dished by themselves; at other times they were used in soup, like cabbage; and on one occasion Mr. Forbes, the American consul in China, to whom I recommended them, taught me to make an excellent omelette, in which they formed one of the ingredients.

In the south of China, that is about Hongkong and Canton, several kinds of the bamboo are very common. There is a yellow variety with beautiful green stripes, painted on its stems as if done by the hand of a most delicate artist. But all these kinds resemble the Indian varieties,—that is, they grow in dense bushes, their stems are not remarkable for their straightness, and the large joints and branches, which are produced on all parts of the stem, give it a rough surface, and consequently render it unsuitable for fine work.

These tropical, jungley-looking bamboos disappear as we go to the more northern latitudes; and in their places we have the *mow-chok*, already mentioned, the *long-sin-chok*, the *hoo-chok*, and one or two others, all with clean stems and feathery branches, suited for the most delicate kinds of work, and all "good for food." These trees are well worth the attention of people who inhabit temperate climates, such as the south of France, Italy, and other parts of the south of Europe. No doubt they would be well worth introduction to some parts of Australia, New Zealand, and the southern portions of the United States of America. In the province of Chekiang the maximum summer heat is from 90° to 100° in the shade, but only a few days in the months of July and August so high ; in winter the thermometer (Fahr.) is rarely so low as 20°. Those interested in this matter may consult my ' Wanderings in China,' and ' Journey to the Tea Countries,' for fuller accounts of the climate of this part of China. With regard to soil and situation, it should be remarked that these trees invariably grow in a rich yellow loam on the slopes of the hills.

I have succeeded in introducing the mow-chok to India, and at no very distant day it may be seen flourishing on the slopes of the Himalaya in the north-western provinces, where the bamboos are very inferior. Several plants were also sent to the Agricultural and Horticultural Society of India, and reached Calcutta in good condition.

Amongst the other productions of these highland valleys, the *ruellia*, formerly noticed, is cultivated extensively for the blue dye which it affords. During the season of its preparation every mountain-stream is coloured and polluted with the refuse liquid drawn off from the tanks, and the stench which fills the air is almost unendurable.

We travelled about thirty *le*—eight or ten miles —across these mountains, which brought us to a little village named Le-tsun, where large quantities of the blue dye just noticed are grown and manufactured. This little highland village is situated at the head of a glen which opens by various windings to the plain of Ningpo. As we had other thirty *le* to go before we reached our boats, we rested ourselves in an old joss-house in order to allow our baggage to come up with us. Here the natives crowded round us in hundreds, evidently delighted to get a view of the far-famed *Hong-mou-jins*—the "red-haired men,"—of whom they had often heard, but rarely if ever seen. We treated them with great kindness, and, I think, left a good impression upon their minds, which may be of use to future tourists in these mountains.

As we had now no more hills to cross, and as the road was good, we got into our mountain bamboo chairs and took our way down the glen towards the plains. The scenery in this glen is more strikingly beautiful than that in any part of the province which has come under my observation, and reminded me forcibly of what I had seen when crossing the Bohea Mountains. High hills rose on each side of us densely covered with the Japan cedar, weeping junipers, and pines; behind, our view was bounded by high mountains, while in front we got now and then glimpses of an extensive fertile plain, richly wooded near the base of the hills, in a high state of cultivation, and teeming with an industrious and happy people.

We arrived just before dark at Ning-kang-jou, a small town near one of the sources of the Ningpo river, where our boats were waiting us. Here we found our old friend Mr. A-chang, who had reached the boats some few minutes before us. We invited him to dine with us again; and before he left us we presented him with an English umbrella, a pencil-case, and some few articles of foreign manufacture which we knew had taken his fancy, and with which he was highly delighted. With a kind invitation to visit him at his little temple, should we ever again come that way, he bade us a hearty farewell.

CHAPTER X.

Collections shipped for India — Success attending this year's importa-
tions — Visit Canton — Method of scenting teas described — Flowers
used in the operation — Their scientific and Chinese names — Their
relative value — Prices paid for them — Manufacture of " caper "
described — Inferior ditto — " Lie capers " — Orange pekoe — High
character of foreign merchants in China — Howqua's garden described — Its plants, ornamental doors, and alcoves, &c. — Polite
notices to visitors worthy of imitation.

THE various collections I had made during the
summer and autumn had been left, from time to
time as they were formed, in the charge of Chinese friends in various parts of the country. Mr.
Meadows, of the British consulate in Ningpo, and
Mr. Wadman, a merchant there, had also taken
charge of some plants which I had planted for
safety in their gardens. It was now of great importance to get all these collections together as
speedily as possible and have them conveyed to
the port of Shanghae, where they could be packed
in a proper manner and shipped to Hongkong,
and from thence to India. This was satisfactorily
accomplished, and, being luckily favoured with fine
weather and a leading wind, I reached Shanghae
in two days, and deposed my collections safely
in the garden of Mr. Beale. A large number of
Ward's cases, having been ordered some time be-

fore, were now ready. These were now filled with earth, and all the plants carefully planted ; at the same time large quantities of tea-seed, chesnuts, and other things of that nature were sown in the soil and left to germinate on the voyage to India. My other collections of the seeds of useful and ornamental trees and shrubs were well dried and packed in a common wooden box.

It is very rare that there is a vessel from Shanghae direct for Calcutta, and consequently all these things had to be transshipped at Hongkong. Living plants are not like bales of merchandize ; they are easily destroyed by the admission of salt water or salt air, and are more likely to be damaged while undergoing transshipment than during a long voyage at sea. As on former occasions, I determined to accompany my collections to Hongkong, and look after the transshipment myself. The formation of this collection had cost me much labour and care ; the unsettled condition of the country rendered it extremely doubtful that I should be equally successful in the following season ; and it was therefore an object of the first importance to endeavour by every means in my power to ensure the safety of that now in hand.

Everything went according to my wishes; Hongkong was reached in safety, the collections were sent on to Calcutta in four different ships, and a few months afterwards I had the very great satisfaction to hear that the whole had arrived at their destination in excellent condition. No fewer

than 23,892 tea-plants, upwards of 300 chesnut-
trees, and a large quantity of other things of great
value in India, now growing on the Himalayas,
were the results of this year's labours. The rice-
paper plant (*Aralia papyrifera*) presented to me
by J. C. Bowring, Esq., of Hongkong, was also
introduced to India, and is now a remarkable
object of great interest in the Calcutta gardens.

When the various consignments had been despatched, I went up to Canton for a few days
before proceeding again to the north, in order if
possible to get some reliable information as to the
mode of scenting tea, which is only understood
and practised at this port with teas destined for
the foreign markets. I had been making inquiries
for some time past, both of foreigners and Chinese,
about this curious process carried on so extensively
at Canton; but the answers and descriptions I received to my questions were so unsatisfactory, that
I gave up all hopes of understanding the process
until I had an opportunity of seeing and judging
for myself. When I reached Canton I was informed the whole process might be seen any day
at that season in full operation in a tea-factory on
the island of Honan. Messrs. Walkinshaw and
Thorburn, two gentlemen well acquainted with
the various kinds of teas sent annually to Europe
and America, consented to accompany me to this
factory, and we took with us the Chinese merchant
to whom the place belonged. I was thus placed
in a most favourable condition for obtaining a

correct knowledge of this most curious subject.
When we entered the tea-factory a strange scene
was presented to our view. The place was crowded
with women and children, all busily engaged in
picking the stalks and yellow or brown leaves out
of the black tea. For this labour each was paid
at the rate of six cash a catty, and earned on an
average about sixty cash a day,—a sum equal to
about threepence of our money. The scene altogether was not unlike that in the great Government Cigar Manufactory at Manilla. Men were
employed giving out the tea in its rough state,
and in receiving it again when picked. With each
portion of tea a wooden ticket was also given,
which ticket had to be returned along with the
tea. In the northern tea-countries the leaves are
carefully weighed when they are given out and
when they are brought back, in order to check
peculation, which is not unfrequent. I did not
observe this precaution taken at Canton. Besides
the men who were thus employed, there were many
others busily at work, passing the tea through
various sized sieves, in order to get out the caper,
and to separate the various kinds. This was also
partly done by a winnowing machine, similar in
construction to that used by our farmers in England. Having taken a passing glance at all these
objects on entering the building, I next directed
my attention to the scenting process, which had
been the main object of my visit,—and which I
shall now endeavour to describe.

In a corner of the building there lay a large heap of orange-flowers, which filled the air with the most delicious perfume. A man was engaged in sifting them to get out the stamens and other smaller portions of the flower. This process was necessary, in order that the flowers might be readily sifted out of the tea after the scenting had been accomplished. The orange-flowers being fully expanded, the large petals were easily separated from the stamens and smaller ones. In 100 parts 70 per cent. were used and 30 thrown away. When the orange is used, its flowers must be fully expanded, in order to bring out the scent; but flowers of jasmine may be used in the bud, as they will expand and emit their fragrance during the time they are mixed with the tea. When the flowers had been sifted over in the manner described they were ready for use. In the mean time the tea to be scented had been carefully manipulated, and appeared perfectly dried and finished. At this stage of the process it is worthy of observing that, while the *tea was perfectly dry, the orange-flowers were just as they had been gathered from the trees.* Large quantities of the tea were now mixed up with the flowers, in the proportion of 40 lbs. of flowers to 100 lbs. of tea. This *dry tea* and the *undried flowers* were allowed to lie mixed together for the space of twenty-four hours. At the end of this time the flowers were sifted out of the tea, and by the repeated sifting and winnowing processes which the tea had afterwards to undergo they were nearly all got rid of. Sometimes a few stray ones are left in the tea, and may be detected even after it arrives in England. A small portion of tea adheres to the moist flowers when they are sifted out, and this is generally given away to the poor, who pick it out with the hand.

The flowers, at this part of the process, had impregnated the tea-leaves with a large portion of their peculiar odours, but they had also left behind them a certain portion of moisture, which it was necessary to expel. This was done by placing the tea once more over slow charcoal-fires in baskets and sieves prepared for the purpose of drying. The scent communicated by the flowers is very slight for some time, but, like the fragrance peculiar to the tea-leaf itself, comes out after being packed for a week or two. Sometimes this scenting process is repeated when the odour is not considered sufficiently strong; and the head man in the factory informed me he sometimes scented twice with orange-flowers and once with the "Mo-le" (*Jasminum Sambac*).

The flowers of various plants are used in scenting by the Chinese, some of which are considered better than others, and some can be had at seasons when others are not procurable. I considered it of some importance to the elucidation of this subject to find out not only the Chinese names of these various plants, but also, by examining the plants themselves, to be able to give each the name by which it is known to scientific men in all

parts of the world. The following list was prepared with great care, and may be fully relied
upon. The numbers prefixed express the relative
value of each kind in the eyes of the Chinese, and
the asterisks point out those which are mostly used
for scenting teas for the foreign markets in the
order in which they are valued ; thus the " Mo-le "
and the " Sieu-hing" are considered the best, and
so on :—

     1. Rose, scented (Tsing moi-qui-hwa).
     1 or 2. Plum, double (Moi-hwa).
     2*. Jasminum Sambac (Mo-le-hwa).
     2 or 3*. Jasminum paniculatum (Sieu-hing-hwa).
     4*. Aglaia odorata (Lan-hwa, or Yu-chu-lan).
     5. Olea fragrans (Kwei-hwa).
     6*. Orange (Chang-hwa).
     7*. Gardenia florida (Pak-sema-hwa).

It has been frequently stated that the *Chloran-
thus* is largely used. This appears to be a mistake,
originating, no doubt, in the similarity of its Chinese name to that of *Aglaia odorata.* The *Chlo-
ranthus* is called " Chu-lan," the *Aglaia* " Lan " or
" Yu-chu-lan."

The different flowers which I have just named
are not all used in the same proportions. Thus, of
orange-flowers there are 40 lbs. to 100 lbs. of tea ;
of *Aglaia* there are 100 lbs. to 100 lbs. ; and of
Jasminum Sambac there are 50 lbs. to 100 lbs.
The flowers of the Sieu-hing (*Jasminum panicu-
latum*) are generally mixed with those of the
Mo-le (*Jasminum Sambac*), in the proportion of
10 lbs. of the former to 30 lbs. of the latter, and
the 40 lbs. thus produced are sufficient for 100 lbs.

of tea. The "Kweihwa" (*Olea fragrans*) is used chiefly in the northern districts as a scent for a rare and expensive kind of Hyson Pekoe—a tea which forms a most delicious and refreshing beverage when taken *à la Chinoise* without sugar and milk. The quantity of flowers used seemed to me to be very large; and I made particular inquiries as to whether the teas that are scented were mixed up with large quantities of unscented kinds. The Chinese unhesitatingly affirmed that such was not the case; but, notwithstanding their assertions, I had some doubt on this point.

The length of time which teas thus scented retain the scent is most remarkable. It varies, however, with the different sorts. Thus, the *Olea fragrans* tea will only keep well for one year; at the end of two years it has either become scentless, or has a peculiar oily odour which is disagreeable. Teas scented with orange-blossoms and with those of the Mo-le will keep well for two or three years, and the Sieu-hing kinds for three or four years. The Aglaia retains the scent longer than any, and is said to preserve well for five or six years. The tea scented with the Sieu-hing is said to be most esteemed by foreigners, although it is put down as second or third rate by the Chinese.

Scented teas for the foreign market are nearly all made in Canton, and are known to merchants by the names of "Scented Orange Pekoe," and "Scented Caper." They are grown in and near a place called Tai-shan, in the Canton province. Mr. Walkinshaw informs me that other descriptions of tea, both black and green, have been scented for the English market, but have been found unsuitable. True "caper" is to black tea what the kinds called "imperial" and "gunpowder" are to green : it assumes a round, shot-looking form during the process of manipulation, and it is easily separated from the other leaves by sifting or by the winnowing machine. It is a common error to suppose that "imperial" or "gunpowder" amongst green teas, or "caper" amongst black ones, is prepared by rolling each leaf singly by the hand. Such a method of manipulation would make them much more expensive than they are. One gathering of tea is said to yield 70 per cent. of orange pekoe, 25 of souchong, and 5 of caper. The quantity of true caper would therefore appear to be very small ; but there are many ways of increasing the quantity by peculiar modes of manipulation, as I shall afterwards show.

In a large factory, such as this at Canton, there is, of course, a considerable quantity of dust and refuse tea remaining after the orange pekoe, caper, and souchong have been sifted out of it. This is sold in the country to the natives at a low price, and no doubt is often made up with paste and other ingredients into those *lie teas* which now-a-days find a market in England. Nothing is lost or thrown away in China. The stalks and yellow leaves which have been picked out by women and children are sold in the country; while the flowers which have done their duty in the scenting process are given to the poor, who pick out the few remaining tea-leaves which had been left by the sieve or winnowing machine. Some flowers, such as those of the Aglaia for example, after being sifted out from the tea are dried and used in the manufacture of the fragrant " joss-stick," so much used in the religious ceremonies of the country.

It appears from these investigations that many kinds of fragrant flowers besides those used by the Chinese would answer the purpose equally well, and therefore in places like India, where tea is likely to be produced upon an extensive scale, experiments in scenting might be made with any kinds of fragrant jasmines, daphnes, aurantiaceous or other plants of a like kind indigenous to the country.

It will be observed from the description just given that the method of scenting teas, like most of the arts in China, is exceedingly simple in its nature and most efficient. It used to be said by those who knew nothing about the matter, that " the flowers were put over a slow fire, with the tea in a separate basket above them, and so the fire drove the scent from the flowers into the tea"! Knowing the immense capacity which *dry* tea has for moisture of any kind, how much more simple and beautiful is the process of allowing it to lie for a space of time mixed up with *undried* flowers!

A few years ago I published a description of the Chinese mode of dyeing green teas to suit our depraved tastes in Europe, and particularly in America, where they are largely consumed. Scenting teas is a very different thing, and nothing can be urged against the taste for them. That this is so in the eyes of the Chinese may be gathered from the fact that, while they *dye* their teas, not to drink, but only to *sell,* they consume and highly appreciate these scented ones.

The price paid for flowers used in the scenting process varies, like everything else, according to the demand or supply in the market. In 1854 and 1855 it was about seventeen dollars per pecul,* but sometimes as much as thirty dollars are paid for the same quantity. In former years—ten or twelve years ago—as much as sixty dollars per pecul used to be paid for flowers. This information was given me some time after I had been examining the method of scenting in the Honan factory, and by another manufacturer, and confirmed me in the opinion I had then formed, namely, that after the tea is once scented with the proportions of flowers mentioned above, it is mixed up with large quantities of unscented tea. Were this not so, the large quantity of flowers used would render the tea much more expensive than it really is. Upon making further inquiries, of different individuals and at different times, I found that my surmises were correct. The results

* 133⅓ lbs.

of the information thus obtained were, that sixty pounds of this highly-scented mixture were capable of scenting one hundred pounds of unscented tea, and no doubt it is sometimes used in even smaller proportions.

In all investigations of this nature one is very apt to be misled by the Chinese; not, perhaps, so much intentionally as from ignorance or carelessness as to whether the information given be correct or otherwise. And having once made an assertion, a Chinese does not like to confess himself mistaken or in the wrong; but this propensity is not confined to the inhabitants of the Celestial Empire. Unless one sees a process with his own eyes, he must in all cases use some discretion when he has to take his information at second hand. With ordinary care, however, and a little common sense, the truth may generally be arrived at, even from the Chinese.

Having satisfied myself as to the mode of scenting teas, I was now anxious to know how the kinds called " Caper " and " Orange Pekoe " are manufactured, as they are quite different in appearance from teas made in the great black-tea provinces of Fokien and Kiang-si. As large quantities of these teas—indeed, the whole which are exported—are made up near Canton, it was not difficult to find out where some of the factories were situated, or to gain admission to witness the process. M. C. Morrison, Esq., her Majesty's Vice-Consul at Canton, whose knowledge of the Chi-

nese language is of a very high order, having
expressed a wish to accompany me, we set out
together, with a Chinese merchant for our guide.
Our guide told us that the manufacture, which
was very extensive, was carried on in a great
many parts of the suburbs of Canton; but that
the most extensive and best hongs were situated
on the island of Honan already mentioned. We
crossed the main river in a boat, and then pulled
up a canal for a short distance which led through
a densely populated suburb.   Here we soon found
ourselves abreast of a number of large tea-hongs,
which our guide informed us were those to which
we were bound.   These hongs were large and
spacious buildings of two stories.   The lower
portion was filled with tea and implements of

Tea Picker.   Canton.

manipulation, while the upper was crowded with hundreds of women and children engaged in picking and sorting the various sorts.

On entering one of these hongs or factories, the first thing to which we directed our attention was the tea which was to be made into "caper." I have already stated that this description of tea is produced near a place called Tai-shan, in the Canton province, a few miles inland from the city. Here it undergoes only the first process of manipulation; that is, it is fired, rolled, and dried, and the colour fixed, but nothing further is done to it. It is then packed up in mat-bags or baskets and sent down to Canton to be made up in the approved manner, and scented for exportation. On examining the tea it presented a very rough appearance, and in the state in which it was, seemed unsuited for the foreign markets. The workmen were busily engaged in remaking it during the time of our visit, and they went to work in the following manner :—

A convenient quantity—about twenty or thirty pounds—was thrown into the drying-pan, which had been heated for the operation. Here it was sprinkled with a basinful of water, and rapidly turned over with the hands of the workman. The dry leaves immediately imbibed the moisture, and became soft and pliable. This softening process prevented them from breaking down into dust, and fitted them, also, to take any form which was considered desirable by the manipulator. The

water used on this occasion stood in a large basin
adjoining the drying-pans, and had a yellow,
dirty appearance, which I was rather at a loss
to account for. At first sight I thought it was
mixed with some ingredient which was intended
to give a peculiar tint or colour to the tea; but
on inquiry it turned out that my conjecture was
wrong. Our guide, on being appealed to for
information on the subject, coolly informed us that
"there was nothing in the water, it was quite
clean, but that the workmen were in the habit of
washing their hands in it!"

As soon as the leaves had become softened
by the moisture and heat in the pan, they were
taken out and put into a strong canvas bag, and
twisted firmly into a round form, resembling a
football. This bag was then thrown down on the
floor, which had been covered with a mat, and a
man jumped upon it with both feet, supporting
himself at the same time by laying hold of a
bamboo pole, which had been erected in a horizontal position for the purpose. The heel, sole,
and toes of his feet were now kept in perpetual
motion in turning and twisting the ball, while the
weight of his body compressed it gradually into a
smaller size. As the bulk of the ball is thus
reduced by pressure, the canvas slackens, and it
is necessary for the workman from time to time
to jump off it and tighten its mouth by giving it
an extra twist with his hands. The balls by this
process of rolling and twisting become at last

very hard and solid, and are then thrown on one side, and allowed to lie in this state for several hours : if this work has been done in the evening, they remain all night. By this system of pressing, twisting, and rolling, the greater portion of the moist leaves take a circular form, which goes on to perfection during the subsequent drying which the leaves have, of course, to undergo, and ends in the production of the round shot-like appearance by which this kind of tea is known.

It is a most curious sight to a stranger who sees the mode of making this tea for the first time. A whole row of these men, nearly naked when the weather is warm, each with a large ball under his feet, which he is twisting and rolling with all his might, is so unexpected a sight in tea-making. The clever sketch (*Frontispiece*) by my friend Mr. Scarth gives a good idea of this curious process.

The best kind of " caper " takes the round form naturally during the manufacture of souchong or congou ; but, as I have already mentioned, only a very small quantity—about five per cent.— could be procured in this way. By far the greatest portion of the caper exported is manufactured in the manner I have just described.

But as I am letting out all the secrets of tea-manufacture, I may just as well notice another mode of making " caper," which is scarcely as legitimate as the former. In one corner of the factory we observed a quantity of tea, exceedingly coarse in quality,—in fact, the refuse of that which we had been examining. All the art of the manipulator, in so far as heating, and pressing, and rolling in the usual way, was not equal to make a good-looking "caper" out of this. The leaves were too old, too large and coarse in their present state. But, although there might be some difficulty, even to a Chinese, in making small leaves into large ones, there was none whatever in making large leaves small; and their mode of doing this was as follows :—These coarse leaves were first of all heated and moistened as the others had been, in order to make them soft and pliable. They were then thrown into square boxes and chopped up for some time, until the size of the leaves was reduced. When this was accomplished to the satisfaction of the operator, they were then made into nice-looking round "caper," suitable for the market.

The origin of the name this tea bears is, no doubt, derived from its resemblance in form to the flower-buds of the caper-bush of the south of Europe. And yet it is rather a curious coincidence that the greater part of *caper* tea finds its market in the *Cape* of Good Hope.

It will probably suggest itself to the reader who has paid any attention to tea-making that large quantities of those kinds of green tea known as "gunpowder" and "imperial" may be manufactured in the same way as "caper," and this is, no doubt, the case, particularly about Canton. And further, it is the simplest thing in the world to

Q

convert "caper" into "imperial" and "gunpowder," and this, too, is often done. Our Chinese
guide informed us, with a peculiar grin on his
countenance, that, when there is a large demand
for green teas, "caper" is converted into "imperial" and "gunpowder" by dyeing it with Prussian blue and gypsum!

The "orange pekoe" of commerce, which is
produced in the same district as the "caper," is
somewhat like congou in make, but the leaf is
much more wiry and twisted, and is of a lighter
complexion. The infusion produced by this tea
has a yellow or orange tint, and hence the name
of orange pekoe which it bears. Like hyson
pekoe amongst green teas, this is made from the
young leaves soon after they unfold themselves in
spring, and hence many of the leaves are covered
with white hairs which are formed at this season
of the year. These hairy leaves are called "pekoe
ends" by the trade. A large quantity of this tea
is gathered and dried by itself, while another portion is taken out of that of which the "caper" is
ultimately made.

Canton enjoys the unenviable notoriety of manufacturing what are commonly called "lie teas"
or "lie capers." These are made out of tea-dust
mixed with other rubbish, and which is taken up and
held together by a glutinous substance consisting
of rice and water. Thin showers of this substance
are thrown over the layers of dust, and, as each
little globule of the fluid comes in contact with it,

a certain number of particles adhere, and in the
course of time are made into little round balls
resembling the caper of commerce. But no one
is, or ought to be, deceived by this. Small quantities of such teas are, no doubt, exported, but it
must be with the knowledge and connivance of
the foreigner himself, whom I shall not honour
with the title of foreign merchant. And I shall
be greatly surprised to find that such a clumsy
fraud affects the respectable broker or dealer in
Europe or America.

During a late tour in India I was told on more
than one occasion, on the authority of " Old In-
dians" who had been home, that it was next to
impossible to get genuine tea in England, now
that the East India Company had no control over
the China trade; and that since the demand had
so much increased, the Chinese were in the habit
of supplying it by substituting the leaves of other
trees and shrubs for that which is genuine.

This idea is simply absurd : as a general rule
the Chinese are doing no such thing; they have
plenty of true tea in the country to supply all
demands, were they twice as great as they are.
And while it may be perfectly true that some
unprincipled adventurers encourage the production of " lie teas" by buying them up, the great
bulk of the teas exported are unadulterated with
other articles. If sloe-leaves and beech-leaves, and
other articles of that kind, are found in the teapot by the consumer, they are much more likely

to have been manufactured in England than in
China.

The foreign merchants in China as a class are
upright and honourable men, and quite incapable
of lending themselves to frauds of this description.
Besides, every house of any standing has a "tea-
taster" who has a perfect knowledge of his business, and who can not only tell true tea from
false, but, in most instances, can tell the identical
district in which the sample presented to him has
been produced.

As it seems only a step or two from the well-
known "Howqua's Mixture" to the less known
Howqua's Garden, I now ask the reader to visit
that with me before we leave Canton.

This garden is situated near the well-known
Fa-tee nurseries, a few miles above the city of
Canton, and is a place of favourite resort both for
Chinese and foreigners who reside in the neighbourhood, or who visit this part of the Celestial
Empire. I determined on paying it a visit in
company with Mr. M'Donald, who is well known
in this part of the world as an excellent Chinese
scholar, and to whom I am indebted for some
translations of Chinese notices, which appeared
very amusing to us at the time, and which, I dare
say, will amuse my readers.

Having reached the door of the garden, we
presented the card with which we were provided,
and were immediately admitted. The view from
the entrance is rather pleasing, and particularly

striking to a stranger who sees it for the first
time. Looking " right ahead," as sailors say,
there is a long and narrow paved walk lined on
each side with plants in pots. This view is
broken, and apparently lengthened, by means of
an octagon arch which is thrown across, and
beyond that a kind of alcove covers the pathway.
Running parallel with the walk, and on each side
behind the plants, are low walls of ornamental
brickwork, latticed so that the ponds or small
lakes which are on each side can be seen. Altogether the octagon arch, the alcove, the pretty
ornamental flower-pots, and the water on each
side, has a striking effect, and is thoroughly
Chinese.

The plants consist of good specimens of southern
Chinese things, all well known in England, such,
for example, as Cymbidium sinense, Olea fragrans,
oranges, roses, camellias, magnolias, &c., and, of
course, a multitude of dwarf trees, without which
no Chinese garden would be considered complete.
In the alcove alluded to there are some nice stone
seats, which look cool in a climate like that of
southern China. The floor of this building is
raised a few feet above the ground-level, so that
the visitor gets a good view of the water and
other objects of interest in the garden. That this
is a favourite lounge and smoking-place with the
Chinese, the following Chinese notice, which we
found on one of the pillars, will testify :—" *A
careful and earnest notice :* This garden earnestly

requests that visitors will spit betle* outside the
railing, and knock the ashes of pipes also outside." Several fine fruit-trees and others are
growing near the walks, and afford shade from
the rays of the sun. On one of these we read
the following :—"Ramblers here *will be excused*
plucking the fruit on this tree." How exceedingly polite!

Near the centre of the garden stands a substantial summer-house, or hall, named "the Hall
of Fragrant Plants." The same notice to smokers
and chewers of betle-nut is also put up here; and
there is another and a longer one which I must
not forget to quote. It is this :—"In this garden
the plants are intended to delight the eyes of all
visitors : a great deal has been expended in planting and in keeping in order, and the garden is
now beginning to yield some return. Those who
come here to saunter about are earnestly prayed
not to pluck the fruit or flowers, in order that
the beauty of the place may be preserved." And
then follows a piece of true Chinese politeness—
"We beg persons who understand this notice to
excuse it!" Passing through the Hall of Fragrant Plants we approached, between two rows of
Olea fragrans, a fine ornamental suite of rooms
tastefully furnished and decorated, in which visitors are received and entertained. An inscription
informs us that this is called "the Fragrant Hall
of the Woo-che tree." Leaving this place by a

---

* Betle-nut is much used by the southern Chinese.

narrow door, we observed the following notice—
" Saunterers here will be excused entering." This
apparently leads to the private apartments of the
family. In this side of the garden there is some
fine artificial rockwork, which the Chinese know
well how to construct, and various summer-houses
tastefully decorated, one of which is called the
" Library of Verdant Purity." Between this part
of the garden and the straight walk already noticed
there is a small pond or lake for fish and water-
lilies. This is crossed by a zigzag wooden bridge
of many arches, which looked rather dilapidated. A
very necessary notice was put up here informing
" saunterers to stop their steps in case of accident."

On the outskirts of the garden we observed
the potting sheds, a nursery for rearing young
plants and seeds, and the kitchen garden. Here
a natural curiosity was pointed out by one of the
Chinese, which, at first sight, appeared singularly
curious. Three trees were growing in a row, and
at about twenty or thirty feet from the ground
the two outer ones had sent out shoots, and fairly
united themselves with the centre one. When
I mention that the outer trees are the Chinese
banyan (Ficus nitida), it will readily be seen how
the appearance they presented was produced. The
long roots sent down by this species had lovingly
embraced the centre tree, and appeared at first
sight to have really grafted themselves upon it.

I am afraid I have given a very imperfect description of this curious garden. Those who know

what a Chinese garden is will understand me well
enough, but it is really difficult to give a stranger
an idea of the Chinese style which I have been
endeavouring to describe. In order to understand
the Chinese style of gardening it is necessary to
dispel from the mind all ideas of fine lawns, broad
walks, and extensive views; and to picture in
their stead everything on a small scale—that is,
narrow paved walks, dwarf walls in all directions,
with lattice-work or ornamental openings in them,
in order to give views of the scenery beyond;
halls, summer-houses, and alcoves, ponds or small
lakes with zigzag walks over them—in short, an
endeavour to make small things appear large, and
large things small, and everything Chinese. There
are some of these ornaments, however, which I
think might be imitated with advantage in our
own gardens. Some of the doorways and openings in walls seemed extremely pretty. In particular I may notice a wall about ten feet high,
having a number of open compartments filled
with porcelain rods made to imitate the stems of
the bamboo. I shall now close this notice with
the modest lines of the Chinese poet, which we
found written in the "Library of Verdant Purity,"
and which seemed to be an effort to describe the
nature of the garden :—

> " Some few stems of bamboo-plants
> A cottage growing round ;
> A few flowers here—some old trees there,
> And a mow * of garden ground."

* A mow is about the sixth part of an acre.

CHAPTER XI.

Visit the port of Foo-chow-foo — Its foreign trade — The advantages
and disadvantages of the port — Steamer "Confucius" — Sail for
Formosa — An amateur watch kept — Sea-sickness of mandarins —
Appearance of Formosa from sea — Land on the island — Rice-
paper plant — The natives —Productions of the island — Suggestions
to the navy in these seas — Sail for Shanghae — Spring and spring
flowers.

In the beginning of March, 1854, having completed my shipments and investigations in the
south, I engaged a passage in a schooner and
sailed for the port of Foo-chow-foo, the capital
city of the province of Fokien, on my way to the
more northerly ports of Shanghae and Ningpo.
My objects in taking Foo-chow-foo by the way
were two-fold. In the first place, I was anxious to
make arrangements for getting a large supply of
tea-seeds from the best black-tea districts about
Woo-e-shan, in the autumn, when they would be
ripe ; and secondly, I determined to try and procure some black-tea manufacturers from the same
districts, through the agency of some influential
friends at this port. The great American house
of Messrs. Russell and Co., by means of energy
and large capital, had opened up a connexion with
these districts the year before, and had shipped
extensively direct from the river Min to America

the same description of black teas which formerly were carried overland across the Bohea mountains to Shanghae and to Canton. Mr. Cunningham, the head of that house at Shanghae, had promised me his assistance in the kindest manner, and Mr. D. O. Clark, who was conducting the business at Foo-chow, also entered warmly into my views on my arrival.

From the opening of Foo-chow in 1843 to the period mentioned, no foreign trade of any importance had been carried on at this port. Several merchants had tried it during these ten years; but as they were men of limited means—not being able to send funds into the country to purchase teas from the manufacturers—their exertions were not attended with success. When the rebels began to disturb and overrun the southern and central districts of the country, and when it seemed doubtful whether the tea-merchants would be able to bring their teas to Canton and Shanghae as formerly, Messrs. Russell and Co., with a clear-sightedness which does them the highest credit, foresaw that, owing to the power of the Government at Foo-chow, that port was likely to remain longer open than any of the others; and as it was no great distance from one great black-tea country—a country which during the days of the East India Company's charter produced the finest teas exported—they determined to make a vigorous effort to open up the trade. Having Chinese on their establishment whom they could thoroughly trust, these men were intrusted with a large amount of capital, and sent inland to the tea country during the manufacturing season, in order to buy up such teas as they required, and transmit their purchases down the river Min to Foo-chow-foo. In the mean time vessels were chartered to go to the same port to load with such teas and convey them to their destination.

The system thus planned and carried out met with the most complete success, and I believe Messrs. Russell and Co. reaped the reward to which they were most justly entitled. Other large houses of capital soon followed the example which had been set them, and now a very large export trade in black teas is carried on at Foo-chow-foo. This is one good result which has arisen out of the rebellion in China, although perhaps it would be difficult to mention another. Had there been no anticipated difficulty in getting down teas to Shanghae and Canton, it is scarcely likely the idea of opening Foo-chow would have occurred to Messrs. Russell and Co.

But it is doubtful if the advantages of the Foo-chow trade are as great as they would seem to be at first sight. No doubt all teas made in the Fokien district, south of the Bohea mountains, and near the source and course of the river Min, can be brought more easily and more cheaply to Foo-chow than to any other port. And moreover, as they come nearly the whole way by water, the chests may be expected to arrive in better order than when they have to be carried for many miles over mountains on the backs of coolies. And further, the new teas will always arrive very early, if this is an advantage.

These circumstances will no doubt be perfectly understood by merchants, and it is for them to say whether the disadvantages which I shall now notice are worth taking into consideration.

1st. The extensive sandbanks at the mouth of the Min, and the rapid currents in the river itself, have been urged by some as fatal objections to its safe navigation. In support of this view it is stated that since the opening of the trade several vessels and cargoes of great value have been completely lost, and insurance offices have been obliged to raise their rates of insurance.

At first sight this seems a very grave objection; but were it worth the merchant's while to conduct a large trade at Foo-chow, the dangers in navigation might be, if not removed entirely, rendered much less than they are, by means of permanent landmarks, buoys, &c. Besides small tug steamers would spring up, whose masters would soon gain a knowledge of the different passages, tides, and currents, and be able to take vessels out to or in from sea, in the most perfect safety. It is a disadvantage, no doubt, to have sandbanks, narrow passages, and rapid currents, but in this instance it does not seem to be insuperable.

2nd. The port of Foo-chow, although nearer to a black-tea district than any of the others open to foreigners, is only nearer to *one district*—that which I have already noticed as being on the south side of the great Bohea mountain-range. The fine districts in Kiang-se, where the Monings or Ningchow kinds are produced, are all on the northern side of these mountains, and could be taken more readily south to Canton, over the Meling Pass, or north to Shanghae. In taking them to the latter place, the whole journey, except about twenty miles, is by water. What are called Hoopak and Hoonan teas can be brought down the Yang-tse-kiang all the way to Shanghae. And finally, with regard to tea, all the green-tea districts are much more accessible from Shanghae than from Foo-chow-foo.

3rd. The country lying between the sea and the great mountain-range in Fokien, in so far as is at present known, has no other articles of export except tea for which there is a demand in Europe and America.

4th. The river Min has its source amongst rugged and barren mountains, thinly populated : it does not lead into the heart of the empire ; and hence it is doubtful if ever there will be an extensive market for foreign goods, such as there is at Shanghae or Canton.

Supposing therefore that it is possible to render the navigation of the Min comparatively safe, it appears that the port of Foo-chow has the advantage of being nearer one black-tea district than any of the other ports in China open to foreign trade. But the other kinds of black tea, and *all* the green ones, can be taken more readily and cheaply to other ports. These other ports have the advantage of other articles of export besides tea. Shanghae, for example, is on the borders of the great Hoo-chow silk country. And lastly, vessels will have to come empty to the Min, owing to the want of a market for imports, while they can go deeply laden, to such ports as Canton and Shanghae, with the manufactures of the west, which can be exchanged for the silk and tea of China. No doubt in the course of time arrangements can be made with the Chinese merchants to receive foreign goods at certain rates at such places as Shanghae, and to pay for such goods in tea, to be delivered at Foo-chow; and in this case there is only the disadvantage of an empty vessel having to be sent to that port.

The advantages and disadvantages of Foo-chow as a great port of trade have thus been fairly stated from an intimate knowledge of the country and its productions, and the merchant is left to draw his own conclusions. My own impression is that it has been rather overrated within the last year or two; that it is absurd to compare it with Shanghae as a commercial emporium, as some have done; but that, owing to there being some large and populous cities on the banks of the Min, such as Foo-chow itself, which is supposed to contain nearly half a million of inhabitants, Yen-pin-foo, Kein-ning-foo, &c., a considerable trade may ultimately be done in imports for the supply of these places. And teas from the south side of the Bohea mountains can always be brought cheaper, in better condition, and earlier in the season, to Foo-chow, than they can be had at any of the other ports.

Having completed the arrangement alluded to at the commencement of this chapter, I was anxious to proceed northward to Chekiang and Kiangnan. On making inquiries as to vessels for the northern ports, I found there was nothing of the kind in port except native craft—boats and wood junks—which were very unsafe, owing to the hordes of pirates which infested all parts of the coast. Owing to the unsettled state of the country and the weakness of Government at this time, it would have been an act of madness to have trusted myself in any of these vessels, unless I had been tired of my life, or had had an inclination to spend some months as a prisoner on some piratical island. As I was not weary of life, and had no fancy for the alternative of being imprisoned with thieves and robbers for my companions, I determined not to go to sea in a native vessel. I was strongly urged to this course by all the foreigners in Foo-chow, but they looked to me like " Job's comforters," for one and all were of opinion that it would be necessary for me to return again to Hongkong—a distance of some four hundred miles, which I had just beat up against the monsoon—before I would be able to get a vessel bound for the northern ports. My lucky star, however, happened to be in the ascendant. One fine morning a Portuguese lorcha came into port, bound north to Ningpo, convoying a number of junks to protect them from pirates. As this vessel was heavily armed, I determined to trust myself in her, and had gone on board to look at her accommodations, and to make arrangements about my passage-money.

" It never rains but it pours," says the proverb, which I cannot help thinking is a gross calumny, particularly on those soft spring showers which were at this time (April) falling on the east coast of China. The proverb proved true, however, in a figurative sense, in this instance, for, before I had made arrangements for a passage in the lorcha, the American steamer " Confucius" made her appearance from Shanghae, and soon came to an anchor amongst the Chinese junks a little below the town. As I suspected the steamer might have been chartered by Messrs. Russell and Co. in Shanghae, to carry some important news, I felt some diffidence in making any inquiries as to her destination. My friend Mr. Clark, however, who knew how anxious I was to get north, mentioned the circumstance to Captain Dearborn, and that gentleman most kindly came forward and offered me a passage without its having been asked. In the mean time, as there were numerous pirates on the coast, of whom the mandarins themselves were afraid, the Government chartered the

steamer to convey money across to the island of
Formosa, where a rebellion was going on, and
where it was necessary to have money to carry on
the war. I had thus an opportunity of paying a
short visit to this beautiful and interesting island.

When we had taken the boxes of money on
board with a guard of mandarins and soldiers, we
got up our anchor and steamed down to the
mouth of the Min. Our decks were covered with
Chinese soldiers, and their baggage, consisting of
baskets and trunks of clothes, arms of various
kinds, such as bows and arrows, short swords,
matchlocks, and bamboo shields ; while mixed up
with these in wild confusion were beds and mandarins' hats, with crystal and white buttons ;
there were also various eatables, such as sugar-
cane, &c., which the soldiers intended to consume
during the voyage. Altogether, the scene thus
presented was a striking one, and one which gave
an idea of Chinese warlike life, not often presented
to the eye of a foreigner.

When we arrived at the mouth of the Min we
anchored for the night, as it was then too late to
cross the sandbanks at the entrance. The coast
here was swarming with pirates, both on land and
at sea ; and although on ordinary occasions a
foreign vessel, and particularly a "fire-ship," *
would have been safe enough, yet loaded as we
were with boxes of sycee silver, the temptation to
these lawless bands was stronger than usual, and

* The name given to steamers by the Chinese.

R

rendered an attack far from unlikely. And had such an attack been made by two or three hundred men, armed with stinkpots and other combustibles, which they generally commence with in cases of this nature, the steamer and all its valuable cargo would have been an easy prize, owing to the small number of foreigners on board. If it ever happen that our mandarin passengers, or any of their *brave* soldiers who were on board at this time, should peruse these lines, I have to beg their pardon, with many low bows, for not taking their valour into consideration.

In addition to the captain, the engineer, and two or three officers belonging to the steamer, there were several passengers on board who had come down from Shanghae for the purpose of seeing the city of Foo-chow. Captain Dearborn very properly proposed that we should all take a share in the protection of the vessel, and that the best way to prevent an attack was to be prepared for one. The Chinese pirate is somewhat like a tiger in his habits, in so far as foreigners at least are concerned. He knows they will fight and defend themselves—he has had several good lessons on this score—and he will rarely attack them if he sees them prepared; but if he can catch them asleep, or take them unawares, he will leap upon them at once, and murder all who show the least resistance.

Knowing these things well, the passengers readily acceded to the proposal which had been

made by the captain. The night from eight p.m.
to four next morning was divided into four watches
of two hours each, and as we numbered in all
about eight or nine persons, there was enough to
have two for each watch. The hours were now
written out on small slips of paper, and thrown into
a hat to be drawn for in the usual way.

When eight bells were struck, Captain Dearborn
and Mr. Sturges, who were lucky enough to draw
from eight to ten, mounted guard, and marched up
and down the deck, armed with a pistol, cutlass,
and matchlock, and ready to repel boarders and
give any alarm if it was necessary. I was unlucky
enough to draw the sleepy watch from twelve to
two. We reported four bells to the chief officer,
struck the intermediate hours, and sung out "all's
well" in the most approved and seamanlike manner. Once or twice during the night it was necessary to warn boats to keep off when it was thought
they were coming too near, but nothing occurred
to create any alarm. Soon after four o'clock
Mr. Floud, the engineer, commenced getting his
steam up, and the steam-pipe began hissing and
snorting and bidding defiance to pirates, however
numerous or however bold.

Leaving the mouth of the river at daylight, we
stood out to sea across the channel in the direction
of the north-west end of Formosa, to which we
were bound. The distance across the channel here
is rather more than 100 miles; and as a stiff
breeze was blowing from the north and a heavy

sea on, our brave Chinese soldiers were doomed to suffer severely from sea-sickness. Huddled about the decks in every direction, unable to move or to eat, and perfectly indifferent to everybody and everything, they presented a most forlorn and wretched appearance. One old mandarin in particular happened to suffer more than any of the others. He was a stout, fat man, rather red in the face, and evidently accustomed to good living on shore. When we started, he was down in the cabin with the others, laughing and joking in the best of spirits; but as soon as we crossed the bar and felt a little motion, he began to put on a most serious countenance, and was evidently most uneasy. At last he could stand it no longer, and rushed up the cabin stairs to the deck. Every now and then we heard a loud groan, which told too plainly of the poor man's sufferings,—sufferings, too, for which no one seemed to have any compassion. The next time I saw him he made a faint attempt to smile, but it ended in a kind of shudder as he rushed past me to the side of the vessel. I confess I pitied the poor fellow, and recommended him to have his bed on deck and to lie down. He took my advice and lay down amongst his retinue, many of whom were nearly as bad as himself,—all distinction for the time being set aside, as they lay on the wet deck of the steamer, with the spray from the ocean dashing over them.

In the afternoon, shortly after we had lost sight

of the shores of China, the high mountains of Formosa came into view. When seen from this position out at sea, the height of the mountains seems greater than that of those in the vicinity of Foo-chow-foo. Judging from the height of mountains well known, I imagine those now in view may be from 3000 to 4000 feet above the level of the sea. Some others in the interior of the island are said to be as high as 10,000 feet, but these did not come under our observation. Night came on as we neared the land, and we were told by the pilot that we must anchor until daylight, as he could not undertake to go in during the dark. In the mean time, the wind had died away, the sea was smooth, and all our Chinese friends, the old mandarin included, were on their legs and in the highest spirits, seemingly astonished at the rapidity with which we had crossed the channel.

Next morning at daylight we entered a river which leads up to an important town called Tamshuy, and dropped our anchor abreast of a small town near its mouth, amongst numerous other junks and small boats which seemed to be trading between China and Formosa. As soon as we had anchored, the mandarins sent their cards to the officials on shore, and soon afterwards left the vessel themselves, promising to return again to make arrangements for landing the treasure.

As this was my first visit to this fine island, and as I knew we had only a short time to stay, I lost no time in going on shore. Before leaving the vessel I had been examining with a spy-glass some large white flowers which grew on the banks and on the hill-sides, and I now went in that direction, in order to ascertain what they were. When I reached the spot where they were growing, they proved to be very fine specimens of Lilium japonicum—the largest and most vigorous I had ever seen. As I was admiring these beautiful lilies, which were growing as wild as the primroses in our woods in England, another plant of far more interest caught my eye. This was nothing less than the rice-paper plant—the species which produced the far-famed rice-paper of China, named by Sir W. Hooker *Aralia papyrifera*. It was growing apparently wild; but the site may have been an old plantation, which was now overgrown with weeds and brushwood. The largest specimens which came under my notice were about five or six feet in height, and from six to eight inches in circumference at the base, but nearly of an equal thickness all up the stem. The stems, usually bare all the way up, were crowned at the top with a number of noble-looking palmate leaves, on long footstalks, which gave to the plant a very ornamental appearance. The under side of each leaf, its footstalk, and the top part of the stem, which was clasped by these stalks, was densely covered with down of a rich brown colour, which readily came off upon any substance with which it came in contact. I did not meet with any plant in flower during my rambles, but it is probable the plant flowers at a later period of the year.* Numerous small plants were coming through the ground in various directions, which a Chinese soldier carefully dug up for me, and which I took with me to Shanghae, and deposited them in Mr. Beale's garden. These, with a few samples of the largest stems I could find, have been sent to England and India; the latter will prove an interesting addition to our museums of vegetable productions. The proportion of pith in these stems is very great, particularly near the top of vigorous growing ones, and it is from this pure white substance that the beautiful article erroneously called " rice-paper " is prepared.

The Chinese call this plant the *Tung-tsaou.* What it was, or to what part of the vegetable kingdom it belonged, was long a mystery to botanists, who were oftentimes sadly misled by imaginary Chinese drawings, as some of those which have been published will clearly show, now that our knowledge has increased. Indeed the only drawing I have seen in Europe, which has any claim to be considered authentic, is that brought from China by the late Mr. Reeves many years ago, and which I have seen in the library of the Horticultural Society of London.

The *Tung-tsaou* is largely cultivated in many parts of the island of Formosa, and with rice and camphor forms one of the chief articles of

* It flowers and seeds during the winter and spring months at Hong-kong and Calcutta.

export. Mr. Bowring, who read a paper upon the rice-paper plant, before the China branch of the Royal Asiatic Society, informs us that the Canton and Fokien provinces are the chief consumers, and that the town of Foo-chow alone is supposed to take annually not less than 30,000 dollars worth of this curious and beautiful production. The cheapness of this paper in the Chinese market, as Mr. Bowring justly remarks, is evidence of the abundance of the plant in its place of growth, and more especially of the cheapness of labour. " That 100 sheets of this material (each about three inches square), certainly one of the most beautiful and delicate substances with which we are acquainted, should be procurable for the small sum of 1¼d. or 1½d., is truly astonishing ; and when once the attention of foreigners is directed to it, it will doubtless be in considerable request among workers in artificial flowers in Europe and America, being admirably adapted to their wants." The larger sheets, such as those used by the Canton flower-painters, are sold for about 1½d. each.

If the Tung-tsaou proves hardy in England, its fine foliage will render it a favourite amongst ornamental plants in our gardens. Judging, however, from its appearance when growing on its native island, and from the temperature of Formosa, I fear we cannot expect it to be more than a greenhouse plant with us.

Before I left China it had been completely naturalised on the island of Hong-kong. A noble plant was growing in the garden at head-quarters house, several very fine ones were observed in Messrs. Jardine's garden at East-point to which Mr. Bowring had introduced it, and younger plants were seen springing up in all directions.

It is really a most striking-looking plant, and highly ornamental. At all times the fine, broad palmate leaves which crown the stem have a noble appearance, and in the winter months its large panicles of flowers make it more interesting.

In going on shore I had landed near an old fort, like many others in China in a most ruinous condition, but still mounting a few old rusty cannon which seemed more for show than for use. The houses of the soldiers inside the fort were, with one or two exceptions, in ruins, and the men told me they had received no pay for a length of time. This was, no doubt, the case over all the island, and was probably the cause of the rebellion which had now broken out in various parts of the country, and which the money we took over was sent to quell.

Leaving the fort and its poverty-stricken guards, I went on to the town, or rather large village, which seems to be the seaport of Tam-shuy. Here I found the authorities receiving those mandarins who had been our fellow-passengers, and giving each a salute of three guns on landing. Some tradesmen were busily employed in fitting up a theatre in which a play was to be performed in the afternoon, also in honour of the new arrivals, and to which we were invited. The houses in the town were generally poor and mean-looking, and there seemed nothing in the shops except the simplest articles of food, such as fish, pork, sweet potatoes and various other vegetables in daily use among the population. However, as I have already remarked, this is only an insignificant seaport, and gives no idea of the more wealthy towns, which are known to exist inland.

As several vessels, which have been shipwrecked at different times on the coast of Formosa, have had their crews barbarously treated by the natives, the impression is abroad that it is far from being safe to land on any part of the island. Judging, however, from the short acquaintance I had with the people, I am inclined to believe the impression to be unfounded; unless, indeed, in cases of shipwreck, when they may not be trusted. But this is the same in China,—and, perhaps, we might instance other places nearer home. Everywhere, both in the town and also in the country, I was civilly and even kindly received by the people. They begged me to enter their houses and sit down, and invariably set tea before me and offered me anything they had in use amongst themselves, —and, during a day's excursion, I did not hear a single disrespectful word from any of those with whom I came in contact.

The natives of Formosa are Chinese, and are under the control of the Governor of Fokien, whose head-quarters are in the city of Foo-chow-foo, on the river Min. In the interior of the island, however, and on its eastern shores, there exists a wild race, who acknowledge no such authority, and of whom little appears to be known. The Chinese tells us, these strange people live in trees like monkeys; but whether this be true or an exaggeration I have no means of stating.

The chief productions and exports of the island are rice and camphor. The rice junks arrive yearly in large numbers at Ningpo from Formosa. The camphor finds its way in native vessels to Amoy, Chinchew, and the Straits, and from thence is exported in large quantities to Europe. Coal is also abundant in many parts, and may at some future period become of great importance to our steam-ships which are now springing up in all directions in these seas.

The hills and valleys, even very near the sea, seem particularly rich and fertile, and I have no doubt that further inland the beauty and fertility are much more striking. Altogether, it is well worth the attention of any government; not with a view to *annexation* or conquest, but to develope its resources, more particularly with regard to coal for our steamers. A new day is beginning to dawn in the east; Japan and China will soon be opened to unfettered commerce; already steamers are making their appearance on these seas and rivers, and it is high time that we should know something of a beautiful island known to be rich and fertile and to have abundant supplies of coal which only require to be dug out of the earth.

We have had a whole fleet of men-of-war—brigs and steamers of all sizes—in China ever since the termination of the last war, and yet how little has been done to extend our knowledge of an island like this, or, with the exception of Japan, and this was only a year ago, of any part to the eastward of China beyond the 32° of north latitude. In the fruitless search made after the Russian fleet in 1855, the knowledge which we ought to have acquired long ago, but which we had not, might have done us good service.

Within the last year or two our vessels of war have had enough to do, and could not be spared on a service of this kind. The disturbances in China and the piracy on the coast have kept the vessels stationed at the different ports fully employed, and well and nobly have they performed their duties ; but some few years ago, I well remember seeing such vessels lying at their anchors with nothing in the world to do for months together, if not for years. In several instances their crews got sick, and when it was too late— when numbers of the hands were dead or dying— the anchors were got up, and the vessels put to sea. Let any one visit the little English burying-ground on the island of Chusan, and he will have a full confirmation of the truth of what I state. Had the commanders of these vessels been ordered to go to sea from time to time, to explore the northern

Chinese coasts and those of Tartary, or to gain a more perfect knowledge of the resources of the islands of Formosa and Japan, a service of great value would have been rendered to commerce, and probably to science, the health of the crews would have been preserved, and numbers of lives saved.

The mandarins we took over to Formosa with the treasure had agreed to pay some two thousand dollars as charter-money for the steamer, and had also promised to give us a sufficient quantity of coal to take us back to the coast of China. It turned out, however, that the said coal had to be sent for some distance inland, and the captain was informed he would have to wait three or four days before he could be supplied. Time is nothing to the Chinese, but it was of great importance to a small tug-steamer. The Chinese were informed that we could not wait; an assertion which they received very coolly, now that themselves and their treasure had been brought safely across the channel. "If we could not wait, we must go; that was all."

During the day of our stay at this port the natives came off in swarms to look at the steamer. They were kindly treated by the officers, and their curiosity was gratified as much as possible. In the afternoon the mandarins brought their friends to see the vessel, and took away their boxes of silver. They were treated with tea and wine, and left us the best of friends. Just before dark, the steam being up, we left them to fight their own battles with the rebel power, and stood out to sea.

Having steamed rapidly all night, we found ourselves next morning at daybreak not a great distance from the entrance to the Min. It had been a stipulation with the Chinese authorities, when they chartered the vessel, that a messenger, who had been sent over in charge of the money, should be brought back, at least as far as the mouth of the river, in order to report that the sycee had been safely delivered and the conditions of the charter fulfilled. This man, whom I happened to meet afterwards, told me when he made his appearance at Foo-chow the authorities were perfectly astonished, and it was a most difficult matter to convince them that he had been further than the mouth of the river. They had calculated on his being absent a week at the least.

As we had now completed the contract undertaken with the mandarins in Foo-chow, and there being nothing else to detain the vessel, we steamed rapidly northward for the port of Shanghae. We were favoured with delightful weather for steaming; there was scarcely a ripple on the water all the way, and as our captain knew every nook and corner of the coast, we had a rapid and delightful voyage, which will long be remembered by that brave band of passengers who mounted guard that night at the mouth of the Min.

It was now spring in the north of China. At this season the weather in the provinces of Kiangnan and Chekiang is most delightful. It is not like an English spring with its easterly winds and cold and cheerless days; nor is it like an Indian one, which is not a spring at all, but rather a hot dry winter, with its leafless trees and burning sand. It is a real genuine spring, which tells one that winter has gone by; the air is cool yet soft, and rendered softer by mild April showers; every tree is bursting into leaf, and how deliciously green these leaves are when they first unfold themselves! The birds are singing in every bush and tree, and all nature seems to rejoice and sing aloud for joy.

In the north of China there are a number of plants which have their flower-buds very prominently developed in autumn, so much so that they are ready to burst into bloom before the winter has quite passed by, or, at all events, on the first dawn of spring. Amongst these *Jasminum nudiflorum* occupies a prominent position. Its yellow blossoms, which it produces in great abundance, may be seen not unfrequently peeping out from amongst the snow, and reminds the stranger in these remote regions of the beautiful primroses and cowslips which grow on the shaded banks of his own land. Nearly as early as this, the pretty daisy-like *Spiræa prunifolia*, the yellow *Forsythia viridissima*, the lilac *Daphne Fortunei*, and the pink Judas-tree, become covered with blossoms, and make our northern Chinese gardens extremely

gay. There are also some good camellias which
flower at this time, but they are generally grown
in pots under such shelter as mat-sheds and other
buildings of a like kind can afford. Two of these
varieties are particularly striking. Their flowers
are of the most perfect form, and they have striped
and self-coloured blossoms upon the same plant.
These are now in Mr. Glendinning's nursery at
Chiswick, and in a year or two will be common in
every collection. The double-blossomed peaches, of
which there are several very distinct varieties now
in England, are perhaps the gayest of all things
which flower in early spring. Fancy, if you can,
trees fully as large as our almond, literally loaded
with rich-coloured blossoms, nearly as large and
double as roses, and you will have some idea of
the effect produced by these fine trees in this part
of the world.

A little later in the season, that is from the
20th of April to the beginning of May, another
race of flowering shrubs and herbaceous plants
succeed those I have named. The most conspicu-
ous amongst them are *Viburnum macrocephalum*
and *dilatatum*, with their large heads of snow-white
flowers; *Spiræa Reevesiana*, and the double variety,
which is more beautiful than the original species;
Weigela rosea, now well known in Europe; Moutans
of various hues of colour; Azaleas, particularly
the lovely little " Amœna;" *Kerria japonica*, the
lilac and white glycines, roses, *Dielytra spectabilis*,

and *Primula cortusoides.* It will easily be believed
that with such a host of Flora's beauties these
Chinese gardens must be gay indeed. But perhaps
the most beautiful sight of all is the *Glycine sinensis*, climbing upon and hanging down from other
trees. I believe I noticed in my former works
the fine effects produced by this climber when in
such situations. I again observed numerous examples this spring, and cannot help drawing attention once more to the subject. The fine plant of
this species upon the Chiswick garden-wall is much
and justly admired; but imagine a plant equally
large, or in some instances much larger, attaching
itself to a tree, or even a group of trees, entwining
itself round the stems, running up every branch,
and weighing down every branchlet; and, in the
end of April or beginning of May, covered with
flowers, some faint idea may be formed of the fine
effects produced by the glycine in its native country. I believe it would not succeed if managed in
this way near London, or anywhere in the north;
but the experiment would be worth a trial in some
parts of Europe, where the summers are warmer
than they are in England. As this description
may meet the eye of readers in the United States
of America, who are as fond of their parks and
gardens as we are of ours, I cannot do better
than recommend the experiment to them. Many
of our northern Chinese plants succeed admirably
in America. China and America are both situated
on the eastern side of large continents, they are

s

equally liable to the extremes of heat and cold, and consequently the shrubs and trees of one country are almost certain to succeed as well in the other, provided they are reared in the same latitudes, and grown in the same kind of soil.

CHAPTER XII.

Return to Chekiang — A journey to the interior — Chinese country fair — Small feet of women — How formed, and the results — Stalls at the fair — Ancient porcelain seal same as found in the bogs of Ireland — Theatricals — Chinese actors — Natural productions of the country —Liliaceous medicinal plant — " Cold water temple " — Start for Tsan-tsin — Mountain scenery and productions — Astonishment of the people — A little boy's opinion of my habits.

On arriving at Shanghae I lost no time in returning again to the tea-districts in the interior of the Chekiang province, in order to make again arrangements for further supplies of seeds and plants for the following autumn. I shall not enter into a description of this part of my duties, as it would be nearly a repetition of some of the earlier pages in this work. But during the summer and autumn I had many opportunities of visiting districts in the interior of the country hitherto undescribed, and to these " fresh fields and pastures new," I shall now conduct the reader.

The eastern parts of the province, in which the islands of the Chusan archipelago and the great cities of Hangchow and Ningpo are included, is now pretty well known,—partly through my own researches, and partly through those of other travellers. The central and western parts of this fine province, however, have scarcely as yet been

s 2

explored by foreigners, and therefore a short account of its inhabitants and productions, as observed by me during a visit this year, may prove of some interest. Having engaged a small boat at Ningpo to take me up to one of the sources of the river, which flows past the walls of that city, I left late one evening with the first of the flood-tide. We sailed on until daylight next morning, when the ebb made strong against us, and obliged us to make our boat fast to the river's bank, and wait for the next flood. The country through which we had passed during the night was perfectly flat, and was one vast rice-field, with clumps of trees and villages scattered over it in all directions. Like all other parts of China, where the country is flat and fertile, this portion seemed to be densely populated. We were now no great distance from the hills which bound the south-west side of this extensive plain,—a plain some thirty miles from east to west, and twenty from north to south. Part of the road was the same I had travelled the year before on my way to the Snowy Valley.

When the tide turned to run up we again got under way, and proceeded on our journey. In the afternoon we reached the hills; and as our little boat followed the winding course of the stream, the wide and fertile plain through which we had passed was shut out from our view. About four o'clock in the afternoon we reached the town of Ning-Kang-jou, beyond which the river is not

navigable for boats of any size; and here I determined to leave my boat, and make excursions into
the surrounding country. It so happened that I
arrived on the eve of a fair, to be held next day
in the little town in which I had taken up my
quarters. As I walked through the streets in the
evening of my arrival great preparations were evidently making for the business and gaieties of the
following day. The shop-fronts were all decorated
with lanterns; hawkers were arriving from all
parts of the surrounding country, loaded with
wares to tempt the holiday folks; and as two
grand theatrical representations were to be given,
one at each end of the town, on the banks of the
little stream, workmen were busily employed in
fitting up the stages and galleries,—the latter being
intended for the accommodation of those who gave
the play and their friends. Everything was going
on in the most good-humoured way, and the people
seemed delighted to see a foreigner amongst them,
and were all perfectly civil and kind. I had many
invitations to come and see the play next night;
and the general impression seemed to be, that I
had visited the place with the sole intention of
seeing the fair.

Retiring early to rest, I was up next morning
some time before the sun, and took my way into
the country to the westward. Even at that early
hour—4 A.M.—the country-roads were lined with
people pouring into the town. There were long
trains of coolies, loaded with fruits and vegetables;

there were hawkers, with their cakes and sweet-meats to tempt the young; while now and then passed a thrifty housewife, carrying a web of cotton cloth, which had been woven at home, and was now to be sold at the fair. More gaily dressed than any of these were small parties of ladies limping along on their small feet, each one having a long staff in her hand to steady her, and to help her along the mountain-road. Behind each of these parties come an attendant coolie, carrying a basket of provisions, and any other little article which was required during the journey. On politely inquiring of the several parties of ladies where they were going to, they invariably replied in the language of the district " Ta-pa-Busa-la,"— we are going to worship Buddha. Some of the younger ones, particularly the good-looking, pretended to be vastly frightened as I passed them on the narrow road; but that this was only pretence was clearly proved by the joyous ringing laugh which reached my ears after they had passed and before they were out of sight.

It is certainly a most barbarous custom that of deforming the feet of Chinese ladies, and detracts greatly from their beauty. Many persons think that the custom prevails only amongst persons of rank or wealth, but this is a great mistake. In the central and eastern provinces of the empire it is almost universal,—the fine ladies who ride in sedan-chairs, and the poorer classes who toil from morning till evening in the fields, are all deformed

in the same manner. In the more southern provinces, such as Fokien and Canton, the custom is
not so universal; boat-women and field-labourers
generally allow their feet to grow to the natural
size. Here is one of a peculiar class of country-
women, to be met with near Foo-chow, from the
talented pencil of Mr. Scarth.

Foo-chow Countrywoman.

Dr. Lockhart, whose name I have already mentioned in these pages, gives the following as the
results of his extensive and varied experience on
this subject.   He says :—

" Considering the vast number of females who
have the feet bound up in early life, and whose
feet are then distorted, the amount of actual disease of the bones is small; the ancle is generally
tender, and much walking soon causes the foot to

swell, and be very painful, and this chiefly when
the feet have been carelessly bound in infancy.
To produce the diminution of the foot, the tarsus
or instep is bent on itself, the os calcis or heel-bone
thrown out of the horizontal position, and what
ought to be the posterior surface, brought to the
ground; so that the ancle is, as it were, forced
higher up than it ought to be, producing in fact
artificial Talipes Calcaneus; then the four smaller
toes are pressed down under the instep, and
checked in their growth, till at adult age all that
has to go into the shoe is the end of the os calcis
and the whole of the great toe. In a healthy constitution this constriction of the foot may be carried on without any very serious consequences;
but in scrofulous constitutions the navicular bone,
and the cuneiform bone supporting the great toe,
are very liable, from the constant pressure and
irritation to which they are exposed, to become
diseased; and many cases have been seen where
caries, softening, and even death of the bone have
taken place, accompanied with much suppuration
and great consequent suffering. Chinese women
have naturally very small hands and feet, but this
practice of binding the feet utterly destroys all
symmetry according to European ideas, and the
limping uncertain gait of the women is, to a foreigner, distressing to see. Few of the Chinese
women can walk far, and they always appear to
feel pain when they try to walk quickly, or on
uneven ground.

" The most serious inconvenience to which women with small feet are exposed," he observes, " is that they so frequently fall and injure themselves. During the past year, several cases of this kind have presented themselves. Among them was one of an old woman, seventy years of age, who was coming down a pair of stairs and fell, breaking both her legs ; she was in a very dangerous state for some time, on account of threatened mortification of one leg, but the unfavourable symptoms passed off, and finally the bones of both legs united, and she is able to walk again.

" Another case was also that of an elderly woman, who was superintending the spring cutting of bamboo shoots in her field, when she fell over some bamboos, owing to her crippled feet slipping among the roots ; a compound fracture of one leg was the consequence, and the upper fragment of the bone stuck in the ground ; the soft parts of the leg were so much injured, that amputation was recommended, but her friends would not hear of it, and she soon afterwards died from mortification of the limb.

" The third case was that of a woman, who also fell down stairs and had compound fracture of the leg ; this case is still under treatment, and is likely to do well, as there was not very much injury done to the soft parts in the first instance."

About eight o'clock I returned to the town, and took the principal temple on my way. The sight which presented itself here was a curious and

striking one. Near the doors were numerous
venders of candles and joss-stick, who were eagerly
pressing the devotees to buy; so eager were they,
indeed, that I observed them in several instances
actually lay hold of the people as they passed; and
strange to say, this rather rough mode of getting
customers was frequently successful. Crowds of
people were going in and coming out of the temple
exactly like bees in a hive on a fine summer's day.
Some halted a few moments to buy their candles
and incense from the dealers already noticed;
while others seemed to prefer purchasing from the
priests in the temple. Nor were the venders confined to those who sold things used only in the
worship of Buddha. Some had stalls of cakes and
sweetmeats; others had warm and cold tea, snuff-
bottles, fans, and a hundred other fancy articles
which it is needless to enumerate. Doctors were
there who could cure all diseases; and fortune-
tellers, too, seemed to have a full share of patron-
age from a liberal and enlightened public. In
front of the altar other scenes were being acted.
Here the devotees—by far the largest portion
being females—were prostrating themselves many
times before the Gods; and each one, as she arose
from her knees, hastened to light some candles
and incense, and place these upon the altar, then
returning to the front, the prostrations were again
repeated, and then the place was given up to
another, who repeated the same solemn farce. And
so they went on during the whole of that day,—

on which many thousands of people must have paid their vows at these heathen altars.

I may here mention, in passing, that I picked up two articles at this place, of considerable interest to antiquaries in Europe. One was a small porcelain bottle, exactly similar in size, form and colouring to those found in ancient Egyptian tombs. The characters on one side are also identical, and are a quotation from one of the Chinese poets— " *Only in the midst of this mountain.*"

I have already alluded to these bottles in one of the earlier chapters, and need say nothing further about them here. They are to be met with not unfrequently in doctors' shops and old stalls; several persons, both in China and England, possess specimens.

The other article I have mentioned is far more curious and interesting. It is a small porcelain seal identical with those found of late years in the bogs of Ireland. On the 6th of May, 1850, Mr. Getty read a very curious and interesting paper on this subject before the Belfast Literary Society, and he has since published it with drawings and descriptions of the different seals. One was found when ploughing a field in Tipperary, another in the county of Down, a third in the bed of the river Boyne, and a fourth near Dublin. That these seals have lain in the bogs and rivers of Ireland for many ages there cannot be the slightest doubt. The peculiar white or rather cream-coloured porcelain of which they are composed, has not been made in China for several hundred years. The Chinese, who laugh at the idea of the bottles being considered ancient which have been found in the tombs of Egypt, all agree in stating that these seals are from one thousand to two thousand years old.

They are very rare in China at the present day. I had the greatest difficulty in getting the few which are now in my possession, although my opportunities of picking up such things were greater than those of most persons in China. It is therefore absurd to suppose that those found in Ireland can have been brought over of late years by sailors, or captains of ships, or even by either of the two embassies to Peking. Here is a sketch of some of those found in China at the present day. Those who are fortunate enough to possess the Irish ones will see an exact resemblance to their own.

Ancient Porcelain Seals.

There is therefore no doubt that those rare and ancient seals found in China at the present day

are identical with those found in Ireland. That
the latter must have been brought over at a very
early period, and that they must have lain for
many ages in the bogs and rivers of that island
seems also quite certain. But when they came
there, how they came, and what were the circumstances connected with their introduction, are
questions which we cannot answer. To do this
satisfactorily we should probably have to consult
a book of history, written, studied, and lost long
before that of the present history of Ireland.

The streets of the town were now crowded with
people; and the whole scene reminded me of a
fair in a country-town in England. In addition
to the usual articles in the shops, and an unusual
supply of fruits and vegetables, there was a large
assortment of other things which seemed to be
exposed in quantity only on a fair-day. Native
cotton cloths, woven by handlooms in the country,
were abundant,—mats made from a species of Juncus, and generally used for sleeping upon,— clothes
of all kinds, both new and second-hand,—porcelain
and wooden vessels of various sorts,—toys, cakes,
sweetmeats, and all the common accompaniments
of an English fair. Various textile fibres of interest were abundant, being produced in large
quantities in the district. Amongst these, and the
chief, were the following : — hemp, jute, China
grass (so called)—being the bark of *Urtica nivea*—
and the Juncus already noticed. A great number
of the wooden vessels were made of the wood of

Cryptomania japonica, which is remarkable for the number of beautiful rings and veins which show to great advantage when the wood is polished.

In the afternoon the play began, and attracted its thousands of happy spectators. As already stated, the subscribers, or those who gave the play, had a raised platform, placed about twenty yards from the front of the stage, for themselves and their friends. The public occupied the ground on the front and sides of the stage, and to them the whole was free as their mountain-air,—each man, however poor, had as good right to be there as his neighbour. And it is the same all over China :— the actors are paid by the rich, and the poor are not excluded from participating in the enjoyments of the stage.

The Chinese have a curious fancy for erecting these temporary theatres on the dry beds of streams. In travelling through the country I have frequently seen them in such places. Sometimes, when the thing is done in grand style, a little tinsel town is erected at the same time, with its palaces, pagodas, gardens, and dwarf plants. These places rise and disappear as if by the magic of the enchanter's wand, but they serve the purposes for which they are designed, and contribute largely to the enjoyment and happiness of the mass of the people.

On the present occasion I did not fail to accept the invitations which had been given me in the earlier part of the day. As I did not intend to

remain for a great length of time I was content to
take my place in the " pit," which I have already
said is free to the public. But the parties who
had given the play were too polite to permit me
to remain amongst the crowd. One of them—a
respectable-looking man, dressed very gaily—came
down and invited me to accompany him to the
boxes. He led me up a narrow staircase and into
a little room in which I found several of his
friends amusing themselves by smoking, sipping
tea, and eating seeds and fruits of various kinds.
All made way for the stranger, and endeavoured
to place me in the best position for getting a view
of the stage. What a mass of human beings were
below me ! The place seemed full of heads, and
one might suppose that the bodies were below, but
it was impossible to see them, so densely were they
packed together. Had it not been for the stage
in the background with its actors dressed in the
gay-coloured costumes of a former age, and the
rude and noisy band, it would have reminded me
more of the hustings at a contested election in
England than anything else. But taken as a
whole, there was nothing to which I could liken
it out of China.

The actors had no stage-scenery to assist them
in making an impression on the audience. This
is not the custom in China. A table, a few chairs,
and a covered platform are all that is required.
No ladies are allowed to appear as actresses in the
country, but the way in which the sex is imitated

is most admirable, and always deceives any foreigner ignorant of the fact I have stated.

In the present instance each actor repeated his part in a singing falsetto voice. The whole interest of the piece must have lain in the story itself, for there was nothing natural in the acting, the sham sword-fights perhaps excepted. One or two of these occurred in the piece during the time I was a spectator, and they were certainly natural enough, thoroughly Chinese and very amusing. An actor rushed upon the stage amid the clashing of timbrels, beating of gongs, and squeaking of other instruments. He was brandishing a short sword in each hand, now and then wheeling round apparently to protect himself in the rear, and all the time performing the most extraordinary actions with his feet, which seemed as if they had to do as much of the fighting as the hands. People who have seen much of the manœuvring of Chinese troops will not call this unnatural acting. But whatever a foreigner might think of such " artistes," judging from the intense interest and boisterous mirth of a numerous audience, they performed their parts to the entire satisfaction of their patrons and the public.

" How-pa-how," said my kind friends, as I rose to take my leave; "is it good or bad?" Of course I expressed my entire approbation, and thanked them for the excellent view I had enjoyed of the performance through their politeness. It was now night—dark—the lanterns were lighted, the crowd still continued, and the play went on. Long after I left them, and even when I retired for the night, I could hear, every now and then, borne on the air the sounds of their rude music, and the shouts of applause from a good-humoured multitude.

The natural productions of this part of China now claim a share of our attention. Much of the level land among the hills in this part of the country, being considerably higher than the great Ningpo plain, is adapted to the growth of other crops than rice. The soil in these valleys is a light rich loam, and is in a state of high cultivation ; indeed, I never witnessed fields so much like gardens as these are. The staple summer crops are those which yield textile fibres, such as those I saw in the fair already described. A plant well known by the name of jute in India—a species of Corchorus—which has been largely exported to Europe of late years from India, is grown here to a very large extent. In China this fibre is used in the manufacture of sacks and bags for holding rice and other grains. A gigantic species of hemp (Cannabis) growing from ten to fifteen feet in height, is also a staple summer crop. This is chiefly used in making ropes and string of various sizes, such articles being in great demand for tracking the boats up rivers, and in the canals of the country. Every one has heard of China grass-cloth,—that beautiful fabric made in the Canton province, and largely exported to Europe and

T

America. The plant which is supposed to produce this (*Urtica nivea*) is also abundantly grown in the western part of this province, and in the adjoining province of Kiangse. Fabrics of various degrees of fineness are made from this fibre, and sold in these provinces; but I have not seen any so fine as that made about Canton. It is also spun into thread for sewing purposes, and is found to be very strong and durable. There are two very distinct varieties of this plant common in Chekiang —one the cultivated, the other the wild. The cultivated variety has larger leaves than the other; on the upper side they are of a lighter green, and on the under they are much more downy. The stems also are lighter in colour, and the whole plant has a silky feel about it which the wild one wants. The wild variety grows plentifully on sloping banks, on city walls, and other old and ruinous buildings. It is not prized by the natives, who say its fibre is not so fine, and more broken and confused in its structure than the other kind. The cultivated kind yields three crops a year.

The last great crop which I observed was that of a species of juncus, the stems of which are woven into beautiful mats, used by the natives for sleeping upon, for covering the floors of rooms, and for many other useful purposes. This is cultivated in water, somewhat like the rice-plant, and is therefore always planted in the lowest parts of these valleys. At the time of my visit, in the beginning of July, the harvest of this crop had just commenced, and hundreds of the natives were busily employed in drying it. The river's banks, uncultivated land, the dry gravelly bed of the river, and every other available spot was taken up with this operation. At grey dawn of morning the sheaves or bundles were taken out of temporary sheds, erected for the purpose of keeping off the rain and dew, and shaken thinly over the surface of the ground. In the afternoon, before the sun had sunk very low in the horizon, it was gathered up again into sheaves and placed under cover for the night. A watch was then set in each of the sheds; for however quiet and harmless the people in these parts are, there is no lack of thieves, who are very honest if they have no opportunity to steal. And so the process of winnowing went on day by day until the whole of the moisture was dried out of the reeds. They were then bound up firmly in round bundles, and either sold in the markets of the country, or taken to Ningpo and other towns where the manufacture of mats is carried on, on a large scale.

The winter crops of this part of China consist of wheat, barley, the cabbage oil-plant, and many other kinds of vegetables on a smaller scale. Large tracts of land are planted with the bulbs of a liliaceous plant—probably a *Fritillaria*—which are used in medicine. This is planted in November, and dug up again in April and May. In March these lily-fields are in full blossom, and give quite a feature to the country. The flowers

are of a dingy greyish white, and not very ornamental.

It seems to me to be very remarkable that a
country like China,—rich in textile fibre, oils of
many kinds, vegetable tallow, dyes, and no doubt
many other articles which have not come under
my notice—should afford so few articles for exportation. I have no doubt that as the country gets
better known, our merchants will find many things
besides silk and tea, which have hitherto formed
almost the only articles exported in quantity to
Europe and America.

When I was travelling in the part of the
country I have been describing, the weather was
extremely hot,—July and August being the hottest
months of the year in China. When complaining
of the excessive heat to some of my visitors, I was
recommended to go to a place called by them the
Lang-shuy-ain, or "cold water temple," situated
in the vicinity of the town in which I was staying.
In this place they told me both air and water were
cold notwithstanding the excessive heat of the
weather. On visiting the place I found it an old,
dilapidated building, which had evidently seen
more prosperous days. Ascending a few stone
steps, I reached the lower part of the edifice, when
I felt at once a sudden change in the temperature,
something like that which one experiences on
going into an ice-house on a hot summer's day.
My guide led me to the further corner of this
place, and pointed to some stone steps which

seemed to lead down to a cave or some such sub-
terranean place, and desired me to walk down. As
it appeared perfectly dark to me on coming from
the bright sunshine, I hesitated to proceed without a candle. On this being brought, I was much
disappointed in finding the steps were only a few
in number and led to nowhere. It appeared that
in the more prosperous days of the temple there
had been a well of clear water at the bottom of
the steps, but now that was choked up with stones
and rubbish. I was able, however, to procure
a little water nearly as cold as if it had been iced.
The stones in this part of the building were also
very cold to the touch, and a strong current of
cold air was coming out of the earth at this particular point. I regretted much not having my
thermometer with me to have tested the difference
of the temperature with accuracy. On the floor of
the temple a motley group of persons was presented to my view. Beggars, sick persons, and
others who had taken refuge from the heat of the
sun were lolling about, evidently enjoying the
cool air which filled the place. It appeared to be
free to all, rich and poor alike. There are some
large clay-slate and granite quarries near this
place; and I afterwards found several springs of
water issuing from the clay-slate rocks quite as
cold as that in the " cold water temple."

Having spent several days in the town of Ning-
kang-jou, I determined to proceed onwards to a
large temple situated amongst the hills to the

westward, and distant, as I was informed, some twenty or thirty le. Packing up my bed and a few necessaries, I started in a mountain chair one morning, after an early breakfast. Leaving the town behind me, the road led me winding along the side of a hill, following the course of the little stream. The scenery here was perfectly enchanting. The road, though narrow, like all Chinese roads, was nicely paved and oftentimes shaded by the branches of lofty trees. Above me rose a sloping hill, covered with trees and brushwood, while a few feet below me was seen the little stream trickling over its gravelly bed and glistening in the morning sun. Now and then I passed a pool where the water was still and deep, but generally the river, which is navigable for large ships at Ningpo, was here not more than ankle deep. Shallow as it was, however, the Chinese were still using it for floating down the productions of these western hills. Small rafts made of bamboo, tiny flat-bottomed boats, and many other contrivances were employed to accomplish the end in view. When the river was so shallow that the boatman could not use his scull, he might oftentimes be seen walking in the river and dragging his boat or raft over the stones into deeper water. As I passed along, I observed several anglers busily employed with rod and line —real Izaak Waltons it seemed—and although they did not appear very expert, and their tackle was rather clumsy, yet they generally succeeded

in getting their baskets well filled.   Altogether,
this scene, which I can only attempt to describe,
was a charming one,—a view of Chinese country-
life, telling plainly that the Chinese, however
strange they may sometimes appear, are, after all,
very much like ourselves.

My road at length left the hill-side and little
stream, and took me across a wide and highly
cultivated valley, several miles in extent, and
surrounded on all sides by hills, except that one
through which the river winded in its course to
the eastward.   I passed through two small towns
in this valley where the whole population seemed
to turn out to look at me.   Everywhere I was
treated with the most marked politeness, and even
kindness, by the inhabitants.   " Stop a little, sit
down, drink tea," was said to me by almost every
one whose door I passed.   Sometimes I complied
with their wishes ; but more generally I simply
thanked them, and pushed onwards on my journey.
In the afternoon I arrived at the further end of
the valley and at the foot of a mountain pass.
As I gradually ascended this winding path, the
valley through which I had passed was entirely
shut out from my view.   Nothing was now seen
but mountains, varying in height and form,—some
about 2000, and others little less than 4000 feet
above the level of the sea,—some formed of gentle
slopes, with here and there patches of cultivation,
—others steep and barren, where no cultivation
can ever be carried on, except that of brushwood,

which the most barren mountains generally furnish. The Chinese pine and Japan cedar were
almost the only trees of any size which I observed
as I passed along. A little higher up I came to
fine groves of the bamboo—the famous *maou-chok*,
already noticed—the finest variety of bamboo in
China, and always found growing in the vicinity
of Buddhist temples.

In a small valley amongst these mountains,
some 2000 feet high, the temple of Tsan-tsing
was at last seen peeping out from amongst the
trees. The building in itself is of a much less
imposing character than others I have seen in this
province and in Fokien; but, like all others of its
kind, it is pleasantly situated in the midst of the
most romantic scenery. In addition to the pines
and bamboos already noticed, were several species
of oaks and chesnuts, the former producing good-
sized timber. But the finest tree of all, and quite
new to me, was a beautiful species of cedar or
larch; which I observe Dr. Lindley, to whom
I sent specimens, calls *Abies Kœmpferi*.

When I entered the court of the temple the
priests seemed quite lost in astonishment. No
other foreigner, it seemed, had been there before,
and many of them had only heard of us by name.
Some of them stood gazing at me as if I were a
being from another world, while others ran out to
inform their friends of my arrival. My request
for quarters was readily granted; and being now
an old traveller, I was soon quite at home amongst

my new friends. Late in the afternoon, long
trains of coolies — men and boys — passed the
temple from a district further inland, loaded with
young bamboo shoots, which are eaten as a vegetable and much esteemed. The news of the
arrival of a foreigner at the temple seemed to fly
in all directions; and we were crowded during the
evening with the natives, all anxious to get a
glimpse of me. Some seemed never tired of looking at me; others had a sort of superstitious
dread mingled with curiosity. One little urchin,
who had been looking on with great reverence
for some time, and on whom I flattered myself
I had made a favourable impression, undeceived
me by putting the following simple question to
his father :—" If I go near him, will he bite me ? "
This, I confess, astonished me; for although I had
no tail,—was not exactly the same colour as they
were,—and did not wear the same kind of dress,—
I did not expect to be taken for a wild animal.
What strange tales must have been told these
simple country people of the *barbarians* during the
last Chinese war ?

CHAPTER XIII.

A dinner audience — Adventure with a priest — Sanatarium for Ningpo missionaries and others — Abies Kæmpferi — Journey to Quanting — Bamboo woods and their value — Magnificent scenery — Natives of Poo-in-chee — Golden bell at Quan-ting — Chinese traditions — Cold of the mountains — Journey with Mr. Wang — A disappointment — Adventure with pirates — Strange but satisfactory signal — Results.

THE bedroom which I expressed a wish to occupy, as it seemed somewhat cleaner than the others, was used during the day by an itinerant tailor, a native of Fung-hwa-heen, who was in the habit of going from place to place to mend or make the garments of his customers. This man willingly removed to other quarters, and gave the room up to me. He was a good specimen of his race, shrewd, intelligent, and formed a striking contrast to the priest for whom he was working. Never in all my travels in China had I met with such poor specimens of the human race as these same priests. They had that vacant stare about them which indicated want of intellect, or at least, a mind of a very low order indeed. They did nothing all day long but loll on chairs or stools, and gaze upon the ground, or into space, or at the people who were working, and then they did not appear to see what was going on, but kept looking

on and on notwithstanding.   The time not spent
in this way was when they were either eating or
sleeping.   They were too lazy to carry on the
services of the temple, which they deputed to a
little boy.   And thus they spent their days, and
in this manner they would float down the stream
of time until they reached the ocean of eternity
and were no more seen.

There were four or five of these men connected
with the old monastery, and two or three boys,
who were being reared to succeed them.   All the
men were apparently imbecile, but the superior
seemed to be in a state approaching to insanity.
I seemed to have an extraordinary attraction for
this man; he never took his eyes off me; wherever I went he followed at a certain distance
behind, stopping when I stopped, and going on
again when I went on.   When I entered the
house he came and peeped in at the window, and
when I made the slightest motion towards him, he
darted off in an instant, but only to return again.
I began to think his actions extraordinary, and to
feel a little uneasy about his ultimate intentions.
The place and the people were all strange to me,
and it might so happen that the man was really
unsafe.   By day there was no fear, as I could
easily protect myself; but what if he fell upon me
unawares at night, when I was asleep!   I therefore sent for Tung-a, one of my servants, and
desired him to go out and make some enquiries
concerning the propensities of the mad priest.

Tung-a returned laughing, and told me there was no danger; the man was not mad, but that it was partly fear and partly curiosity which made him act in the manner he was doing, and further, that I was the first specimen of my race he had seen.

During the time I was at dinner, and for some time after, in addition to some of the more respectable who were admitted into the room, the doors and windows were completely besieged with people. Every little hole or crevice had a number of eager eyes peeping through it, each anxious to see the foreigner feed. Having finished my dinner and smoked a cigar, much to the delight of an admiring audience, I politely intimated that it was getting late, that I was tired with the exertions of the day, and that I was going to bed. My inside guests rose and retired, but it seemed to me they only went outside to join the crowd, and they were determined to see the finale; they had seen how I eat, drank, and smoked my cigar, and they now wanted to see how and in what manner I went to bed. My temper was unusually sweet at this time, and therefore I had no objection to gratify them even in this, providing they remained quiet and allowed me to get to sleep. A traveller generally does not spend much of his time over the toilet, either in dressing or undressing, so that in less time than I would take to describe it I was undressed, the candle was put out, and I was in bed. As there was nothing more to be seen the crowd left my window, and as

they retired I could hear them laughing and
talking about what they had seen.

The chamber in which the head-priest, whom I
have described, was wont to repose after the
fatigues of the day, was behind the one occupied
by me, and it appeared it was necessary to come
through mine in order to get into it. I had examined the chamber and learned to whom it
belonged in the course of the evening. Not
caring to be disturbed by having my door opened
and a person walking through my room after I
was in bed and asleep, I had suggested to the
priest the propriety of going to bed about the
same time as I did. When the crowd therefore
had left my windows, I heard one or two persons
whispering outside and still lingering there. I
called out to them and desired them to go away to
their beds. "Loya, Loya!"* a voice cried, "the
Ta-Hosan (high-priest) wants to go to bed."
"Well," said I, "come along, the door is not
locked." "But he has not had his supper yet,"
another voice replied. "Tell him to go and get it
then, as quickly as possible, for I do not wish to
be disturbed after I go to sleep."

The fatigue of climbing the mountain-pass, and
the healthy fresh air of the mountains, soon sent
me to sleep, and I dare say the priest might have
walked through the room without my knowing
anything about it. How long I slept I know not,

* Mode of addressing mandarins and high government officers—a
term of respect.

for the room was quite dark ; but I was awakened
by the same voices which had addressed me before,
and again informed that the Ta-Hosan wanted to
come to bed.

" Well, well, come to bed and let me have no
more of your noise," said I, being at the time half-
asleep and half-awake ; and going off sound again
immediately I heard no more. Next morning,
when I awoke, the day was just beginning to
dawn, and daylight was streaming through the
paper window and rendering the tables and chairs
in the apartment partially visible. The proceedings of the evening seemed to have got mixed up
somehow with my dreams, but as they became
gradually distinct to the mind, and separated, I
began to wonder whether my friend the priest had
occupied his bedroom during the night. The door
was closed and seemed in the same state in which
I left it when I went to bed, and I could hear no
sound of anything breathing or moving through
the thin partition-wall which divided our rooms.
In order to satisfy myself I gently opened the
door and looked in. But no priest was there.
The bed had been prepared, and the padded cover-
let carefully folded for his reception, but all remained in the same condition, and showed plainly
that no one had occupied the room during the
night.

Tung-a now made his appearance with my
morning cup of tea. It turned out on inquiry
that the poor old priest could not get over his

superstitious dread of me; he was anxious to get
to his own bed, and had striven hard to accomplish his object; but it was quite beyond his
power. It was now easy enough to account for
his conduct at my window the night previous.
When it was found he could not conquer his fears
a brother priest gave him a share of his bed, and I
had been left to the undisturbed repose which I
greatly required.

The valley of Tsan-tsin, as I have already
stated, is high up amongst the mountains, some
1500 or 2000 feet above the level of the sea. It
is completely surrounded by mountains, many of
them apparently from 3000 to 4000 feet high.
Even in the hot summer months, although warm
during the day in the sun, the evenings, nights,
and mornings, are comparatively cool. At this
time of the year the southwest monsoon is blowing, but ere it reaches the valley it passes over a
large tract of high mountains, and consequently
gets cooled on its course. This appears to be the
reason why the country, even at the foot of the
mountains here, is cooler than further down in the
Ningpo valley.

I have frequently thought this would make an
admirable sanitary station for the numerous missionaries and other foreigners who live at Ningpo.
Could the Chinese authorities be induced to allow
them to build a small bungalow or two in the
valley, they might thus have a cool and healthy
retreat to fly to in case of sickness. It is easy of

access even to invalids, and could be reached in a day and a half, or at most two days from Ningpo.

I have already noticed a new cedar or larch-tree named *Abies Kœmpferi* discovered amongst these mountains. I had been acquainted with this inte-

Larch Tree.

resting tree for several years in China, but only in gardens, and as a pot plant in a dwarfed state. The Chinese, by their favourite system of dwarfing, contrive to make it, when only a foot and a half or two feet high, have all the characters of an aged cedar of Lebanon. It is called by them the *Kin-le-sung*, or Golden Pine, probably from the rich yellow appearance which the ripened leaves and cones assume in the autumn. Although I had often made enquiries after it, and endeavoured to get the natives to bring me some cones, or to take me to a place where such cones could be procured, I met with no success until the previous autumn, when I had passed by the temple from another part of the country. Their stems, which I measured, were fully five feet in circumference two feet from the ground, and carried this size, with a slight diminution, to a height of 50 feet, that being the height of the lower branches. The total height I estimated about 120 or 130 feet. The stems were perfectly straight throughout, the branches symmetrical, slightly inclined to the horizontal form, and having the appearance of something between the cedar and larch. The long branchless stems were, no doubt, the result of their growing close together and thickly surrounded with other trees, for I have since seen a single specimen growing by itself on a mountain side at a much higher elevation, whose lower branches almost touched the ground. This specimen I shall notice by-and-by.

I need scarcely say how pleased I was with the discovery I had made, or with what delight, with the permission and assistance of the good priests, I procured a large supply of those curious cones sent to England in the winter of 1853.

U

I now lost no time in visiting the spot of my last year's discovery. The trees were there as beautiful and symmetrical as ever, but after straining my eyes for half-an-hour I could not detect a single cone. I returned to the temple and mentioned my disappointment to the priests, and asked them whether it was possible to procure cones from any other part of the country. They told me of various places where there were trees, but whether these had seed upon them or not they could not say. They further consoled me with a piece of information, which, although I was most unwilling to believe it, I knew to be most likely too true, namely, that this tree rarely bore cones two years successively, that last year was its bearing year, and that this one it was barren. A respectable looking man, who was on a visit to the temple, now came up to me and said that he knew a place where a large number of trees were growing, and that if I would visit the temple to which he belonged he would take me to this spot, and that there I would probably find what I wanted. I immediately took down the name of his residence, which he told me was Quan-ting, a place about twenty le distant from the temple in which I was domiciled, and at a much higher elevation on the mountains. After making an appointment for next day he took his leave of me with great politeness, and returned to his home.

Having procured a guide for Quan-ting, I set out early next day to visit my new acquaintance.

Leaving the temple of Tsan-tsing, our way led up a steep pass, paved with granite stones. On each side of the road were forests of fine bamboos—the variety called by the Chinese *Maou*, the finest I ever saw. The forests are very valuable, not only on account of the demand for the full-grown bamboos, but also for the young shoots, which are dug up and sold in the markets in the early part of the season. Here, too, were dense woods of *Cryptomeria, Cunninghamia lanceolata*, oaks, chesnuts, and such like representatives of a cold or temperate climate.

On the road up the mountain pass I met long trains of coolies, heavily laden with bamboos, and on their way to the plains. The weight of the loads which these men carry is perfectly astonishing; even little boys were met carrying loads which I found some difficulty in lifting. All these people are accustomed to this work from their earliest years, and this is no doubt one of the reasons why they are able to carry such heavy loads.

This fine bamboo may be regarded as a staple production amongst these mountains, and one of great value to the natives. In the spring and early summer months its young shoots furnish a large supply of food of a kind much esteemed by the Chinese. At that time of the year the same long trains of coolies which I had just met carrying the trees, may then be seen loaded with the young shoots. The trees in the autumn and the

young shoots in spring, are carried down to the
nearest navigable stream, where they are put on
rafts, or in small flat-bottomed boats, and conveyed
a few miles down until the water becomes deep
enough to be navigated by the common boats of
the country. They are then transferred into the
larger boats, and in them conveyed to the populous towns and cities in the plain, where they
always find a ready sale. Thus this valuable tree,
which is cultivated at scarcely any expense, gives
employment and food to the natives of these
mountains for nearly one-half the year. All the
way up the mountain passes the axe of the wood-
man was heard cutting down the trees. In many
parts the mountains were steep enough for the
trees to slide down to the road without any more
labour than that required to set them in motion.

When I reached the top of this pass I got into
a long narrow valley—the valley of Poo-in-chee—
where the road was nearly on a level. This
valley must be nearly 1000 feet higher than
Tsan-tsing, or between two and three thousand
feet above the level of the plain. At the top of
the mountain-pass, and just before entering this
valley, some most glorious views were obtained.
Behind, before, and on my left hand, there was
nothing but steep and rugged mountains covered
with grass and brushwood, but untouched by the
hand of man, while far down below in a deep
dell, a little stream was dashing over its rocky
bed and hurrying onwards to swell the river in

the plain with its clear, cool waters. A little further on, when I looked to my right hand, a view of another kind, even grander still, met my eye. An opening in the mountain exposed to view the valley of Ningpo lying far below me, and stretching away to the eastward for some thirty miles, where it meets the ocean, and appeared bounded by the islands in the Chusan Archipelago. Its cities, villages, and pagodas were dimly seen in the distance, while its noble river was observed winding through the plain and bearing on its surface hundreds of boats, hurrying to and fro, and carrying on the commerce of the country. The picture was grand and sublime, and the impression produced by it then must ever remain engraved on my mind.

The village of Poo-in-chee is a straggling little place and contains but few inhabitants. Many of these mountaineers—indeed, the greater part of them—had never seen a foreigner in their lives. As I approached the village the excitement amongst them was very great. Every living thing—men, women, and children, dogs, and cats —seemed to turn out to look at me. Many of them, judging from the expression on their countenances, were not entirely free from fear. "I might be harmless, but it was just as possible I might be a cannibal, or somewhat like a tiger." In circumstances of this kind it is always best to take matters coolly and quietly. Observing a respectable-looking old man sitting in front of one of the best houses in the village, I went up to him and politely asked him if he " had eaten his rice." He called out immediately to a boy to bring me a chair, and begged me to rest a little before I proceeded on my journey. As usual, tea was brought and set before me. As I chatted away with the old man, the natives gathered confidence and crowded round us in great numbers. Their fears soon left them when they found I was much like one of themselves, although without a tail. Everything about me was examined and criticised with the greatest minuteness. My hat, my clothes, my shoes, and particularly my watch, were all objects which attracted their attention. I took all this in good part, answered all their questions, and I trust when I left them their opinion of the character of foreigners had somewhat changed.

Another mountain-pass had now to be got over, nearly as high as the last one. When the top of this was gained, I found I was now on the summit of the highest range in this part of the country. Our road now winded along the tops of the mountains at this elevation for several miles, and at last descended into the Quan-ting valley, for which I was bound. This was somewhat like the Poo-in-chee valley just described, and apparently about the same elevation.

Having reached the temple, I had no difficulty in finding my acquaintance of the previous day, Mr. Wang-a-nok, as he called himself. It now

appeared he was a celebrated cook — the Soyer
of the district—and had been engaged on this
day to prepare a large dinner for a number of
visitors who had come to worship at the temple.
He told me he would be ready to accompany me
as soon as the dinner was over, and invited me
to be seated in the priest's room until that time.
As there was nothing in the temple of much
interest, I preferred taking a stroll amongst the
hills. Before I set out I made inquiry of Wang
and the priest whether there were any objects of
interest in the vicinity more particularly worth
my attention. I was told there was one place of
more than common interest, which I ought to see,
and at the same time several persons offered to
accompany me as guides. We then started off to
inspect the new wonder, whatever it might turn
óut to be.

A short distance in the rear of the temple my
guides halted at the edge of a little pool, which
was surrounded with a few willows and other
stunted bushes. They now pointed to the little
pool, and informed me this was what they had
brought me to see. " Is this all ? " said I, with
features which, no doubt, expressed astonishment;
" I see nothing here but a small pond, with a
few water-lilies and other weeds on its surface."
" Oh, but there is a golden bell in that pool," they
replied. I laughed, and asked them if they had
seen it, and why they did not attempt to get it
out. They replied that none of them had seen

it, and that it was impossible to get it out; but that it was there, nevertheless, they firmly believed. I confess I was a good deal surprised, and was half inclined to think my friends were having a good-humoured joke at my expense, but again, when I looked in their faces, I could detect nothing of this kind expressed in any of their countenances. Much puzzled with this *curiosity*, and not being able to gain any information calculated to unravel the mystery, I determined to keep the subject in mind, and endeavour to get an explanation from some one who was better informed than these countrymen appeared to be.

A short time after this I happened to meet a Chinese gentleman who had travelled a great deal in many parts of his own country, and whose intelligence was of a higher order than that of his countrymen generally. To this man I applied for a solution of the *Kin-chung,* or golden bell. When I had described what I had seen at Quanting, he laughed heartily, and informed me that it was simply a superstition or tradition which had been handed down from one generation to another, and that the ignorant believed in the existence of such things although they did not endeavour to account for them. He further informed me such traditions were very common throughout China, particularly about Buddhists' temples and other remarkable places visited by the natives for devotional purposes. Thus, at the falls in the Snowy Valley, which I have already

noticed, there was said to be a *Heang-loo*, or
incense burner, of fabulous size, which no one had
ever seen or were likely to see ; and a large white
horse was said to reside somewhere in the mountain called T'hae-bah-san, which rises to the height
of 2000 feet behind the old monastery of Tein-
tung. All these were simply traditionary stories,
which are believed by the vulgar and ignorant,
but, as my informant said, are laughed at by men
of education and sound sense.

Not being able to find the golden bell, and as
the sight of the spot where it was supposed to be
had not produced the impression which my companions and guides had supposed it would, they
dropped off, one by one, and returned to the
temple, while I was left alone to ramble amongst
the wild scenes of these mountains. There was,
however, little time to spare, and I was most
anxious to secure the services of Mr. Wang the
moment he had finished his culinary operations.
I, therefore, returned to the temple, and arrived
there soon after the group who had taken me to
see the golden bell. I found them explaining to
the priests and other visitors how disappointed I
had been, and how incredulous I was as to the
existence of the said bell itself.

The temple of Quan-ting has no pretensions as
regards size, and appeared to be in a most dilapidated condition. In one of the principal halls I
observed a table spread and covered with many
good things, which were intended as an offering

to Buddha. The expected visitors, who appeared
to be the farmers and other respectable inhabitants of the neighbourhood, were arriving in considerable numbers, and each one as he came in
prostrated himself in front of the table.
As the valley in which the temple is placed is
fully 3000 feet above the sea, I felt the air most
piercingly cold, although it was only the middle
of October, and hot enough in the plains in the
daytime. So cold was it that at last I was
obliged to take refuge in the kitchen, where Mr.
Wang was busy with his preparations for the
dinner, and where several fires were burning.
This place had no chimney, so the smoke had
to find its way out through the doors, windows, or
broken roof, or, in fact, any way it could. My
position here was, therefore, far from being an
enviable one, although I got a little warmth from
the fires. I was, therefore, glad when dinner was
announced, as there was then some prospect of
being able to get the services of Mr. Wang. The
priests and some of the visitors now came and
invited me to dine with them, and, although I was
unwilling, they almost dragged me to the table.
In the dining-room, which was the same, by-
the-bye, in which they were worshipping on my
arrival, I found four tables placed, at one of which
I was to sit down, and I was evidently considered
the lion of the party. They pressed me to eat
and to drink, and although I could not comply
with their wishes to the fullest extent, I did the

best I could to merit such kindness and politeness. But I shall not attempt a description of a Chinese dinner which, like the dinner itself, would be necessarily a long one, and will only say that, like all good things, it came to an end at last, and Mr. Wang having finished his in the kitchen and taken a supply in his pockets, declared himself ready for my service.

Our road led us up to the head of the valley in which the temple stands, and then it seemed as if all further passage was stopped by high mountain barriers. As we got nearer, however, I observed a path winding up round the mountain, and by this road we reached the top of a range of mountains fully a thousand feet higher than any we had passed, or 4000 feet above the sea. When we reached the top the view that met our eyes on all sides rewarded us richly for all the toil of the morning. I had seen nothing so grand as this since my journey across the Bohea mountains. On all sides, in whichever direction I looked, nothing was seen but mountains of various heights and forms, reminding one of the waves of a stormy sea. Far below us, in various directions, appeared richly cultivated and well wooded valleys; but they seemed so far off, and in some places the hills were so precipitous, that it made me giddy to look down. On the top where we were there was nothing but stunted brushwood, but, here and there, where the slopes were gentle, I observed a thatched hut and some spots of culti-

vation. At this height I met with some lycopods,
gentians, and other plants not observed at a
lower elevation. I also found a hydrangea in a
leafless state, which may turn out a new species,
and which I have introduced to Europe. If it
proves to be an ornamental species it will probably
prove quite hardy in England.

We had left the highest point of the mountain
ridge, and were gradually descending, when on
rounding a point I observed at a distance a sloping hill covered with the beautiful object of our
search—the *Abies Kœmpferi*. Many of the trees
were young, and all had apparently been planted
by man ; at least, so far as I could observe, they
had nothing of a natural forest character about
them. One tree in particular seemed the queen
of the forest, from its great size and beauty, and
to that we bent our steps. It was standing all
alone, measured 8 feet in circumference, was fully
130 feet high, and its lower branches were nearly
touching the ground. The lower branches had
assumed a flat and horizontal form, and came out
almost at right angles with the stem, but the
upper part of the tree was of a conical shape,
resembling more a larch than a cedar of Lebanon.
But there were no cones even on this or on any
of the others, although the natives informed us
they had been loaded with them on the previous
year. I had, therefore, to content myself with
digging up a few self-sown young plants which
grew near it ; these were afterwards planted in

Ward's cases and sent to England, where they arrived in good condition.

I now parted from my friend Mr. Wang, who returned to his mountain home at Quan-ting, while I and my guide pursued our journey towards the temple at which I was staying by a different route from that by which we had come. The road led us through the same kind of scenery which I have endeavoured to describe — mountains; nothing but mountains, deep valleys, and granite and clay-slate rocks—now bleak and barren, and now richly covered with forests chiefly consisting of oaks and pines. We arrived at the monastery just as it was getting dark. My friends, the priests, were waiting at the entrance, and anxiously inquired what success had attended us during the day. I told them the trees at Quanting were just like their own—destitute of cones. "Ah!" said they, for my consolation, "next year there will be plenty."

I cannot agree with Dr. Lindley in calling this an *Abies*, unless cedars and larches are also referred to the same genus. It is apparently a plant exactly intermediate between the cedar and larch; that is, it has deciduous scales like the cedar and deciduous leaves like the larch, and a habit somewhat of the one and somewhat of the other. However, it is a noble tree; it produces excellent timber, will be very ornamental in park scenery, and I have no doubt will prove perfectly hardy in England.

I had been more successful in procuring supplies of tea and other seeds and plants for the
Himalayas than I had been in my search for the
seeds of the new tree just noticed. Large supplies
had been got together at Ningpo at various times
during the summer and autumn, and these were
now ready to be packed and shipped for India.
For this purpose it was necessary to proceed to
Shanghae ; but to get there in safety was no easy
matter at this time, owing to the numerous bands
of pirates which were then infesting the coasts.
The Chinese navy either would not, or perhaps
it would be more correct to say they durst not,
make the attempt to put them down. Hence,
while these lawless gentry were ravaging the
coast, the brave Chinese admirals and captains
were lying quietly at anchor in the rivers and
other safe places where the pirates did not care
to show themselves.

In going up and down this dangerous coast I was
greatly indebted to Mr. Percival, the managing
partner of Messrs. Jardine Matheson and Co.'s
house at Shanghae, and to Mr. Patridge, who
had the charge of the business of that house at
Ningpo. By their kindness I was always at
liberty to take a passage in the " Erin," a boat
kept constantly running up and down in order to
keep up the communication between the two ports.
This boat was well manned and armed, and, moreover, she was the fastest which sailed out of
Ningpo. The Chinese pirates knew her well :

they also knew that her crew would fight, and that they had the means to do so, and although she often carried a cargo of great value, I never knew of her being really attacked, although she was frequently threatened.

On this occasion, as usual, I availed myself of Mr. Patridge's kindness, and had all my collections put on board of the " Erin." My fellow-passengers were the Rev. John Hobson, the Shanghae chaplain, and family, and the Rev. Mr. Burdon, of the Church Missionary Society, who had also secured passages in the " Erin " in order to escape falling into the hands of the pirates.

Leaving Ningpo at daybreak, with the ebb-tide and a fair wind, we sailed rapidly down the river, and in three hours we were off the fort of Chinhae, where the river falls into the sea. As we passed Chinhae anchorage a number of boats got up their anchors and stood out to sea along with us, probably with the view of protecting each other, and getting that protection from the " Erin " which her presence afforded. When we had got well out of the river, and opened up the northern passage, a sight was presented to view which was well calculated to excite alarm for our safety. Several piratical lorchas and junks were blockading the passage between the mainland and Silver Island, and seizing every vessel that attempted to pass in or out of the river. These vessels were armed to the teeth, and manned with as great a set of rascals as could be found on the coast of China.

These lawless hordes went to work in the following manner. They concealed themselves behind
the islands or headlands until the unfortunate junk
or boat they determined to pounce upon had got
almost abreast of them, and too far to put about
and get out of their way. They then stood boldly
out and fired into her in order to bring her to;
at the same time hooting and yelling like demons
as they are. The unfortunate vessel sees her position when too late; in the most of instances resistance is not attempted, and she becomes an easy
prize. If resistance has not been made, and no
lives lost to the pirate, the captain and crew of the
captured vessel are treated kindly, although they
are generally plundered of everything in their
possession to which the pirates take a fancy.

The *jan-dows*, as the pirates are called, have
their dens in out-of-the-way anchorages amongst
the islands, and to these places they take their
unfortunate prizes, either to be plundered or to be
ransomed for large sums by their owners at Ningpo,
according to circumstances. Negociations are immediately commenced; messengers pass to and fro
between the outlaws at the piratical stations, only
a few miles from the mouth of the river, and the
rich ship-owners at Ningpo; and these negociations are sometimes carried on for weeks ere a
satisfactory arrangement can be made between the
parties concerned. And it will scarcely be credited
—but it is true nevertheless—that within a few
miles from where these pirates with their prizes are

at anchor there are numerous Chinese "men-of-war" (!) manned and armed for the service of their country.

Many of the boats which had weighed anchor as we passed Chinghae put about and went back to their anchorage. The little "Erin," however, with several others, stood boldly onwards in the direction of the piratical fleet, and were soon in the midst of it. At this time some of them were engaged in capturing a Shantung junk which had fallen into the trap they had laid for her. We were so near some of the others that I could distinctly see the features of the men, and what they were doing on the decks of their vessels. They seemed to be watching us very narrowly, and in one vessel the crew were getting their guns to bear upon our boat. They were perfectly quiet, however; no hooting or yelling was heard, and as these are the usual preludes to an attack it was just possible they were prepared to act on the defensive only.

The whole scene was in the highest degree exciting; their guns were manned, the torch was ready to be applied to the touchhole, and any moment we might be saluted with a cannon-ball or a shower of grape. Our gallant little boat, however, kept on her way, nor deviated in the slightest degree from her proper course. The steersman stood fast to the helm, the master— Andrew, a brave Swede—walked on the top of the house which was built over three-parts of the

x

deck, and the passengers crowded the deck in front of the house. Every eye was fixed upon the motions of the pirates.

When our excitement was at the highest pitch the pirates hoisted a signal, which was a welcome sight to our crew, and although I have, perhaps, as much bravery as the generality of people, I confess it was a welcome sight to myself. The signal which produced such results was neither more nor less than a Chinaman's jacket hoisted in the rigging. I believe any other article of clothing would do equally well. It will not be found in Marryat's code, but its meaning is, " Let us alone and we will let you." This amicable arrangement was readily agreed to ; a jacket was hoisted in our rigging as a friendly reply to the pirates, and we passed through their lines un-harmed.

During the time they were in sight we observed several vessels from the north fall into their hands. They were in such numbers, and their plans were so well laid, that nothing that passed in daylight could possibly escape. Long after we had lost sight of their vessels we saw and pitied the un-suspecting northern junks running down with a fair wind and all sail into the trap which had been prepared for them.

We experienced head-winds nearly the whole way, and, consequently, made a long passage, and had frequently to anchor. I rather think Andrew attributed this luck to the two clergymen we had

on board; but if he did he may be excused, for
wiser heads than his have had their prejudices on
this point. Whatever luck we had as regards the
weather we were certainly most fortunate in getting so well out of the hands of the pirates, and
in fairness this ought to be taken into consideration.

CHAPTER XIV.

Season's collections shipped for India — Ancient porcelain vase —
Chinese dealers — Joined by two friends — Inland journey — City
of Yu-yaou — Fine rice district — Appearance and conduct of
natives — Laughable occurrence with an avaricious boatman — Soil
and rocks of district — Village of Ne-ka-loo and Chinese inn —
Shores of the' bay of Hang-chow — Salt and its manufacture —
Curious moonlight journey — Rapid tides — Passage junk — Voyage
across the bay — Chinese sailors — Arrive at Kan-poo.

DURING the succeeding winter and spring months
I was engaged in packing and dispatching to India
and Europe the numerous collections of plants,
seeds, and other objects of natural history which I
had formed in the summer and autumn. Large
quantities of implements used in the manufacture
of tea were also sent to India at this time, destined
for the government plantations in the Himalayas
and Punjab. I had been unceasing in my endea-
vours to procure some first-rate black-tea makers
from the best districts in the interior of the provinces of Fokien and Kiangse, but up to this time
I had not succeeded. This was by far the most
difficult part of my mission, but as the services of
such men were absolutely necessary in order to
carry on the great tea experiment which the
government of India had in hand, I determined
not to leave China until I had accomplished the

object in view. As all the details concerning tea-plants, implements, and manufactures, may not have the same interest to the reader as they had to myself I shall skip a few pages of my journal and go on to where the narrative is more interesting.

In the month of April, 1855, I paid another visit to the old city of Tse-kee. My boat was moored in a canal near the north gate of the city, and I had been a prisoner for several days on account of a heavy and continuous fall of rain. One morning, soon after daylight, and before the boatmen or my servants were out of bed, a Chinese merchant, who made a living by selling old books and curiosities, paid me a visit, and informed me he had an ancient porcelain vase for sale which was well worthy of my attention. The heavy rain was beating on the roof of the boat, which prevented me from having the politeness to open it and ask the man inside. I therefore opened the little sliding window and called out that I would pay him a visit when fine weather came. This proceeding, however, would not satisfy him, and he insisted that I should go with him at once. To encourage me he pointed to his large Chinese boots studded with heavy nails, and said if I had a pair of them to put on they would protect me from the wet and mud in the streets. I had nothing of the kind, but as I had been making from time to time large collections of ancient porcelain vases and other works of art of an early period, I felt a

strong inclination to see this one, and therefore
consented to accompany him to his house. On the
way the rain fell in torrents ; many parts of the
streets were ankle deep in water, and as the houses
are not furnished with gutters, as with us, to carry
off the rain, it pours down upon the head of the
unlucky passenger without mercy.

When we reached the house my conductor called
out to his wife to bring me some warm tea, and as
I was sipping this he produced his vase. It was a
beautiful specimen of its kind, very fine in form,
of a blue colour, and richly enamelled with houses,
flowers, and Chinese characters, in gold. It was
no doubt ancient, and quite perfect. The Chinese
as a people are first-rate physiognomists : they can
tell at a glance whether their wares take one's
fancy, and vary their prices accordingly. I had
long been accustomed to this, and invariably in
my dealings with them tried to prevent them from
reading any admiration or anxiety in my countenance when I intended to buy. When the vase in
question was exposed to my admiring gaze its
owner gazed intently into my face and asked me
in a triumphant manner what I thought of it ? I
told him it was pretty good, and perfect, but that
it was too large for me, and then asked in a careless way what its value was. He hesitated for
some few seconds, evidently not quite certain what
sum to name ; at last he said that the true price
was eighty dollars, but that if I wanted it he would
let me have it for sixty—a sum equal to about 20*l*.

according to the rate of exchange at the time. Being a pretty good judge of the value of such things I knew the price asked was absurd, and did not make him an offer, although he pressed me very hard to do this. At the same time I had made up my mind to have the vase. The vendors of these ancient works of art in China have rarely any fixed price, and will not scruple to ask ten times the true value, which, if they are lucky enough to get, they do not scruple to laugh at the simpleton who gives it.

On my way back to my boat a man came up to me in the street and, greatly to my surprise, put a pencil note into my hand. This was from two friends, Messrs. Walkinshaw and Smith, who had found out on their arrival in the province that I was sojourning near Tse-kee, and had determined to join me for the sake of seeing a little of the country. As Mr. Walkinshaw had a good collection of ancient vases, and was almost as fond of collecting as I was, he expressed a wish to see the one I have just been describing. When the rain cleared off we went into the city and called upon my friend of the morning. The vase was again produced, and was much admired by Mr. Walkinshaw. We could not succeed in inducing its owner to part with it at the time, but some months afterwards I bought it for nine dollars, and it now adorns Mr. Walkinshaw's drawing-room in Canton ; or rather it did so some time ago.

Having nothing more to do in the Ningpo dis-

trict until the autumn I determined to pay a visit
to the great silk country of Hoo-chow, and to the
hills on the western side of the plain of the Yang-
tse-kiang, a country which was entirely new to me.
My two friends had employed their time well during the few days they had to spare about Ningpo.
They had visited the snowy valley and waterfalls,
and various other places of interest which I have
already noticed in these pages, and they were now
ready to go northward to Shanghae.

In leaving Ningpo for Shanghae we determined
to take the inland route, *via* Kan-poo (or Cam-poo),
a town situated on the shores of the bay of Hang-
chow, and about midway between that city and the
seaport of Chapoo. Having engaged boats we left
Ningpo with the first of the flood-tide and proceeded up the northern branch of the river in the
direction of the ancient city of Yu-yaou.

In our passage up the river there was nothing
seen worthy of particular notice. We were favoured with a fair wind between Ningpo and Yu-
yaou, and reached that city in about twenty-four
hours from the time of starting. As our boatmen
expected to be paid back-fare, and as that fare
would be allowed them for the same number of
days taken to accomplish our journey, they had no
interest in getting quickly onward. On the contrary, they looked on the fair wind we had experienced as a great misfortune. We reached Yu-
yaou several hours before nightfall, but our boatmen having evidently made up their minds to stay

there for the night objected to proceed onwards.
They gave as a reason that night was coming on,
and they did not know the way after dark.   Unfortunately for their logic it was only about four
o'clock in the afternoon, and, consequently, we
had four hours of daylight before us.   I therefore
told them that what they said might be perfectly
true—I doubted it myself—yet we could go on
until it became dark and then we would stop for
the night.   To this they demurred for some time,
but eventually, by coaxing and threatening, they
were induced to proceed onwards.

Previous to this discussion we had landed and
paid a visit to the city.   It consists of two portions, or rather there are two cities, one on the
south side of the river and the other on the north.
The city on the south side appears to be very ancient, and is now in ruins; its walls are broken
down and covered with weeds and brushwood.
The one on the north side, although old, is of a
more modern date, and appeared to be in a flourishing condition.   Its walls enclose a hill about
300 feet in height, on which there is a temple dedicated to a minister of state who flourished in the
Ming dynasty.   In as far as I know, the city is
not famous for anything particular in the arts,
and we saw nothing of importance as we passed
through its streets.

After passing the city our boats left the main
stream and turned into a canal on its left bank.
When we had proceeded a few miles along the

canal we came to another on a higher level, and had our boats drawn up an inclined plane by means of two rude windlasses. Here a fresh difficulty awaited us. This canal was so full, owing to the late rains, that our boats could not pass under the bridges without having the roofs taken off. As it was now nearly dark, we made up our minds to remain here for the night, and make a fresh start early next morning.

The natives in the surrounding villages now came flocking to our boats in great numbers. They seemed a more respectable set than most of the country Chinese with whom I have been in the habit of mixing. They were well clothed, apparently well fed, and had a cleanly appearance about them, which, it must be confessed, is rather rare in country districts in China. Their houses, too, were large and well-built; many of them were neatly whitewashed with lime, and had a sort of comfortable look about them which expressed in language unmistakeable that their owners were " well to do in the world."

In this part of the country the staple article of summer-cultivation was rice. The land seemed exceedingly fertile, and this no doubt had something to do with the well-being of the inhabitants. I have observed this frequently exhibited in a most marked manner in China. Wherever the country is fertile, or when it produces an article of great value in commerce, such as silk or tea for example, there the natives as a general rule have more comfortable houses, are better fed and better clothed than they are in other places. In those bleak and barren mountain-districts, both inland and on the seacoast, where the land yields barely a remunerative crop, the natives are generally ragged and dirty in appearance, while their dwellings are mean hovels which scarcely afford protection from the inclemency of the weather.

The manners of the people we were now amongst were quite in keeping with their outward appearance. As they crowded round our boats they were exceedingly polite and courteous, and gave us any information we required as to our journey through the country, and the state of the canals and bridges.

It was now past seven o'clock in the evening, and dinner being ready we sat down to enjoy our evening meal. This proceeding seemed highly interesting to our Chinese visitors, who now crowded round our boat and were peeping through every crevice where a view of what was going on within could be obtained. They were, no doubt, quite as much surprised at the operation of eating with knives and forks as country-people at home would be if they saw a Chinese family sit down with their chop-sticks.

The Chinese are early in their habits—they go to bed early and rise early in the morning—so we were soon left by the crowd which surrounded our boats, to enjoy our dinner in peace and quietness. At daybreak on the following morning we took

our provisions and baggage out of the largest boat,
which could not pass under the bridge, and dis-
charged it. Here a laughable occurrence took
place which I must notice. One of the men belonging to the boat was an old man, very obsti-
nate and rather despotic in his bearing both to the
other boatmen and to ourselves. In China an old
man has great privileges in this respect. He can
do many things which a younger man must not
attempt, and is generally looked up to and humoured in many of his foibles. Now it so happened that this old man had made up his mind to
be as long as possible on our upward journey, in
order that he might have the same allowance of
time and money for his journey back to Ningpo,
and it was he who had given us so much trouble at
Yu-yoau. But fair winds and other circumstances
had disappointed him, and instead of spending
about three days in bringing us thus far, he had
been only one day and two nights. As we had
been one of these nights lying at the bridge, and
as his way back was down stream, we calculated
that he would easily reach Ningpo in a day and
night, even if the wind was contrary. He was
therefore paid for three days in full, which appeared to us to be most ample. But this did not
satisfy the old man ; he had calculated on being
six days in our service, and six days' pay he was
determined to have, nor would he listen to reason
or any explanation.

We had borrowed a table and three chairs from

Mr. Wadman in Ningpo, and had promised to send them back in the old man's boat, in which they had been used. These he threatened to sell to make up the amount—a mode of proceeding which I well knew he durst not adopt. We then bade him good-bye, and with the money which he had refused we proceeded on our journey in the smaller boats.

We had not gone very far when our friend made his appearance,—having come by a near cut across country,—and begged in the humblest manner that we would let him have his money. He was quite satisfied now, and he "would not sell the chairs." As a slight punishment, we paid no attention to his request for some time, and allowed him to follow the boats for about a mile. We then paid him the sum which he had formerly refused, and added for his consolation that had he taken it at first he would have received a present besides—a lesson which, if it was lost on him, had a good effect on our other men.

As we proceeded the canal became fuller, and my boat, which was the next largest, was stopped by a bridge. There was nothing for it but taking out all my luggage, and sending it onwards in a small sand-pan, which luckily was easily procured. My boatmen were quite satisfied with the allowance made to them for their homeward journey, and wished me fair winds and a prosperous journey, adding that if I returned to Ningpo they would be happy to have a fresh engagement.

As we were only a few miles distant from the end of the canal—a place called Ne-ka-loo—we sent the boats on, and determined to walk across the country ourselves. On our way we passed through a large village named Te-sye-mun, remarkable for a neat and well-finished mausoleum erected in the dynasty of the Mings for a minister of state—the same, I believe, to whom the temple is dedicated on the hill inside of the city of Yu-yaou.

The low country through which we passed had the same rich appearance which I have already mentioned, but the hills, which seemed jutting into it in all directions, were comparatively barren. They were chiefly composed of porphyritic granite mixed with crystals of quartz of a very coarse description.

About midday we arrived at the little village of Ne-ka-loo, which is situated on the shores of the bay of Hang-chow, and took up our quarters in a Chinese inn. Our landlord seemed a bustling, good sort of a man, and did everything in his power to make us comfortable. He informed us the passage-junks by which we had to cross the bay had not arrived from Kan-poo, but would probably make their appearance in the afternoon, and if we would agree to pay six dollars we could have a junk to ourselves, and could start to cross the bay at eleven o'clock that night, when the flood-tide came in. Assenting to this arrangement, we left our servants to prepare an early dinner in

" our inn," and went down to make an inspection
of the shores of the bay.

Between the village of Ne-ka-loo and the bay
there is a wide mud-flat, three or four miles in
extent, having several wide and substantial embankments stretching across it and running parallel with the bay. It appeared as if the bay had
been much wider at some former period than it is
at the present day. Large portions of land have
been from time to time reclaimed from the sea,
and the embankment furthest inland is now a
long way from the shore. Outside of this the
land is now under cultivation, and annually yields
heavy crops of grain. As we approached nearer
to the bay, we observed the flats covered with
a white crystalline substance, which on a nearer
view proved to be salt. Here there is but little
vegetation of any kind, and the whole face of the
country presents a most barren aspect.

Salt is made in large quantities all along the
shores of the bay in the following manner :—A
thin layer of the surface-soil is raked up, loosened,
and then saturated with sea-water. As the water
evaporates, the operation is repeated several times
in succession until the clay or mud has absorbed
as much salt as it is capable of doing. This salt-
clay is then collected together into large round
mounds, and this part of the process is finished.
The second part of the process consists in sepa-
rating the salt from the mud. This is done by
throwing the latter on the top of a rude filter, and

pouring water over it. The water takes the salt out of the mud and carries it down through the filter into a hole below. Sometimes the mud is stamped upon by the feet of the workmen in order to remove the whole of the saline particles with which it is mixed.

When the salt has been removed in this way from the mud, the latter is thrown out of the filter and dried, in order to act in the same way again. The brine when it has passed through the filter into the well below is perfectly clear, and of course highly saline. In this state it is taken out of the well and conveyed in bullock-carts to the place where it is to be boiled. Here it is poured into large square boilers with bamboo frames covering the surface of the liquid. On these frames the salt adheres as it crystallizes.

Large quantities are also made without the aid of fire or the boiling-house. The saline mixture described above is poured thinly into shallow wooden trays, and in this state exposed to the sun. If the day is hot the water soon evaporates and leaves the salt with which it was mixed at the bottom of the trays. The salt made by boiling or by evaporation in the sun does not seem to undergo any mode of purifying as with us, but in this rough state is put into baskets and carried to the market.

Salt is a government monopoly in China. All the land here, with the salt-mounds, boiling-houses, &c., belongs to the government. Everywhere,

however, along these flats, and in many parts of
the sea-coast, a large smuggling trade is carried
on under the eye of the authorities, who do not
seem to interfere, or only now and then.

While engaged in making these investigations
a Chinese sailor came running towards us from the
shore, and informed us that the passage-junk had
arrived. Her captain had been obliged to anchor
a considerable way out for want of water, but
would come close in-shore when the flood-tide
made in the evening. We therefore returned at
once to our inn in order to have dinner and to
make preparations for our voyage across the bay.
In the mean time our landlord had got together a
number of coolies and three chairs to carry us and
our luggage across the flats.

About eight o'clock in the evening we left the
inn, and took our way to the junk. It was a fine
moonlight night, and every object around us was
sparkling as if covered with gems. The chairs in
which we performed this part of the journey were
the most uncomfortable things of the kind I had
ever been in. The bearers, instead of slipping
along in that easy way in which such persons
generally go, jogged along like two rough buffaloes. As we proceeded the country had a most
curious appearance by moonlight. Soon after leaving the village there was scarcely a tree to be
seen, and after passing the second embankment
vegetation — except some salt-loving plants — entirely disappeared. Everywhere the ground was

Y

whitened with a coating of salt, and had a most
wintery look about it; indeed had it not been for
the soft and warm air which fanned us as we went
along, and reminded us of summer, it would have
been no stretch of imagination to believe the
ground was covered with snow.

The night was so beautifully clear, that we
could see our long train of coolies a great way off,
toiling along with our luggage towards the shores
of the bay. Now and then one would break down
and get left in the rear, and then he might be
heard shouting to his companions to wait until he
came up with them. Here and there we passed
rude-looking bullock carts or waggons which are
used to convey the salt-brine to the boiling-houses,
and sometimes to carry passengers' luggage, or
merchandize, from the junks to Ne-ka-loo. The
whole scene reminded me forcibly of a journey
across the isthmus of Suez, which I had made in a
clear moonlight night such as this was.

As we neared the shore, the ground seemed
much broken up by deep water-courses, caused no
doubt by the rapid tides for which the bay is
famed. The atmosphere, too, became thick with a
kind of misty haze, so that we could see but a
very short distance either before or behind. Our
coolies were now heard shouting out to each other
in order that they might keep together, which was
a difficult matter in the circumstances in which we
were placed. To me there did not seem to be a
landmark of any kind to direct our course, al-

though, no doubt, our coolies, who were well accustomed to the road, saw with very different eyes. Those furthest ahead now began to shout loudly to the sailors in the junk, which was supposed to be somewhere near, but as yet not visible from the spot where we had halted. The signal was heard and replied to by the people on board, who seemed close at hand, and in another minute we were standing on the brink of the bay.

When we reached the water's edge we observed our junk aground a little below the spot where we stood, and were informed the flood-tide would make immediately, when she would be brought to the bank to receive us and our luggage. In a few minutes an extraordinary sound of rushing water was heard coming up the bay, and almost at the same moment the tide began to flow with a rapidity which was quite alarming. This was the " Eagre," or as it is called in India, the " Bore," which often makes its appearance on the Bay of Hang-chow at full and change of the moon, and is sometimes most dangerous to boats and junks which are caught in its full strength. In the present instance our junk was in a kind of creek, or at the mouth of a canal, and in this position was perfectly safe. She floated instantly and moved up to a position close to the bank on which we were standing. The sailors seemed to manage her admirably, and it certainly required both activity and experience to bring her up as they did. As soon as the vessel was in her proper position, she was kept in it

Y 2

by two strong stakes—one near the bow, and the other near the stern—which went from the deck right through her keel. These stakes by their own weight fall firmly into the mud, and while they secure the vessel, at the same time they allow her to rise with the tide.

This mode of navigation, curious though it may seem at first sight, is very safe and almost indispensable where the tides run so rapidly. It will be observed that the vessel was at first aground on a mud-flat, which gradually rose towards the banks in the form of an inclined plane. As soon as the tide rose sufficiently to enable her to float, she was propelled in the proper direction by poling. If she grounded again before she made the bank, the stakes were let down, and she was secured for a second or two until she floated again. And so she was propelled forward, and kept in her position in this way, until the bank was reached, and she was finally secured. All this occupies less time than it takes to describe it, particularly during spring-tides; but if the sailors waited until they had plenty of water to carry them inshore at once, in many instances the force of the flowing tide would render the junk unmanageable, and carry her right up the bay.

When the junk had been brought into her proper position alongside the bank where we were standing, she was secured by strong cables made fast at stem and stern, and then tied to wooden stakes which were driven firmly into the bank on the water's edge. She was now considered secure, and able to withstand the strong rush of water which seemed to be carrying everything before it.

Before these preparations were completed the tide was rushing up the bay with fearful rapidity, and rising much faster than I had ever witnessed before. In less than a quarter of an hour it rose some fourteen or fifteen feet, and seemed as if it would soon overflow the banks and cover the lowland on which we were standing. At the same time it poured its water into the creeks and ditches which its former violence had torn open, and every now and then we could hear the dull, heavy sound of mud-banks tumbling into the stream. Although there was no danger when we were standing still, we felt glad when the junk had been properly moored so that we could get on board.

The junks which navigate this dangerous bay are generally loaded with pigs when coming from the north side, and consequently are frequently in a most filthy condition. Dr. Medhurst, of the London Missionary Society at Shanghae, gives the following graphic description of what he experienced when crossing in a pig-laden junk :—
" It was night before we arrived on board the junk, which immediately got under weigh. It was only then that we became alive to our uncomfortable position. The grunting and stink of the pigs, together with the smoking and jabbering of the men, affected a variety of the senses in a most

disagreeable manner. We found the berths that
had been assigned us already occupied by about a
dozen individuals, but upon remonstrance made we
got one of the berths cleared for our reception, in
which we had to make our beds, immediately
under the pigs, and in close contiguity to a dozen
Chinamen, who lay about on the floor one over
the other, almost as filthy and unceremonious as
the pigs themselves. The stench and heat was
almost unsupportable, and the horrid groaning and
struggling of the porcine multitude over head,
rendered sleep almost impossible. To increase
our troubles we had a contrary wind, and as the
navigation of the Tséen-tang (owing to the tides
in the Bay of Hang-chow altering the position of
the sands almost every day) is at all times difficult,
we had the additional pleasantness of a probable
shipwreck in a windy night, without a single boat
in which we could have reached the shore. By
God's good providence, however, we were preserved during the night, and in the morning found
ourselves only a few miles from the place where
we embarked, with the wind right ahead. By
dint of great exertion in skulling, the boatmen
brought the vessel to the south side of the bay
about midday. By this time we found that the
tide was just ebbing, which caused our vessel to
ground far from land, and made it necessary for
us to wait until the tide had run all out and made
again, before we could get at all nearer the shore.
In the mean time we sent a man to wade through

the mud and water, in order to call a couple of chairs and coolies to convey us and our baggage across the mud-flats to Ne-ka-loo."

Having engaged the junk for ourselves, we were not quite so badly off as our missionary friends, and had no pigs to annoy us. When we got on board we went below to see the berths in the cabin which were set apart for our accommodation, but they appeared so filthy and stunk so horridly that we were glad to get on deck again. The cabin was also full of smoke, and everything we came in contact with left its mark on our hands or our clothes. It was now determined to have our beds spread down on the deck of the vessel, where, as it was partly covered, we could sleep with more comfort than in the filthy cabin.

We weighed anchor, or rather we "cast off" about midnight, and stood across the bay. The wind was light and fair, the water was perfectly smooth, and everything seemed to promise a safe and speedy passage. As this part of the bay was sometimes frequented by numerous small piratical craft, I was doubtful about going to sleep, but the boatmen assured me there was no fear from an attack at this time, and as these people are exceedingly timid an assurance of this kind from them was deemed satisfactory.

For some time after we were under way I sat on the foredeck of the vessel contemplating the beauty and stillness of the scene around me. The

moon was shining dimly through a thick haze, not
a sound was heard, except now and then a sail
flapping against the mast and the rippling noise
which the water made against the bows. Notwithstanding the beauty and stillness of the scene
around me I soon began to feel very sleepy, and
went and lay down on my couch. How long I
had slept I know not, but I was suddenly awakened
by being pitched bed and all to the lea side of the
deck, when I was brought up by the bulwarks, a
part of which were under water. It was now
" all hands in-sail." The scene had undergone
a complete and it appeared a rapid change ; the
moon had set ; it was now dark and blowing half
a gale, and the waters of the bay which were so
smooth a few hours before were now rolling along
in deep waves capped with foam.

On account of the numerous sand-banks and
rocks and rapid tides in this bay, its navigation at
all times is exceedingly dangerous if the vessels
are driven but a short way out of the proper
course. But the Chinese are excellent sailors on
their own coasts and in their own vessels. On the
present occasion the helm was instantly put down,
and the vessel came up to the wind. The crew
then ran forward to the masts, the sails were
lowered and reefed, and we kept our course again.
The sails had to be reduced from time to time as
the wind freshened ; but as it was fair we were
flying through the water with great rapidity, and
had the satisfaction of knowing that we should be

soon across the bay. As we approached the
northern shores we got under the shelter of the
land, and the sea became perfectly smooth.

The distance across the bay at this point is
about twenty miles, and this we accomplished in
about three hours. At daylight in the morning
we found ourselves " high and dry" in the mud
alongside of several other trading junks, which,
like ourselves, had run in here at high-water.
We crossed the mud-flat between the vessel and
the shore on men's shoulders,—a fine, stout fellow
carried me and deposited me dry and safely on the
sands—and then walked on to the ancient city of
Kan-poo, which we found situated about a mile
from the beach.

CHAPTER XV.

The Tsien-tang river — Its eagre or " bore " — Appearance it presents — Effects it produces — Superstitions of the natives — City of Kanpoo — Mentioned by Marco Polo —Its decay as a maritime port — Another source of wealth — Its inhabitants — Village of Luh-le-heen — Engage canal boats — Pass through borders of silk country — City of Yuen-hwa — Supposed emporium for " *Yuen-fa* " silk — Geology of isolated hills — City of Ping-hoo — Way to manage Chinese crowds — Shops and gardens — A dangerous position — Arrive at Shanghae.

THE Tsien-tang river, which flows past the city of Hang-chow-foo and empties itself into the bay we had just crossed, is formed of two branches, which unite at the old town of Yen-chow, about one hundred and twenty miles from its mouth. The more southerly branch has its numerous sources amongst the mountains bordering on Fokien, and amongst some hills north-west of the town of Chang-shan, where the three provinces of Chekiang, Kiangse, and Gnan-hwuy meet. The other branch rises in the north-west, amongst the green-tea hills of Hwuy-chow. On former occasions * I had journeyed to the source of both these branches, and found them navigable for country flat-bottomed boats for upwards of two hundred miles from Hang-chow. These boats bring down all the tea

* See ' Journey to the Tea Countries of China and India.'

and other articles produced amongst these inland provinces to Hang-chow, where they are transferred to boats of another class on the canals. Owing to the numerous rocks, sandbanks, and rapid tides eastward of the city, the lower part of the river and head of the estuary is rarely trusted by vessels of any class, large or small. Everything is sent onward by the canals, which here form a network all over the vast plain of the Yang-tze-kiang.

The Eagre, or as it is called in India, the " Bore " of the Tsien-tang river is famous in Chinese history. It is one of the three wonders of the world, according to a Chinese proverb, the other two being the demons at Tang-chau and the thunder at Lung-chau. As in other countries, the Eagre makes its appearance generally on the second or third day after the full or change of the moon, or at what are called " spring tides," and particularly in spring and autumn, about the time the sun is crossing the line. Should it so happen that strong easterly gales blow at these times the Eagre rolls along in all its grandeur, and carries everything before it. Dr. Macgowan, the well-known medical missionary at Ningpo, gives the following graphic account of it which he witnessed during a visit to Hang-chow-foo.

" Between the river and the city walls, which are a mile distant, dense suburbs extend for several miles along the banks. As the hour of flood-tide approached crowds gathered in the streets running

at right angles with the Tsien-tang, but at safe
distances. My position was a terrace in front of
the *Tri-wave* temple, which afforded a good view
of the entire scene. On a sudden all traffic in the
thronged mart was suspended; porters cleared the
front street of every description of merchandise,
boatmen ceased lading and unlading their vessels,
and put out into the middle of the stream, so that
a few minutes sufficed to give a deserted appearance to the busiest part of one of the busiest cities
in Asia. The centre of the river teemed with
craft, from small boats to large barges, including
the gay 'flower-boats.' Loud shouting from the
fleet announced the appearance of the flood, which
seemed like a glistening white cable stretched
athwart the river at its mouth, as far down as the
eye could reach. Its noise, compared by Chinese
poets to that of thunder, speedily drowned that of
the boatmen, and as it advanced with prodigious
velocity—at the rate, I should judge, of twenty-
five miles an hour—it assumed the appearance of
an alabaster wall, or rather of a cataract four or
five miles across and about thirty feet high, moving bodily onward. Soon it reached the advanced
guard of the immense assemblage of vessels awaiting its approach. Knowing that the Bore of the
Hoogly, which scarce deserved mention in connection with the one before me, invariably overturned
boats which were not skilfully managed, I could
not but feel apprehensive for the lives of the floating multitude. As the foaming wall of water

dashed impetuously onwards they were silenced,
all being intently occupied in keeping their prows
towards the wave which threatened to submerge
everything afloat : but they all vaulted, as it were,
to the summit with perfect safety. The spectacle
was of greatest interest when the Eagre had
passed about half-way among the craft. On one
side they were quietly reposing on the surface of
the unruffled stream, while those on the nether
portion were pitching and heaving in tumultuous
confusion on the flood; others were scaling, with
the agility of salmon, the formidable cascade.

"This grand and exciting scene was but of a
moment's duration ; it passed up the river in an
instant ; but from this point with gradually dimin-
ishing force, size, and velocity, until it ceased to
be perceptible, which Chinese accounts represent
to be eighty miles distant from the city. From
ebb to flood-tide the change was almost instanta-
neous. A slight flood continued after the passage
of the wave, but it soon began to ebb. Having
lost my memoranda I am obliged to write from
recollection : my impression is that the fall was
about twenty feet; the Chinese say that the rise
and fall is sometimes forty feet at Hang-chow.
The maximum rise and fall at spring-tides is
probably at the mouth of the river, or upper part
of the bay, where the Eagre is hardly discover-
able. In the Bay of Fundy, where the tides rush
in with amazing velocity, there is at one place a
rise of seventy feet, but there the magnificent

phenomenon in question does not appear to be known at all. It is not, therefore, where tides attain their greatest rapidity, or maximum rise and fall, that the wave is met with, but where a river and its estuary both present a peculiar configuration.

* * * * *

" A very short period elapsed between the passage of the Eagre and the resumption of traffic ; the vessels were soon attached to the shore again, and women and children were occupied in gathering articles which the careless or unskilful had lost in the aquatic mêlée. The streets were drenched with spray, and a considerable volume of water splashed over the banks into the head of the grand canal, a few feet distant." *

Such is the appearance which is presented, and some of the effects which are produced by this tidal phenomenon. By the superstitious and ignorant among the natives it is accounted for in the following manner. One Wú-Tsz'-si, who lived about five hundred years before our era, had the misfortune to offend his sovereign, who politely made him a present of a sword, by which he understood he was to remove himself from the presence and from the world at the same time. When this object was accomplished his body was thrown into the Tsien-tang river, and afterwards became the god of the Eagre. His indignation and rage for such treatment while on earth is now

* Transactions of the China branch of the Royal Asiatic Society.

exhibited periodically by the violence of the tidal wave, which sweeps everything before it on its course, breaks down the river's banks, and floods the adjoining lands. Monarchs of almost every dynasty have honoured him with titles; temples have been erected to his memory; and prayers and sacrifices are periodically offered by the people in order to appease his anger.

At the entrance of the Bay of Hang-chow, or Chapoo, as it is sometimes called, although there is no Bore, the spring-tides are well known to navigators as very rapid and dangerous. Sir R. Collinson, when in the H. C. steamer " Phlege-thon," trying to find a passage to Hang-chow-foo, found he had a tide running " eleven and a half knots when nineteen miles distant from the Cha-poo hills and two from the shore. Traversing the river, which at this point is about fifteen miles wide, there was no continuous channel found, although there were some deep spots. When the ' Phlegethon' was exposed to this tide she had an anchor down with a whole cable (having pre-viously lost an anchor and cable in endeavouring to hug up), was under her full power of steam with sails set, and was still driving."

On the north side of the Bay of Hang-chow the Yang-tze-kiang, one of the largest rivers in the world, empties itself into the ocean. Year by year it brings down large quantities of alluvial matter and deposits it at its mouth. While this annual deposit is in some places gradually and rapidly rising and forming islands,* much of it is apparently swept by the rapid tides into the bay of Hang-chow, where it stops up the passages for navigation, makes former seaports into mere inland towns, and gives a new direction to the traffic of the country.

Kan-poo, the old city at which we had now arrived, is an example of what I have now stated. It is thought by some, and with pretty good reason, that this place is the same as that mentioned in Marco Polo's travels under the name of Kanfoo. In his day it was the seaport of Hang-chowfoo, and was frequented by ships from India and other parts of the world. Now the sands and alluvial deposit of the Yang-tze-kiang, and the rapid tides of the estuary, have destroyed its maritime importance, and instead of receiving ships freighted with the riches of India, and dispatching them full of the silk and other products of the country, it is an insignificant inland town with a few passage junks which keep up a communication with the opposite shore, whose principal articles of freight are Chinese passengers and pigs.

Kan-poo is between twenty and thirty miles to the eastward of Hang-chow-foo. Some fifty miles further east, and near the mouth of the bay, the city of Chapoo has sprung up into con-

---

* In 1843, when I first visited these parts, there was a sand-bank barely visible at high water. That is now covered with trees, inhabited, and forms an excellent mark to navigators.

siderable importance, and has taken the place of
Kan-poo as the seaport of the provincial capital.
But there is scarcely any foreign trade carried on
at Chapoo. No ships bring "merchandise from
India." It is chiefly remarkable for the large
trade done in wood, brought up from the province
of Fokien, and also as being the only port in the
empire that trades with Japan.

It is just possible that long before the days of
Marco Polo Hang-chow-foo itself was a seaport;
then as the river gradually became unsafe Kan-
poo sprang up, which in its turn again gave place
to Chapoo. And it seems equally certain that in
the course of time—that time may yet be far distant—if the depositions at the mouth of the bay
continue, Chapoo itself will have to give way to
some place nearer the sea.

The city of Kan-poo seems a very ancient place,
judging from the appearance of its wall and ramparts. They are built of large square stones, much
worn by time, and are rather in a dilapidated condition. Overgrown in many places with long
grass, reeds, and brushwood, and much broken,
they have a hoary look about them which insensi-
bly carries the mind back to bygone ages, and to
generations which have long since passed away.
They appeared to be nearly three miles in circumference, but the space enclosed is not nearly
covered with houses, and also includes many gardens and green fields. In our walks through the
city we found it contained a number of clean re-

z

spectable-looking houses, but its streets reminded us of a quiet country-town, and had none of that bustling activity which is visible at a flourishing Chinese seaport.

Although the shifting sands and rapid tides of the estuary have long ago cut off communication with the sea, yet the old city has a mine of wealth within itself, which it is likely long to retain. It is situated on the border of a rich silk country, and large quantities of this valuable article are annually produced, both for home consumption and for export. The natives were now (June 1st) busily employed in reeling the first crop of coccoons. In almost every other house in some of the streets the clack, clack, clack, of the winding-machine fell upon our ears as we passed along. We frequently stopped to examine this part of the process, which will be found fully described in a subsequent chapter, if the reader condescends to accompany me through the centre of the great silk country to the silk-towns of Nan-tsin and Hoo-chow-foo. We did not observe any other articles of manufacture in Kan-poo worthy of notice. The natives seemed clean and comfort-ably-looking in their appearance, and treated us very civilly. We were not inconvenienced by those crowds of noisy vulgar-looking fellows who generally surround foreigners when they make their appearance in their inland towns.

In order to engage canal-boats to continue our journey we walked onward to a place named Luh-le-heen, distant from Kan-poo between two and three miles. Here a canal terminates which is connected with those which ramify all over the plain of the Yan-tze-kiang, and here we found travelling-boats from all quarters of the country ready to be engaged. There is a canal which leads from the city to this point, and by this means we brought up our servants and luggage. At Luh-le-heen the two canals are separated by an embankment, and goods or luggage has to be carried across on men's shoulders.

Luh-le-heen is a small bustling village on the banks of the canal, chiefly remarkable for the number of tea-shops and other houses of refreshment it contains. Judging from the crowds of people we saw in these places, a thriving trade must be done by their proprietors; but it must be taken into consideration that most of their customers spend very small sums. In tea-shops in China a cup of tea can be had for about the third part of a farthing of our money, and oftentimes for less than that, so that a shop of this kind may be crowded from morning to evening and not a large sum of money taken after all during the day.

We found no difficulty in engaging boats to take us onwards to Shanghae, and having had our luggage carried into them over the embankment, we sculled away, and soon left the canal village far behind us. Our route now lay along the borders of the silk district, and everywhere we saw groves

z 2

of mulberry trees in cultivation in the fields. A few hours brought us to a large city, named Yuen-hwa, containing a population estimated at 100,000 persons. As this city is also on the borders of the great silk country, it is probably here where that description of silk called Yuen-fa is produced. This, however, is only conjecture, although probably a correct one. A few isolated hills were observed near this city which formed a boundary on the south to the immense alluvial plain which now stretched away far to the north and eastward from Yuen-hwa. The Rev. Dr. Medhurst, when on a missionary tour, examined these hills, and states they are composed of a " red kind of igneous rock, mixed with large portions of quartz. It seemed to be a schistose formation of disintegrated granite combined with porphyry."

In the afternoon of the following day after we had left Yuen-hwa, we arrived off the city of Ping-hoo, having called in by Chapoo, a town which my two friends were anxious to see. Although Ping-hoo is not a very great distance from Shanghae, it does not seem to have been often visited by foreigners, and the people are very wild and unruly. This is, no doubt, partly owing to the large boat-population which the place contains, being situated on the bank of a central canal, which communicates with all parts of the country. Having determined to visit the place in passing, in order to endeavour to make some purchases of articles of *virtu*, and to visit some nursery gardens

near the west gate, I warned my friends of the
unruly mob which we would probably find outside the walls, and begged them to endeavour, if
possible, not to lose temper. There is nothing
more dangerous than losing one's temper with a
Chinese rabble. Keep in good humour, laugh and
joke with them, and all will go on well; they may
be noisy and boisterous in their mirth, but generally they will do nothing further to annoy you;
but once lose temper, and show that you are
angry either by word or deed, and ten to one you
will soon find yourself in a dangerous position.
There are more than one whom business or other
matters has made a sojourner in the Celestial
Empire, who can bear witness to the truth of this
statement.

When we landed from our boats a large crowd
collected around us and followed us into the city,
increasing as we went along. Every now and
then a little urchin ran past to give warning on
ahead, so that we found the whole street aware of
our approach, and every door and window crowded
with anxious faces. All went on quite well, however, although the crowd contained some mis-
chievous-looking fellows in its ranks. When we
entered a shop the scene outside was quite fearful.
The street was very narrow and literally crammed
with human beings, all anxious to see us and to
find out what we were buying. In more than one
instance the pressure was so great as to endanger
the fronts of the shops; and, anxious as the

Chinese are for trade, I believe the poor shopkeepers were heartily glad when they got rid of us.
We picked up two or three interesting specimens
of ancient porcelain, and, had time and the crowd
permitted, we would have got many more. We
had entered the city at the east gate, near the
canal, and as its main street runs from the east to
the west gate, we proceeded in the direction of the
latter. Its shops are but poor in general, and as a
city I believe it is not remarkable for any particular branch of manufacture, but many retired
wealthy people live within its walls.

Outside the west gate were the nursery gardens
I was desirous of visiting. I had been here on
more than one occasion formerly, but had generally avoided raising a crowd by coming round
the moat which surrounds the city in my boat, and
stepping out of it into the gardens unseen except
by two or three persons. On these occasions, ere
a crowd could gather, I had finished my business
and was off. In the present instance, however,
the dense mass of beings followed us closely, and
went into the gardens along with us, to the great
danger of numerous pretty flowers and flowerpots
which stood in the way. All were, however,
though boisterous, in perfect good humour, and,
although we found it very annoying to be followed
and crowded in this way wherever we went, and
prevented from well examining the various things
which came in our way, yet we bore with it as
well as we could and took everything in good

part. Nothing new or rare being found in the gardens to reward us for the visit we had paid to them, and as it was getting late in the afternoon, we determined to return at once to our boats, from which we were distant about two miles. In order to get relieved from the crowd we did not again enter the city, but went back through its northern suburb in the direction of the east gate. This movement in a great measure accomplished the intended object, and most of the people who had followed us thus far, with the intention of returning with us through the city, left and went home. A small portion, however, continued to follow us until we came to the north gate, when I remonstrated with them by saying that surely they had seen enough of us, and that we were anxious to have a quiet walk after all the noise and inconvenience we had been subjected to. After this they seemed afraid to follow us any further, but we had soon reason to repent having stopped them. Our road led us for some distance close under the city walls. Two or three rascally-looking fellows, the scum of the crowd, entered by the north gate and got upon the top of the ramparts, and soon showed evil intentions towards us. Several stones were thrown by unseen hands, and from the position we were in, our situation was far from being an agreeable one. Hemmed in as we were by the city wall on one side and houses on the other, moreover the street thus formed being very narrow, we were placed entirely at the

mercy of our assailants. At last a large brick
came tumbling down, and struck the ground close
to our feet. It was well-aimed, and had it struck
the mark it is probable that one of our little party
would have been killed on the spot. We were
perfectly powerless. We neither could see those
by whom we were attacked, nor could we get out
of their way. Several respectable Chinese remonstrated with their unruly countrymen, and we
hurried onwards in order to get out of our awk-
ward position as soon as we possibly could. Fortunately, we soon came to a cross-street which led
away from the wall, and we were then out of
danger.

We reached our boat without any further adventure, and were glad to push out into the
stream, having had quite enough popularity for
one day. Having described the country between
Ping-hoo and Shanghae in a former work,* I need
not say anything further about it here. A few
hours brought us to the upper part of the Shanghae river, and we reached that city on the third of
June, much pleased, on the whole, with our inland
journey.

* 'Three Years' Wanderings in China.'

CHAPTER XVI.

Leave Shanghae for the silk country — Melancholy results of the Shanghae rebellion — Country and productions about Cading — Indigo and safflower — Bamboo paper-making — Insects — Lakes and marshy country — Visit the town of Nan-tsin in the silk districts — Its shops and inhabitants — Producers of raw silk and silk merchants — Description of silk country — Soil — Method of cultivating the mulberry — Valuable varieties — Increased by grafting and not by seeds — Method of gathering the leaves — Hills near Hoo-chow-foo — Temples and priests.

On the evening of the eighth of June I took my departure from Shanghae, en route for the great silk district for which the province is famed all over the world, and for the mountainous country which lies to the westward of the plain of the Yang-tse-kiang. As my boat proceeded rapidly up the Soochow branch of the river, I soon approached the ground where the imperialists had their principal camp during the siege of the city, and where so many hundreds of poor wretches were executed after the city was evacuated. It was a calm and beautiful evening. The sounds of civil warfare and of a camp teeming with barbarous soldiers, which had been so often heard a few months before, had now passed away,—the sword had been converted into the ploughshare— and the husbandman was quietly engaged in the cultivation of his fields, now enriched with the blood and bodies of his countrymen.

As I passed the site of the old camp I sat on the outside of my boat smoking my cigar in the cool air of the evening, and musing upon the events of the preceding years. The wind at the time blew softly from the south, and before it reached the river on which I was sailing it had to pass over the site of the old encampment. The first puff that reached me almost made me sick, and it has nearly the same effect on me even now when I think of it as I write. Although I had seen none of the executions which had taken place a short time before, I did not require any one to inform me that this was the "field of blood." Here hundreds of headless bodies scarcely covered, or only with an inch or two of earth, lay in a state of decomposition, and the stench from them filled and polluted the air. Here, then, was the end of the Shanghae rebellion, which, at one time, was so much lauded and encouraged by foreigners at that port. The country was devastated for miles round, the city lay in ruins, thousands of the peaceful inhabitants were rendered homeless and friendless, and the authors of this state of things, who used to strut about dressed in the richest silks and satins (which they plundered from the shops and houses of the wealthy), smoke opium, and make a profession of regard for the Christian religion, were now either skulking fugitives, or had atoned with their blood for their crimes.

I was heartily glad when my boat had passed the place into purer air. As my boatmen sculled all night, in the morning we were thirty miles distant from Shanghae and within sight of the walls of Cading, an old city which I passed some years ago, when on my way to Soo-chow-foo. Here I remained for several days, inspecting the natural productions of the country. As this city and the surrounding country is frequently visited by missionaries and other residents in Shanghae, a foreigner is a common sight to the natives, who do not crowd round him as they do in more inland towns. I could, therefore, pursue my investigations in town and country without being molested in any way whatever.

The surrounding country, although a plain, is somewhat higher and more undulating in its general character than that about Shanghae. The land is exceedingly fertile and admirably adapted for Chinese cotton cultivation, and consequently we find that cotton is the staple production of the district. But there are many other articles besides which are worthy of notice. The Shanghae indigo (*Isates indigotica*) is largely cultivated in the Ke-wang-meow district, a few miles to the south. The " Hong-wha," a variety of safflower (*Carthamnus tinctorius*), was found for the first time in fields near Cading. This dye, I was informed, was held in high esteem by the Chinese, and is used in dyeing the red and scarlet silks and crapes which are so common in the country and so much and justly admired by foreigners of every nation. Although I had not met with the safflower in cultivation in any other part of the country, my servants informed me that large quantities were annually produced in the Chekiang province near Ningpo. At this season (June 10th) the crop of flowers had been gathered, and all the plants removed from the land, except some few here and there on the different farms which had been left for seed. The seed was not yet ripe, so that I could not get a supply, but I determined to return that way and secure a portion to send to the Agricultural and Horticultural Society of India, in order to compare the Chinese with the Indian safflower. I believe they have turned out to be alike, or nearly so. Large quantities of fruit and vegetables are also produced in the vicinity of the city. I observed orchards of apple-trees, which is rather a rare sight in this district. The variety of apple was a small one, about as big as our golden pippin, but excellent in flavour; indeed, the only kind worth eating in this part of China. Melons of several different kinds were also extensively cultivated : when they are ripe the markets are literally crowded to overflowing with them, and they are eaten by the natives much in the same way as apples are with us; in fact they seem to be, so to speak, the apples of the country.

In the canals near the city there were large quantities of bamboos partially covered with mud, so as to be pressed under water. These, I believe, were intended to be made into paper after they had been soaked for some time. The whole of the process of making paper from the bamboo did not come under my notice while travelling in the country, but I believe it is carried out somewhat in the following manner :—After being soaked for some time in the way I have noticed, the bamboos are split up and saturated with lime and water until they become quite soft. They are then beaten up into a pulp in mortars, or where water-power is at hand, as in the hilly districts, the beating or stamping process is done by means of stampers, which rise and fall as the cogs which are placed on the axis of the water-wheel revolve. When the mass has been reduced to a fine pulpy substance it is then taken to a furnace and well boiled until it has become perfectly fine, and of the proper consistency. It is then formed into sheets of paper.

Bamboo-paper is made of various degrees of fineness according to the purposes for which it is intended. It is not only used for writing upon, and for packing with, but a large quantity of a coarse description is made for the sole purpose of mixing with the mortar used by bricklayers.

In the fields about Cading I found two fine species of carabus, under stones, which were highly prized by entomologists at home. On the first discovery of these insects I showed them to a group of children who were with me, and offered to buy all they brought me at the rate of thirty cash for each perfect specimen. I dare say they considered me insane or foolish, and I thought I could detect a look of pity on some countenances; but the motley group by which I was surrounded was soon scattered in all directions, engaged in turning over stones, lumps of loose earth and rubbish, and eagerly looking for the insects I wanted. The news was soon communicated to the old women in the villages, who were as anxious as the children, and many were the disputes and tumbles they had when scrambling for these beetles.

By this means I soon procured as many specimens of these insects as I required, and then the difficulty was to induce my crowds of collectors to leave off collecting. I have already stated that the natives always believed I was collecting insects for medicine, and, therefore, had no idea of some forty or fifty of each kind being enough.

Leaving Cading I pursued my journey to the westward in the direction of Tsing-poo. Soon after dark I found myself on the borders of an extensive sheet of water. My boatmen refused to proceed farther that night, telling me they could not find their way in the dark, and that if the wind rose we would be placed in a dangerous position. As this part of the country was unknown to me I considered it best to allow the men to have their own way, and so we brought up for the night.

When I awoke at daybreak on the following morning we were already under way, and sailing with a fair wind across the lake. It was not difficult to perceive the justice of the remarks made by the boatmen the evening before; indeed, it seemed a difficult matter to find our way in broad daylight. This is a most extraordinary part of the country : the lake, or rather lakes, extend in all directions for many miles, sometimes so narrow as to have the appearance of canals, and then again expanding into large sheets of water. Everywhere the shores are low, and have a most irregular outline formed by a succession of reed-covered capes and deep bays.

After sailing for a distance of six or eight miles we came to what appeared at first sight to be a canal leading out of the lake. It proved, however, to be merely a neck of water which led into another lake equal in size to that which we had just crossed. And so we went on during the whole day through this dreary region. The low marshy shores seemed to be thinly inhabited, although in the neighbourhood of the richest and most populous part of the Chinese empire; indeed, almost the only sign of the place being inhabited by human beings was, strange to say, the numerous coffins and graves of the dead, which were continually coming into view as we sailed along. It is not improbable, however, that many of these had been brought from other districts to those *lucky* spots and laid down, or interred

according to circumstances, by the surviving relatives.

The lakes themselves had a much more lively
appearance than those dreary shores. The white
and brown sails of boats like our own were observed in great numbers making for the mouths
of the various canals which form the highways to
the large towns and cities in this part of China.
Those seen going in a southerly direction were
bound for Hang-chow-foo, and the towns in that
district; those sailing northwards were on their
way to Soo-chow-foo, while those going in the
same direction as ourselves were for the silk
country and its rich and populous cities.

The water of the lakes was as smooth as glass,
and in many places very shallow. Various species
of water-plants, such as *Trapa bicornus*, Nympheas,
&c., were common, while here and there I came
upon the broad prickly leaves of *Euryale ferox*
covering the surface of the water.

In the afternoon the scenery began to assume
an appearance somewhat different from that of
the morning. The country was evidently getting
higher in level and more fertile and populous.
To the westward I thought I could detect a real
boundary to the waters, but I did not feel quite
certain of this as I had been deceived several
times during the day. About five P.M. we arrived
at a place named Ping-wang or Bing-bong, as it
is pronounced in the dialect of the district. This
proved to be a small bustling town on the edge of

VIEW ON THE GRAND CANAL, WITH MULBERRY-TREES ON ITS BANKS.

the lakes, and rather important from the central position which it occupies. Fine navigable canals lead from it to all the important towns of this large and fertile plain. A very fine one leads on to the city of Hoo-chow to which I was bound. On one side it has a substantial paved pathway, which is a high road to foot-passengers, and is also used by the boat-people in tracking their boats and junks. I was now able to leave my boat to be sculled slowly along, and walk along the banks of the canal.

I had reached the eastern borders of the great silk country of China—a country which in the season of 1853–54 exported upwards of 58,000 bales of raw silk.

The mulberry was now observed on the banks of the canal, and in patches over all this part of the country. The lakes which I had passed through, and which I have endeavoured to describe, were now left behind, and a broad and beautiful canal stretched far away to the westward, and led to the great silk-towns of Nan-tsin and Hoo-chow-foo. Hitherto the country had been completely flat, but now some hills at a great distance on my right-hand came into view. These I afterwards ascertained were the Tung-t'ing-shans, situated on the T'ai-hu Lake—one of the largest lakes in China, which covers a considerable extent of country between the cities of Hang-chow-foo and Soo-chow-foo. As we passed along the country seemed exceedingly rich and fertile; and mulberry-plantations met the eye in every direction. A great quantity of rice was also produced on the lower lands. The natives seemed well to do in the world, having plenty of work without oppression, and enough to procure the necessaries and simple luxuries of life. It was pleasant to hear their joyous and contented songs as they laboured amongst the mulberry-plantations and rice-fields.

In the evening we arrived at Nan-tsin, and as I was anxious to see something of this celebrated silk-town by daylight, I determined on remaining there for a few days. Early next morning I was up and on my way to see the town. Even at this early hour—five A.M.—the roads were full of people; for like other nations the Chinese hold their markets in the morning. The streets in the town were lined with vegetables of all kinds, and the fruits of the season were abundant and cheap, particularly water-melons, peaches, plums, &c. Butchers' stalls groaned under loads of fat pork; there was an abundance of fresh and salt fish; ducks, geese, and fowls, were there in hundreds, and, indeed, everything was there which could tempt the eye of the Chinese epicure, except cats, rats, and young puppies, and these are not appreciated in this part of the country.

Frogs are in great demand in all the Chinese towns, both in the north and south, wherever I have been, and they were very abundant in Nan-tsin. They abound in shallow lakes and rice fields, and many of them are very beautifully

coloured, and look as if they had been painted by
the hand of a first-rate artist. The vendors of
these animals skin them in the streets in the most
unmerciful and apparently cruel way which I have
already described.

There are many good streets and valuable shops
in Nan-tsin, but they are very much like what I
have seen and described in other cities in China.
What struck me most was the large quantity of
raw silk which was here exposed for sale. Soon
after daylight the country people began to arrive
with their little packets of silk, which they intended to sell to the merchants. The shops for
the purchase of this article appeared to be very
numerous in all the principal streets. Behind the
counter of each shop stood six, eight, and sometimes more, clean, respectable-looking men, who
were silk inspectors, and whose duty was to examine the quality of the silk offered for sale, and to
name its value. It was amusing to notice the
quietness of these men compared with the clamorous crowds who stood in front of their shops
with silk for sale. Each one was expatiating on
the superior quality of his goods and the lowness
of the offer that had been made to him. Many of
the vendors were women, and in all instances they
were the most noisy. The shopmen took everything very quietly, and rarely offered a higher
price than they had done in the first instance.
But notwithstanding all the noise and bustle
everything seemed to go on satisfactorily, and

2 a 2

when the money was paid the people went off in
high spirits, apparently well satisfied with the
sales they had effected.

From the observations which I made at this
time on the farms and markets in this the great
silk country of China, it appears that, however
large in the aggregate the production of silk may
be in the country, this quantity is produced not by
large farmers or extensive manufactures, but by
millions of cottagers, each of whom own and cultivate a few roods or acres of land only. Like bees
in a hive each contributes his portion to swell the
general store. And so it is with almost every
production in the celestial empire. Our favourite
beverage, tea, is produced just in the same way.
When the silk has thus been bought in small samples from the original producers, it is then the
business of the native inspectors and merchants to
sort it and arrange it into bales of similar quality
for home consumption or for exportation.

Nan-tsin is not a walled city, and politically it
is a place of small importance. But it is a place
of great wealth and size, extending for miles on
each side of the canal, and far back into the
country. I believe there is a larger trade in silk
done here than even in the city of Hoo-chow-foo
itself. The people generally seemed to have
plenty of work, and judging from their clean,
healthy, and contented appearance, they are well
paid for their labour.

During my walk in the town I was surrounded

and followed by hundreds of the natives, all anxious to get a view of the foreigner. But except the inconvenience of the crowd I had nothing to complain of, for all were perfectly civil and in the best humour.

I spent the next few days in the vicinity of Nan-tsin, and as it may be considered the centre of the great silk country of China, I shall endeavour now to give a description of the cultivation and appearance of the mulberry trees.

The soil over all this district is a strong yellow loam, well mixed and enriched by vegetable matter; just such a soil as produces excellent wheat crops in England. The whole of the surface of the country, which at one period has been nearly a dead level, is now cut up, and embankments formed for the cultivation of the mulberry. It appears to grow better upon the surface and sides of these embankments than upon level land. The low lands, which are, owing to the formation of these embankments, considerably lower than the original level of the plain, are used for the production of rice and other grains and vegetables. It is therefore on the banks of canals, rice fields, small lakes and ponds, where the mulberry is generally cultivated, and where it seems most at home. But although large quantities of rice and other crops are grown in the silk districts, yet the country, when viewed from a distance, resembles a vast mulberry garden, and when the trees are in full leaf, it has a very rich appearance.

The variety of mulberry cultivated in this district appears to be quite distinct from that which is grown in the southern parts of China and in the silk districts of India. Its leaves are much larger, more glossy, and have more firmness and substance than any other variety which has come under my notice. It may be that this circumstance has something to do with the superior quality of the silk produced in the Hoo-chow country, and is worthy of the notice of silk growers in other parts of the world.

This peculiar variety is not reproduced by seed, and hence all the plantations are formed of grafted trees. Each plant is grafted from a foot to two feet above the ground, and rarely higher. The trees are planted in rows from five to six feet apart, and are allowed to grow from six to ten feet high only, for the convenience of gathering the leaves. In training them they are kept open in the centre; the general outline is circular, and they are not unlike some of those dwarf apple-trees which are common in European gardens. The accompanying sketch gives a good representation of the habit and form of one of those trees which has attained its full size.

The different methods of gathering the leaves in these districts are curious and instructive, and show clearly that the cultivators well understand the laws of vegetable physiology. Leaves are not taken at all from plants in their young state, as this would be injurious to their future productive-

ness. In other instances a few leaves only are
taken from the bushes, while the remainder are

Mulberry Tree.

allowed to remain upon the shoots until the
summer growth is completed. In the latter case
the leaves are invariably left at the *ends* of the
shoots.

When the bushes have attained their full size,
the young shoots with the leaves are clipped close
off by the stumps, and shoots and leaves carried
home together to the farm-yard to be plucked
and prepared for the worms. In the case of
young trees the leaves are generally gathered by

the hand, while the shoots are left to grow on until the autumn. At this period all the plantations are gone over carefully; the older bushes are pruned close in to the stumps, while the shoots of the younger ones are only shortened back a little to allow them to attain to the desired height. The ground is then manured and well dug over. It remains in this state until the following spring, unless a winter crop of some kind of vegetable is taken off it. This is frequently the case. Even in the spring and summer months it is not unusual to see crops of beans, cabbages, &c., growing under the mulberry trees.

During the winter months the trees are generally bare and leafless. Those persons who are accustomed to live in countries with marked seasons, where the winters are cold, and where the great mass of vegetation is leafless, would not be struck with this circumstance in the silk country of China. But the view one gets in this country in the summer months, after the first clipping of the shoots, is curious and striking. As far as the eye can reach, in all directions, one sees nothing but bare stumps. It looks as if some pestilential vapour had passed over the plain and withered up the whole of these trees. And the view is rendered still more striking by the beautiful patches of lively green which are observed at this time in the rice-fields and on the banks of the canals. This system of clipping close in to the stumps of the old branches gives the trees a curious and deformed appearance. The ends of the branches swell out into a club-like form, and are much thicker there than they are lower down.

The following sketch explains the state in which those trees are seen after they have been deprived of their stems and leaves.

Mulberry Tree.

After I had completed my inspection of the country near the town of Nan-tsin, I proceeded onwards to the west in the direction of Hoo-chow-foo. A few hours' sail on a wide and beautiful canal brought me within view of the mountain ranges which form the western boundary to the great plain of the Yang-tse-kiang, through which I had been passing for several days. The most striking hill which came first into view was crowned by a seven-storied pagoda. It had a large tree by its side, equally striking in the distance, and which had probably been planted when the pagoda was built. I afterwards ascertained this to be the "maidenhair-tree" (*Salisburia adiantifolia*), a tree which attains a large size in this part of China, and is extremely ornamental.

As I neared Hoo-chow the general aspect of the country appeared very different from that through which I had been travelling for upwards of one hundred miles. The general level seemed higher, and little well-wooded hills adorned the surface of the country. I visited these hills as I went along for the purpose of examining their vegetation. In most cases I found pretty temples near their summits, surrounded with trees. From these spots the most charming views were obtained of the great mulberry plain, the city of Hoo-chow, and the mountain ranges which form the background towards the west.

In one of the temples which I visited I found a priest who was a native of Ningpo, the town to which my servants belonged. He received us most cordially, and appeared glad to have an opportunity of talking with his townsmen, and getting all the news from his native place, which he had not visited for several years. In one of the cells of this temple we were shown a priest

who had been submitting to voluntary confinement
for nearly three years.   It is not unusual to find
devotees of this kind in many of the Buddhist
temples of China.   Although they never come out
of their cells until the time of their confinement
expires, they have no objection to see and con-
verse with strangers at their little windows.   The
person whom we visited at this time received us
with Chinese politeness, asked us to sit down on a
chair placed outside his little cell, and gave us tea,
on the surface of which various fragrant flowers
were swimming.

CHAPTER XVII.

Enter the city of Hoo-chow-foo — Method of managing Chinese crowds — Description of the city — Richness of the shops — Fans and silks — Rich dresses of the people — Raw silk and hongs — Flowered crapes — Chinese play and audience — How I perform my part! — Leave the city — Charming scenes in the country — Thrown silk — Silk villages and their inhabitants — Temple of Wan-shew-si and its priests — Taou-chang-shan pagoda — Glorious views from the pagoda hill.

On the 17th of June I reached the city of Hoo-chow-foo—the City of the Lakes and the capital of the principal silk-country of China. According to Chinese accounts, this city is about six miles in circumference, and contains about a hundred thousand families. Both of these statements are probably exaggerated, as the walls did not appear to me to be more than three, or at most four, miles round. As I was anxious to see something of the interior of the city, I sent one of my men to procure a sedan-chair, for the day was excessively warm. The chairmen soon made their appearance, but as their demands for hire were so exorbitant, I refused to comply with them and determined to walk—a proceeding which, although not so comfortable, would enable me to see more of the shops and people.

Entering at the south gate, I proceeded in a northerly direction, and examined all the principal

streets on my way. Thousands of people followed
me as I went along. They were very uproarious,
but good-humoured withal, and appeared delighted
with the opportunity of seeing a " Pak Quei-tze,"
or white devil—a term by which foreigners are
designated in this civilized part of the world.
Although this term was sometimes used in a tone
of contempt or insult, showing that those who
used it fully understood its meaning, yet generally
it was not so. Upon one occasion some friends
of mine remonstrated with some of these polite
people, and endeavoured to explain to them that
the term was one to which we were not exactly
entitled, and that it was not very agreeable. In
reply the Chinese expressed surprise and regret
for having used the term and thus given offence ;
but innocently asked if we were not white devils ;
and if not, what we were, and by what name they
should call us !

Alone as I now was, and surrounded by thousands of Chinese in one of their inland cities, it
was absolutely necessary to keep my temper under
the most complete control. In circumstances of
this kind, if one laughs and jokes with the crowd,
and takes everything in good part, all will generally go well, for the Chinese are upon the whole
good-humoured and polite ; but if he by any chance
loses his temper, he will most certainly get the
worst of it, and most likely will be hooted and
pelted with stones. I had had some experience in
the management of Chinese crowds, and therefore

continued to be in the sweetest possible frame of mind in the midst of the thousands who followed me through the city as if I had been a wild animal or " white devil " indeed.

As I threaded my way slowly along, in addition to the dense crowds that followed and preceded me, every window and doorway was crowded with curious-looking faces all anxious to get a view of the foreigner. It was curious to mark the varied expression in the different countenances. In some there was a look of contempt, in others wonder was strongly depicted; but in the vast majority there was wonder mingled with fear, as if I was in reality a being from another world. Keeping onward in a northerly direction, and diverging now and then to the right or left, according as an object of interest met my eye, I arrived at last at the north gate of the city. Here I ascended the ramparts in order to get a good view. Outside the walls I observed a large dense suburb, with a pretty pagoda and a canal leading through it in the direction of the T'ai-hu lake. Throwing my eyes over the city, the roofs of the houses seemed nearly all of the same height; indeed this is a striking characteristic of all Chinese towns which I have visited. One rarely sees any difference in the height of the houses except when a temple, a pagoda, or a watch-tower disturbs the monotony of the view. I believe the Chinese have a strong prejudice against one house being raised higher than the others.

I now walked round the ramparts from the
north to the east gate, and then crossed the town
from east to west in the same leisurely way I had
done from south to north. A fine broad stream,
or rather canal, crosses the city from south to
north, and forms the chief highway for the boat-
traffic, for boats are the carriages in this part of
China and canals are the highways. This stream
was crowded with boats of all sizes; some were
discharging goods and passengers at the jetties
on its banks, while others were hurrying onward
deeply laden with goods and passengers for other
parts of the country.

The city near the south gate by which I entered
had rather a poor appearance, but the centre,
and particularly the northern side, appeared rich
and densely populated. Many of the shops were
crowded with articles of great beauty and value.
The fronts of Chinese shops are not shut up as
ours are; the interior is fully exposed to passers-
by, so that I got an excellent view of their contents without the inconvenience of going inside.
The silk fans struck me as being more gorgeous
and handsome than any I had seen in other towns.
Manufactured crapes and silks were also plentiful,
and judging from the dresses of the people of both
sexes, these goods must be in great demand. I
have visited many Chinese towns, and I must say
I never saw the people as a whole better dressed
than those of Hoo-chow. Every person I met
above the common working coolie was dressed in

silks or crape, and even the coolies have at least one silk dress for holyday wear.

Although the fans and silks of Hoo-chow struck me particularly when walking through the town, it abounds also in all kinds of articles in common use amongst the people. Embroidered shoes, hats, caps, umbrellas, tobacco-pipes made of bamboo and nicely painted, porcelain of all kinds, and indeed every conceivable article in demand amongst the natives.

But in Hoo-chow, as at Nant-sin, the great trade of the place is in raw silk. Near the north gate many large hongs were pointed out to me where this trade is carried on most extensively. Here the silk is sorted, stowed, and made up into parcels, which are afterwards despatched to Shang-hae, and offered for sale to foreign merchants. It is estimated that about four-fifths of the silk produced in this district is exported to Europe and America; but considering the large quantity consumed by the people themselves, I doubt if the proportion exported is so large.

The greater part of the silks and crapes used in this part of China are manufactured in the adjoining towns of Soo-chow and Hang-chow. Flowered crape, however, a very beautiful production, is made in Hoo-chow. The process of manufacture is thus described by the Rev. Mr. Edkins in the ' North China Herald :'—

" Two men were engaged at a loom in a cottage on the side of a stream. One sat at the end of the loom moving five pedals, and directing the shuttle and all that needed to be done with the threads that lay horizontal on the frame. The other was perched overhead to superintend the pattern. This he did by means of vertical threads tied up in bundles, a large number of which, distributed transversely through the threads of the horizontal frame beneath him, were at his disposal. These he raised according to the requirement of the pattern, and thus caused that elevation in the threads on the frame below that constituted the flowered part of the piece."

Like their countrymen all over China, the Hoochow people are fond of the drama. During my visit to the city a fine play was going on in one of the temples near the north gate. I had many pressing invitations, from individuals in the crowd who were following me, to go and see the play. But having seen many of these exhibitions on former occasions, I had no wish to see this one, more particularly as I knew well that all the rabble in the town are generally collected about such places. My companions, however, rather outwitted me, and gained their point before I was aware of it. Having a kind of mania for collecting ancient works of Chinese art, such as porcelain vases, bronzes, enamels, and such things, I had been making many enquiries regarding them as we went along, and had already made several purchases of considerable interest. I was now told by a person in the crowd that he would take me to an old curiosity-shop hard by, where I would see some fine things such as I wanted. Without suspecting anything, I desired him to lead the way, and I followed him. To my surprise, and I must confess to my amusement too, for I was in a capital humour, I found myself in a few minutes ushered into the temple square, where two or three thousand heads were gaping intently up to a platform covered with actors, who were in the midst of what appeared to be a most interesting melodrama, judging from the effect it had upon the audience. I saw at once I had been duped, and, looking for my guide and conductor, found that he had disappeared, no doubt fully satisfied with the part he had played. My part was now to enjoy the joke and take it in good part, which I did not fail to do. I was now pressed on all hands for my opinion of the merit of the performance, which I declared was inimitable. Nor was there any flattery intended in this expression of opinion, for I doubt much if such a performance could have been got up out of the Celestial Empire.

It was some time before a large portion of the crowd found out that a foreigner was amongst them, so intent were they upon the performance, and longer still before the eyes of the actors saw me. By degrees, however, the news spread, and all eyes were turned from the stage to where I was standing. At first the actors seemed surprised at the want of that attention to which they had been accustomed, then they discovered the cause, and, if possible, were more astonished than their audience. In vain the prompter and leader of the band urged them to go on; their "occupation was gone" until the greater attraction was removed. Prudence now suggested that, having thus come unexpectedly upon the scene and played my part, it would be as well to withdraw while there was time. I now bowed very politely to the most respectable of the people who were standing near me, and expressed my delight and thanks for what I had seen. I then edged quietly out of the crowd, a few of whom followed me, while the greater part remained to enjoy the rest of the performance, which I have no doubt was concluded in a most satisfactory manner.

The day was now far advanced, and as I had been surrounded by noisy, although good-humoured, crowds since the morning, I was excessively tired. I therefore made the best of my way back to the southern suburbs, where I had left my boat in a retired creek surrounded on all sides by mulberry-trees. But even here I could not get the quiet I wished for. Numbers followed me to where my boat was moored, and pestered me with all sorts of questions. It was generally believed by them that I had come from Shanghae for the sole purpose of buying silk, nor could my assurances to the contrary convince them they were mistaken.

In order to get rid of inquisitive crowds I now gave orders to my boatmen to leave our moorings

and go on to the southwards; but did not tell
them to what point we were bound. By this
means the crowds were quite puzzled, and returned
to their homes inside the city. In passing under
one of the bridges here, and often both before and
after this when in the same position, the head
boatman warned us not to speak; for, said he, "if
you do so, something evil will happen to us afterwards." There is a superstition amongst them,
to the effect that those who speak while passing
under a bridge will be punished by being involved
in a quarrel.

After passing out of the creek I found myself
on a broad and beautiful canal which leads to the
southwards in the direction of Hang-chow-foo. As
it was my intention to remain for some days in the
vicinity of Hoo-chow, we soon found a small creek
on the east side of this canal, which led up to the
bottom of a richly-wooded hill. Having sculled
the boat up there, we made her fast to the grassy
bank of the creek, and, while dinner was getting
ready, I went on shore.

It was a lovely evening—the 18th of June—the
sun was just setting behind the high mountain-
ranges to the westward, and although the day had
been oppressively warm, the air was now comparatively cool and enjoyable. I was in the midst of
most charming scenery, and although only about
two miles distant from a crowded and bustling
city, everything was perfectly quiet and still.
Overhead the rooks were seen returning home for

the day, and here and there on a solitary bush
or in a grove of trees the songsters of the woods
were singing their last and evening song of praise.
Mulberry-trees, with their large rich green leaves,
were observed in all directions, and the plantations
extended all over the low country and up to
the foot of the hills. The hills here were low
and isolated, and appeared as if they had been
thrown out as guards between the vast plain,
which extends eastwards to the sea, and the mountains of the west. For the most part they were
covered with natural forests and brushwood, and
did not appear to have ever been under cultivation. In some parts their sides were steep—almost
perpendicular — while in others the slope was
gentle from their base to the summit. Here and
there some rugged-looking granite rocks reared
their heads above the trees, and were particularly
striking.

Looking to the hills, there all was nature pure
and unadorned, just as it had come from the hands
of the Creator ; but when the eye rested on the
cultivated plain, on the rich mulberry-plantations,
on the clear and beautiful canals studded with
white sails, the contrast was equally striking, and
told a tale of a teeming population, of wealth and
industry.

I remained for three days amongst these hills,
and employed myself in examining their natural
productions, and in making entomological collections. In some grassy glades in the woods I fre-

quently came upon little bands of natives engaged
in making thrown silk. A long, narrow framework of bamboo of considerable length was constructed, and over this the threads were laid in
the state in which they came from the reel. At
the end of the frame collections of these threads
were attached to a number of round brass balls
about the size of marbles. A rapid motion was
communicated to the balls by a smart stroke between the palms of the hands. The workmen
went along the line of balls with the quickness
of lightning, striking one after the other and
keeping the whole in motion at the same time,
until the process of twisting the silk was completed.

The little silk-villages at the base of these hills
were all visited by me at this time, and although
the natives were much surprised at the presence
of a foreigner amongst them, yet generally they
were polite and hospitable. The same features of
wealth and comfort which I had already remarked
in other parts of the silk-country were apparent
here. The people were well dressed, had good
substantial houses to live in, and, judging from
their appearance, they were well fed. Nearly all
the respectable farm-houses were surrounded with
high walls. In addition to keeping their families as
private as possible, the object of having the houses
constructed in this way was probably for safety to
their property, which is often very valuable during the silk season. I am not aware that these

districts are much infested with thieves, but the respectable Chinese country farmer is generally very timid in his nature, and would much rather incur considerable expense in making his house secure than run any risk of having it plundered, or to be obliged to defend it.

When I had completed my examination of this part of the country, and made some interesting entomological collections, I bade adieu to the hospitable villagers. My object was now the pagoda I had seen in the distance when nearing Hoochow, with the large tree growing by its side, both together forming the most striking landmark in this part of China. It was only two or three miles west from where I had been sojourning for the last few days, and about two miles from the south gate of the city. By means of canals and small creeks I was enabled to get my boat nearly to the foot of the hill on which the pagoda stands. It being late in the evening when we arrived there, I slept near a small village at the head of the creek, and made arrangements to ascend the hill early next morning.

Some time before daybreak my servant Tung-a brought me a cup of tea, which I drank and then made preparations for our journey. It seemed we had anchored at the place to which worshippers come in their boats when they are going to the temple and pagoda. We found an excellent paved road leading up to the monastery of Wan-sheu-si, which is situated in a romantic hollow, a little

below the hill on whose summit the pagoda stands.
The soil of these hills is sandy and barren, and
contrasts unfavourably with that in the rich plains
below. Avenues and clumps of pines (*Pinus sinensis*), many of which had no doubt been planted
by the priests, lined the ascent, and gave it a very
pretty appearance. As we ascended by the windings of our mountain-road, we often lost sight of
the plain which we had left, and were surrounded
on all sides by hills.

Half-an-hour's walk brought us near the doors
of the monastery of Wan-sheu-si, a large and imposing building, or rather collection of buildings,
founded about a thousand years ago by a certain
Fuh-hu-shan-si—the "Tamer of the Tiger." His
picture is still preserved in the monastery, and
represents him seated on a tiger, whose ferocity
he had completely tamed, and who now was content to carry him over hill and dale and obey his
commands!

The priests here—about thirty in number—received me with great ceremony and kindness, and
ordered tea and cakes to be set before me. I was
also taken to see two hermits who were undergoing voluntary solitary confinement for a period
of three years. One of them had been nearly two
years shut up in his cell, and consequently had
another year to remain there before he could come
out again and mix with the world.

After partaking of the tea which the good
priests had kindly set before me — and very re-

freshing it was after my morning walk — I proceeded up the hill towards the pagoda. Here I was received by a solitary priest and a little boy who seemed his servant. The priest took me into a small room in which was a bed, a table, and a few books—all he possessed in the world, so he told me. He informed me, in answer to my questions, that the pagoda was called Taou-chang-shantā. It appeared to be ancient, for the adjoining temple, which had probably been built about the same period, was now in a very ruinous condition. Being curious to know what the tree was which, with the pagoda, formed such a striking sight when seen from a distance, I paid it a visit and found it was the maidenhair-tree (*Salisburia adiantifolia*).

If the pagoda and maidenhair-tree were striking from a distance, the view from the top of the hill where they stood was equally so, and of quite a different character. The bustling city of Hoochow-foo, with its walls, rampart, and broad and beautiful canals lay at my feet. Looking eastward the country was perfectly flat as far as the eye could reach—it is one vast rich and fertile mulberry-garden. On the west the prospect was bounded by a long range of mountains, very irregular in height, form, and general outline, and some of them very high. The T'ai-hu lake with its islands—the Tung-ting-shans—were seen to the north, and far away on the horizon to the southeast the little hills near Chapoo are just visible on a clear day.

I gazed long with rapture upon the wonderful
scene which lay beneath and around me. Many
views which I have had both before and since that
time, when travelling in the Himalayas, have been
perhaps more grand and sublime, owing to the
stupendous height of these mountains, but as a
view of marvellous richness and loveliness that
from the top of Taou-chang-shan stands unrivalled.

CHAPTER XVIII.

Ascend the Lun-ke river — A musical Buddhist high priest — Hoo-
shan monastery — Its silk-worms — Mode of feeding them —
General treatment — Their aversion to noise and bright light —
The country embanked in all directions — A farmer's explanation of
this — Town of Mei-che — Silk-worms begin to spin — Method of
putting them on straw — Artificial heat employed — Reeling process — Machine described — Work-people — Silk scenes in a
monastery — Industrious Buddhist priests — Novel mode of catching
fish — End of silk season — Price of raw silk where it is produced.

I SPENT a week in the midst of this beautiful
scenery, and experienced nothing but kindness
and civility from the hundreds of natives with
whom I came daily in contact. During this time
I gained a good deal of information regarding the
hilly districts to the westward, which I intended
to penetrate before I left this part of the country.
I found that a river of considerable size flowed
up to the west gate of the city, and apparently
emptied itself into the net-work of canals which
cover this extensive plain; and I was informed
that it was navigable for upwards of twenty miles
to boats much larger than the one I was travelling
in. My object now was to get my boat into that
river, and as all these rivers and canals are connected this was accomplished without the least
difficulty. We returned to the south gate of Hoo-

chow, where we found a wide canal leading round
the walls to the west gate. Following this canal
we soon skulled round, and found ourselves on a
wide and deep river which takes its rise amongst
the hills in the far west. It is called Lun-ke by
the natives, and probably one of its most distant
sources is near the celebrated Tein-muh-shan—a
mountain said to be the highest in this part of
China.

In sailing up this river I observed that the
plantations of mulberry still formed the staple
crop of the country on all the flat lands which
were raised above the surface of the rice-fields.
About sixty le west of Hoo-chow-foo I observed a
large monastery not very far from the banks of
the river, and as it seemed situated in the midst of
rich and luxuriant vegetation, I determined to
moor my boat to the banks of the river, and
remain in the neighbourhood for a few days. As
I was going up the road in the direction of the
temple I met an old respectable-looking priest
carrying a kind of flute or flageolet in his hand,
which he induced now and then to give out
not unmusical sounds. His head was shaven
after the manner of the priests of Buddha; but
the three nails on his left hand were each about
two inches in length, denoting that he did not
earn his bread by the sweat of his brow, and that
in fact he was one of the superiors in the order to
which he belonged. This old gentleman met me
in the most dignified manner, and did not express

the least surprise at seeing a foreigner so far from home. He asked me to accompany him home to his temple, and when we arrived there he introduced me to his own quarters and desired his servants to set tea and cakes before me. He then led me over all the halls and temples of the monastery, which, although very extensive, were in a most dilapidated condition. They were too much like buildings of this kind in other parts of the country to require any further notice.

If there was little to notice in these temples with reference to Buddhism and its rites, there were objects of another kind which soon attracted my attention. The halls and outhouses of the monastery seemed to be converted for the time into a place for feeding silk-worms. Millions of these little animals were feeding in round sieves, placed one above another in open framework made for this purpose. So great was the number of the worms that every sieve—and there must have been many hundreds of them—was crammed quite full. In one large hall I observed the floor completely covered with worms. I shall never forget the peculiar sound which fell upon my ear as I opened the door of this hall. It was early in the morning, the worms had been just fed, and were at the time eagerly devouring the fresh leaves of the mulberry. Hundreds of thousands of little mouths were munching the leaves, and in the stillness around this sound was very striking and peculiar. The place too seemed so strange—

a temple—a place of worship with many huge idols, some from twenty to thirty feet in height, looking down upon the scene on the floor. But to a Chinese there is nothing improper in converting a temple into a granary or a silk-worm establishment for a short time if it is required, and I suppose the gods of the place are supposed to look down with approbation on such scenes of peaceful industry.

When from the large number of worms it is necessary to feed them on floors of rooms and halls, there is always a layer of dry straw laid down to keep them off the damp ground. This mode of treatment is resorted to from necessity, and not from choice. The sieves of the establishment, used in the framework I have already noticed, are greatly preferred.

Whether the worms are fed on sieves or on the floor they are invariably cleaned every morning. All the remains of the leafstalks of the mulberry, the excrement of the animals, and other impurities, are removed before the fresh leaves are given. Much importance is attached to this matter, as it has a tendency to keep the worms in a clean and healthy condition. The Chinese are also very particular as regards the amount of light which they admit during the period the animals are feeding. I always observed the rooms were kept partially darkened, no bright light was allowed to penetrate. In many instances the owners were most unwilling to open the doors, for fear, as they said, of disturbing them; and they invariably cautioned me against making any unnecessary noise while I was examining them.

At this time nearly all the labour in this part of the country was expended on the production of the silk-worm. In the fields the natives were seen in great numbers busily engaged in gathering the leaves; boats on the rivers were fraught with them; in the country market-towns they were exposed for sale in great quantities, and everything told that they were the staple article of production. On the other hand, every cottage, farm-house, barn and temple, was filled with its thousands of worms which were fed and tended with the greatest care.

This part of the country is very populous, villages and small towns are scattered over it in every direction, and the people have the same clean and respectable appearance which I had already remarked in other parts of the silk districts. In making my observations on the rearing of the silk-worm I visited many hundreds of these towns and villages, and never in one instance had any complaint to make of incivility on the part of any one.

After staying a few days in the vicinity of the temple of Hoo-shan—for such was its name— I gave my boatmen directions to move onwards further up the river. We passed a number of pretty towns and villages on its banks, and arrived at last at a place called Kin-hwa, where I remained for two days, and employed myself in making entomological collections and examining the productions of the district. We then went onwards to a small town calted Mei-che, which was as far as the river was navigable for boats, and from thirty to forty miles west from Hoo-chow-foo.

Here I moored my boat at a little distance from the town, and determined to remain in the neighbourhood long enough to examine everything of interest which might present itself. Although the country was comparatively level near the banks of the stream, yet I was now surrounded on all sides by hills, and the flat alluvial plain of the Yang-tse-Kiang was quite shut out from my view. In its general features it was rather curious and striking. Everywhere it was cut up into ponds and small lakes, and wide embankments of earth seemed to cross it in all directions. At the first view it was difficult to account for this state of things, and I could not get any satisfactory reason for it, either from my servants or boatmen. I knew well, however, that the Chinese have a good and substantial reason for everything they do, and determined to apply to some farmer as the most likely person to enlighten me. One day when out on an excursion in the country I met an intelligent-looking man, and to him I applied to solve the difficulty.

" These embankments," said he, " which you now see cutting up the country in all directions, were formed many hundred years ago by our forefathers in order to protect themselves and their crops from being washed away by the floods. The vast plain, through which you have come from Shanghae, is scarcely any higher in level than where we now stand, for you will observe the tide ebbs and flows quite up to Mei-che. With this slow drainage for our mountain streams to the eastward we have frequently a large body of water pouring down upon us from the west, which overflows the river's banks and carries everything away before it. The embankments which you observe running in all directions are intended to check these floods, and prevent them from extending over the country."

Upon giving the matter a little consideration I had no doubt that the explanation given by the Chinese farmer was the correct one, and that however strange these embankments might appear they were necessary for the safety of this part of the country.

Mei-che is a long town on the banks of the stream, and as the river is no longer navigable for the low-country boats a considerable business is done here in hill productions, which are brought down for sale. They are put on board of boats here, and conveyed in them to the towns in the plains.

This town appears to be almost the western boundary of the great silk country. Here the mulberry plantations, although pretty numerous, do not form the staple crop of the district, nor do

2 c

they seem to grow with such luxuriance as they
do further to the east about Hoo-chow and Nan-
tsin.   Large quantities of rice and other grains
now take the place of the mulberry.   In the mountains to the west considerable quantities of tea are
produced, and fine bamboos which are sent down
to the low country are made into paper.   A mountain called Tein-muh-shan, celebrated amongst the
Chinese for its height and for its temples, lies to
the west of this, and further west still is the great
green-tea country of Hwuy-chow, which I examined
during my former visit to China.

On my way up from Hoo-chow-foo to Mei-che,
and about the 23rd of June, I observed that many
of the worms had ceased to feed and were commencing to spin.   The first indication of this
change is made apparent to the natives by the
bodies of the little animals becoming more clear
and almost transparent.   When this change takes
place, they are picked, one by one, out of the
sieves, and placed upon bundles of straw to form
their cocoons.   These bundles of straw, which are
each about two feet in length, are bound firmly
in the middle ; the two ends are cut straight and
then spread out like a broom, and into these ends
the worms are laid, when they immediately fix
themselves and begin to spin.   During this process I observed the under side of the framework
on which the bundles of straw were placed surrounded with cotton cloth to prevent the cold
draught from getting to the worms.   In some

instances small charcoal fires were lighted and
placed under the frame inside the cloth, in order
to afford further warmth. In some of the cottages
the straw covered with spinning worms was laid
in the sun under the verandahs in front of the
doors.

In a few days after the worms are put upon the
straw they have disappeared in the cocoons and
have ceased to spin. The reeling process now
commences, and machines for this purpose were
seen in almost every cottage. This apparatus
may be said to consist of four distinct parts, or
rather, I may divide it into these for the purpose
of describing it. There is, first, the pan of hot
water into which the cocoons are thrown; second,
the little loops or eyes through which the threads
pass; third, a lateral or horizontal movement, in
order to throw the silk in a zigzag manner over
the wheel; and lastly the wheel itself, which is
square. Two men, or a man and woman, are
generally employed at each wheel. The business
of one is to attend to the fire and to add fresh
cocoons as the others are wound off. The most
expert workman drives the machine with his foot
and attends to the threads as they pass through
the loops over on to the wheel. Eight, ten, and
sometimes twelve cocoons are taken up to form
one thread, and as one becomes exhausted, another
is taken up to supply its place. Three, and sometimes four, of such threads are passing over on to
the wheel at the same time. The lateral or zig-

zag movement of the machine throws the threads in that way on the wheel, and I believe this is considered a great improvement upon the Canton method, in which the threads are thrown on in a parallel manner.

The water in the pan into which the cocoons are first thrown is never allowed to boil, but it is generally very near the boiling point. I frequently tried it and found it much too hot for my fingers to remain in it. A slow fire of charcoal is also placed under the wheel. As the silk is winding, this fire is intended to dry off the superfluous moisture which the cocoons have imbibed in the water in which they were immersed.

During the time I was in the silk country at this time I was continually visiting the farmhouses and cottages in which the reeling of silk was going on. As silk is a very valuable production, it is reeled with more than ordinary care, and I observed that in almost all instances a clean, active, and apparently clever workman was entrusted with the care of the reeling process.

The old temple at Hoo-shan, which I visited again on my way down, was in a state of great excitement and bustle. The quantity of silk produced here was very large, and all hands were employed in reeling and sorting it. The priests themselves, who generally are rather averse to work of any kind, were obliged to take their places at the wheel or the fire. But as the silk was their own they seemed, notwithstanding their

CURIOUS METHOD OF FISHING.

Page 375.

habitual indolence, to work with hearty goodwill. My old friend the Superior, however, was exempt from labour. When I called, and found all the verandahs and courts in a bustle, he was quietly smoking his pipe and sipping his tea with his favourite flageolet by his side. I remained with him during the heat of the day, and in the evening he walked down with me to the river side where my boat was moored. He readily accepted an invitation to come on board, and while there took a great fancy to a copy of 'Punch' and the 'Illustrated London News.' I need not say I made him a present of both papers, and sent him away highly delighted. My boat now shot out into the stream, and as we sailed slowly down I could hear the wild and not unpleasing strains of my friend's flageolet as he wended his way homewards through the woods.

On our way down the river that night we came upon some people fishing in a manner so curious that I must endeavour to describe it. The boats used for this purpose were long and narrow. Each had a broad strip of white canvas stretched along the right side, and dipping towards the water at an angle of from thirty to forty degrees. On the other side of the boat a net, corresponding in size with the white cloth, was stretched along above the bulwarks. A man sat in the stern of each boat and brought his weight to bear on the starboard side, which had the effect of pressing the white canvas into the water and raising the net on the opposite side. A small paddle was used for propelling the boat through the water. This will be well understood by a glance at the accompanying sketch.

As we approached these strange fishermen, I desired my boatmen to take in our sail, and as my boat lay still on the smooth surface of the water, I watched their proceedings with much interest. It was a fine, clear night, and I could see distinctly the white canvas shining through the water, although several inches beneath its surface. The fishermen sat motionless and silent, and scarcely noticed us when we joined them, so intent were they upon their work. We had not remained above a minute in the position we had taken up, when I heard a splash in the water, and distinctly saw a fish jump over the boat and get caught by the net on its opposite side. The object in constructing the boats in the manner I have described was now apparent. It seemed that the white canvas, which dipped like a painted board into the water, had the effect of attracting and decoying the fish in some peculiar manner, and caused them to leap over it. But as the boats were low and narrow, it was necessary to have a net stretched on the opposite side to prevent the fish from leaping over them altogether and escaping again into the stream. Each fish, as it took the fatal leap, generally struck against the net and fell backward into the boat.

My boatmen and servants looked on this curious

method of catching fish with as much interest as I did myself, and could not refrain from expressing their delight rather noisily when a poor fish got caught. The fishermen themselves remained motionless as statues, and scarcely noticed us, except to beg we would not make any noise, as it prevented them from catching fish.

We watched these fishermen for upwards of an hour, and then asked them to sell us some fish for supper. Their little boats were soon alongside of ours, and we purchased some of the fish which we had seen caught in this extraordinary and novel manner.

On the following morning, when I awoke, I found myself quietly at anchor close by the west gate of Hoo-chow-foo, my boatmen having worked all night. I spent the next few days in the country to the northward bordering on the T'ai-hoo lake, and partly near the town of Nan-tsin, being anxious to see the end of the silk season. About the eighth, or from that to the tenth of July, the winding of the cocoons had ceased almost everywhere, and a few days after this there was scarcely a sign of all that life and bustle which is visible everywhere during the time that the silk is in hand. The clash of the winding-machines, which used to be heard in every cottage, farmhouse, and temple, had now ceased; the furnaces, pans, and wheels, with all the other parts of the apparatus in common use during the winding season, had been cleared away, and a stranger

visiting that country now could scarcely have believed that such a busy bustling scene had been
acting only a few days before.

During my peregrinations in the silk country I
made many inquiries amongst the natives as to
the price of raw silk in the districts where it is
produced. An inquiry of this kind is always
rather difficult in a country like China, where
the natives are too practical to believe one is
making such an inquiry merely for the purpose
of gaining information. On several occasions
the reply to my question was another, wishing to
know whether I wanted to buy. Most of the
natives with whom I came in contact firmly believed my object in coming to the silk-country
was to purchase silks; and neither my assurances
to the contrary nor those of my servants, who
were generally appealed to on the subject, were
sufficient to make them change their opinion. I
believe, however, the information I gleaned from
various quarters at different times will be found
to be tolerably correct. At Mei-che the price
was said to range from twelve to eighteen dollars
for 100 taels of silk. At Hoo-chow and Nan-
tsin, where the silk is of a superior quality, the
prices in 1855 were from eighteen to twenty-two
dollars for 100 taels. The price of raw silk, like
that of everything else, no doubt depends in a
great measure upon the supply and demand, and
varies accordingly.

CHAPTER XIX.

Leave the silk country — Adventure at Nanziang — A visit from thieves — I am robbed of everything — Unsuccessful efforts to trace the robbers — Astonished by another visit from them — Its objects — My clothes and papers returned — Their motives for this — A visit to the Nanziang mandarin — Means taken to catch the robbers — Two are caught and bambooed — My visit to the mandarin returned — Arrive at Shanghae — Report the robbery to her Majesty's Consul — A portion of the money recovered — The remainder supposed to be kept by the mandarins.

HAVING now finished my inspection of the silk-districts I commenced my journey eastwards, in the direction of Shanghae, where I had some important work awaiting me. I have already stated in a former chapter that it was my intention to call again at Cading on my way in order to procure some seeds which were not ripe when I passed through that place *en route* to the silk-country. On the evening of the third day I arrived at a small town named Nanziang, a few miles to the west of Shanghae, and not very far from Cading, without having any adventures worth recording in these pages. I could not help thinking over the journey I had undertaken, and the quiet and successful manner in which it had been accomplished. Everywhere I had been treated with civility and kindness by the natives;

I had had no trouble whatever with the authorities; and no complaints had been made by them on account of my transgressing the boundary-line drawn out for the restriction of barbarians, or " white devils," as they so politely term us. While congratulating myself upon these results my boat grounded in the midst of the Nanziang canal, and as at least a hundred were in the same predicament ahead of us it was impossible for us to proceed on our journey. My boatmen informed me that it would be necessary to remain where we were until the flood-tide came in, which would be about two or three o'clock in the morning. I was obliged to be contented with this arrangement, and went on shore for a walk while my servants were engaged in preparing dinner.

Between nine and ten o'clock in the evening we retired to rest. As the night was excessively close and warm I allowed the little glass windows in the sides of my boat to remain open in order to admit a little fresh air. These windows were so small that no one could enter the boat by them or take out any of the boxes which lay upon my floor or table. I had, therefore, no suspicion of there being any danger from the arrangement, which added considerably to my comfort. As all the people in the boat, as well as myself, were early risers, and had plenty to do during the day, we were soon fast asleep.

About two in the morning I was awakened by a loud yell from one of my servants, and I sus-

pected at once that we had had a visit from
thieves, for I had frequently heard the same
sound before. Like the cry one hears at sea
when a man has fallen overboard this alarm
can never be mistaken when once it has been
heard. When it had saluted my ear on former
occasions it had proceeded from other boats or
places in which I did not feel so great an interest as I perhaps ought to have done. I do
not know how to describe it; it sounds like
something between fear and defiance, and indi-
cates that were the thieves bold enough to fight
the defenders of property would probably run,
or if the thieves are inclined to run the others
might possibly follow them. In the present
instance, and before I had time to inquire what
was wrong, one of my servants and two of the
boatmen plunged into the canal and pursued the
thieves. Thinking that we had only lost some
cooking utensils, or things of little value that
might have been lying outside the boat, I gave
myself no uneasiness about the matter, and felt
much inclined to go to sleep again. But my
servant, who returned almost immediately, awoke
me most effectually. "I fear," said he, opening
my door, " the thieves have been inside the boat,
and have taken away some of your property."
" Impossible," said I, " they cannot have been here."
" But look," he replied, " a portion of the side of
your boat under the window has been lifted out;
I shall light a candle and have it examined."

Turning to the place indicated by my servant I could see, although it was quite dark, that there was a large hole in the side of the boat not more than three feet from where my head had been lying. At my right hand, and just under the window, the trunk used to stand in which I was in the habit of keeping my papers, money, and other valuables. On the first suspicion that I was the victim I stretched out my hand in the dark to feel if this was safe. Instead of my hand resting on the top of the trunk, as it had been accustomed to do, it went down to the floor of the boat, and I then knew for the first time that the trunk was gone. At the same moment my servant Tung-a came in with a candle and confirmed what I had just made out in the dark. The thieves had done their work well—the boat was empty. My money, amounting to more than one hundred Shanghae dollars, my accounts and other papers, including, gentle reader, this journal which has been amusing and instructing you — all, all, were gone. The rascals had not left me even the clothes I had thrown off when I went to bed.

But there was no time to lose; and in order to make every effort to catch the thieves, or at least get back a portion of my property, I jumped into the canal, and made for the banks. The tide had now risen, and instead of finding only about two feet of water—the depth when we went to bed—I now sank up to the neck, and found the stream very rapid. A few strokes with my arms soon

brought me into shallow water, and to the shore.
Here I found the boatmen rushing about in a
frantic manner, examining with a lantern the
bushes and indigo vats on the banks of the canal,
but all they had found was a few Manilla cheroots
which the thieves had dropped apparently in their
hurry. After looking carefully in all directions
nothing more could be found. A watchman with
his lantern, and two or three stragglers, hearing
the noise we made, came up and enquired what
was wrong, but when asked whether they had
seen anything of the thieves shook their heads
and professed the most profound ignorance.

The night was pitch dark, everything was perfectly still, and with the exception of the few stragglers already mentioned, the whole town seemed
sunk in a deep sleep. We were, therefore, perfectly
helpless, and could do nothing further. Calling
my people together I desired them to put out the
light and to lie down amongst the long grass
which grew on the banks of the canal. In this
position they were desired to remain perfectly
quiet, and should any person come prowling about
he was to be seized without question or warrant.
I thought it just possible the thieves might have
left some of their plunder in the hurry, and that,
when all was quiet, they might return in order to
secure it. Having thus formed my plans and set
the watch I returned, in no comfortable frame of
mind, to my boat, leaving orders to be called
should anything of importance take place.

Dripping with wet, and rather low-spirited on account of the misfortune which had befallen me, I lay down on my couch without any inclination to sleep, as may easily be imagined. It was a serious business for me to lose so much money, but that part of the matter gave me the least uneasiness. The loss of my accounts, journals, drawings and numerous memoranda I had been making during three years of travel, which it was impossible for anyone to replace, was of far greater importance. I tried to reason philosophically upon the matter; to persuade myself that as the thing could not be helped now it was no use being vexed with it; that in a few years it would not signify much either to myself or anyone else whether I had been robbed or not; but all this fine reasoning would not do.

I may have lain about an hour in this pleasing frame of mind, brooding over my ill luck, my people were still on shore, the night was very dark, and everything was perfectly quiet and still. Footsteps were now heard coming down the pathway on the opposite side of the canal from that on which my men were posted. Although we did not expect anything to turn up from that quarter we were all attention, and when we could see two figures halt abreast of our boat our excitement was at a very high pitch. "Louda, louda,"* cried one of them, addressing the head boatman. My men immediately started up from their concealment on

---

* A term always applied to the captain or head man of the boat.

the opposite side and demanded what our visitors wanted. " Louda," said the same voice, with the greatest coolness, and as if he was transacting a very ordinary piece of business, " come over here and receive the ' white devil's ' trunks and clothes."

My first impulse on hearing this conversation was to rush out of the boat and endeavour to seize these men, who I had no doubt were the thieves. But common-sense told me that any endeavour to do this in the darkness would surely fail, and might endanger the safety of the things they had brought back. It also struck me that, as the most valuable part of my property was of no use to them, I might possibly recover my books and papers. These considerations induced me to remain quiet in the boat and allow the Chinese to manage matters in their own way.

When my men reached the opposite side of the canal the thieves had disappeared, but had left on the banks my boxes and clothes. On these being brought into my cabin the first thing I examined was the box in which I kept my money and papers. I saw at the first glance that the padlock had been wrenched off, but the lid was now fastened carefully down with a piece of twine. On cutting this I observed that a small box inside in which I had kept my money had also been cut open, and the dollars were all gone. But everything else in the trunk, although bearing evident marks of having been under the examination of the thieves, had been carefully put back. My

accounts, books, journals, and all that I valued
most, had been returned to me. Many things,
such as knives, pencils, &c., which are highly
valued by the Chinese, were left untouched; and
even the very padlock of the trunk had been put
carefully inside. It was the same with my clothes.
Coats, waistcoats, trousers, and even the necktie
which I had thrown on the table when I went to
bed—everything was returned except the dollars.

This proceeding on the part of the robbers surprised me greatly, and although I regretted the
loss of the money I was truly thankful that I
had come off so well. What an extraordinary
people the Chinese are, and how difficult to understand! The thieves of any other nation would
never have thought of bringing back what they
did not want; if they do not appropriate the
whole of their booty they either destroy it or
throw it away. Chinese thieves are much more
considerate and civilized; they return what does
not suit their purpose to keep!

It is not difficult for a person acquainted with
the manners and government of the Chinese to see
the propriety and convenience of such a proceeding. In China almost every man is responsible in
some way or another for the acts of his neighbour.
If a disturbance takes place in a shop or private
dwelling the owner of the place is liable to be
called upon for an account of it by the authorities;
if a fight occurs in the public street the people in
the neighbourhood are held responsible; and in

this manner every man is made responsible, to a certain extent, for what goes on around him. In this state of things it will easily be perceived that the gentry who robbed me acted wisely in bringing back all articles which, while they were of no use to them, might have led in some way to their detection. And, no doubt, this was the motive by which they were actuated, and not any regard for my convenience. But I felt truly grateful to them nevertheless, and in this frame of mind I retired again to rest after having secured the windows of the boat and set one of the men to watch.

As soon as daylight appeared I dressed myself and took my servant and one of the boatmen to the house of the highest mandarin in the town, in order to inform him what had happened to us during the night, and to ask him to take steps for the detection of the thieves and the recovery of the money. When we reached his Ya-mun, we were told by his servants that he was not yet awake. On explaining to them that my business was urgent, they promised to carry my message to their master, and politely showed me into the audience hall.

I had not been here for more than five minutes, when the mandarin himself appeared, dressed in his official robes, which he had apparently thrown very hurriedly on. As he entered the hall he made me several most polite bows, which, as in duty bound, I did not fail to return. As is usual in such cases, we had a long discussion as to who should occupy the seat of honour on the left side of a raised table at the end of the hall. He succeeded at last in getting me into it, and then ordered tea and pipes to be brought and set before us.

We now entered upon the business which had brought me to pay this visit. I told him that I had been travelling for some time in the interior of the country, and that I had never been plundered or molested in any way until I had come to Nanziang, which was under his jurisdiction. He expressed his great regret and indignation, and told me he was sorry to say that there were more thieves and bad characters about his district than that of any other magistrate in this part of China. I then hinted that no time ought to be lost in endeavouring to trace the thieves, and called my servants, who were outside, to explain particularly how and where the robbery had taken place.

An inferior officer was now sent for, and directed to send off runners in every direction to obtain information, and if possible to capture the thieves. Another was sent to accompany me down to where my boat was lying, to examine the manner in which the thieves had entered it, and to make inquiries amongst the people in the neighbourhood. Having thus put things in train, I bade good-by to the mandarin, and took my leave with an invitation to call upon him again in the evening, or on the following morning, when he might be able to give me some information regarding the recovery of my property.

When we reached my boat, the officer who accompanied me made a minute examination of the mode in which the thieves had effected an entrance. I now observed what I was not aware of before, that a portion of the boat under the window was made to lift out; the thieves, no doubt well aware of this, had only to lift out the window, undo the fastenings inside, and take out a board larger than the window itself, and quite large enough to admit a man or to remove any of my boxes. After examining these matters, and taking down on paper a list of all the articles taken away, those returned to me, and the missing dollars, the officer took his leave in order to prosecute his inquiries.

The news of the robbery by this time had spread over all the town. Hundreds of people came to look at the boat, and to make inquiries as to the truth of what they had heard.

In the afternoon the mandarin whom I had visited in the morning came to return my visit, and to inform me the police had caught one of the thieves. On inquiring if they had recovered the money an evasive answer was given, which I did not much like; so I repeated the question. He then told me that the money would be forthcoming in due time, but that it would be necessary to beat the man with the bamboo that night, and that I should be informed in the morning what success

had attended this operation.   Before taking his
leave he expressed a wish that I would not leave
Nanziang until the next afternoon, when he
trusted all would be arranged to my satisfaction.
He was very averse to my making any complaint
to the English authorities in Shanghae about what
had happened.

Early next morning, one of my boatmen who
had been in the town informed me, apparently
with great satisfaction, that two of the thieves had
been caught and bambooed, and that it was
reported the money had been recovered.   As I did
not intend troubling the authorities until the
evening, I walked across the country to Cading, in
order to procure samples of some seeds which I
had marked when there some weeks before.

On returning to my boat in the evening, I
despatched my servant to the office of the authorities, with a message stating that I had remained
for two days with the prospect of having my property recovered, but that it was my intention now
to proceed to Shanghae, and report the matter to
the English consul.   A very polite message came
back stating that the thieves were to be treated
with another bambooing that night, and asking me
to wait the results.   Thinking that the mandarins
were trifling with me, and that more would be
gained by my absence than presence, I returned
my compliments, stating I could wait no longer,
and that as soon as the money was recovered I
would feel obliged if it was sent to the care of Her

Majesty's consul in Shanghae.   My servants and boatmen assured me it had been recovered, and that the mandarins could pay it if they liked.

As Nanziang was within the boundary line within which foreigners are supposed to range, I reported the circumstance to Mr. Robertson, Her Majesty's consul, and requested he would be good enough to assist me in getting back the money. Had the thieves not been found this perhaps would have been scarcely attended with any success; but as I felt certain the Nanziang mandarins had my property in their own hands, I was rather loth to let it remain there.

A few weeks after this I received from the vice-consul, Mr. Harvey, a handkerchief containing thirty-five dollars, a number of small new three-penny pieces, which I used to carry for giving away amongst the children, a brass ring and seal, and various other little things which I had not missed until they were restored to me. The remainder of the money was no doubt retained by the worthy mandarins to pay for their civility and entertainment.   The labourer is worthy of his hire!

CHAPTER XX.

Tea-makers from Fokien and Kiangse engaged for India — Ning-chow
tea country — Formerly produced green teas — Now produces black
— How this change took place — Difficulty in getting the men off
— One of them arrested for debt — All on board at last and sent on
to Calcutta — Coast infested with pirates — Ningpo missionaries
robbed — Politeness of the pirates — Their rendezvous discovered—
Attacked and destroyed by the 'Bittern' — A mandarin in difficulty
— The English "don't fight fair" — Liberality of the Chinese and
English merchants — Captain Vansittart's reward.

On my arrival at Shanghae I found that the
efforts I had been making in order to secure the
services of some firstrate black-tea manufacturers
for the Government Plantations in the Himalayas
had been successful.   Eight men, natives of Fokien, and well acquainted with the method of
making the finest teas of Tsin-tsun and Tsong-gan
—districts situated on the south side of the great
Bohea mountains, famous for the superior quality
of their black teas—had been engaged by Mr.
Clark at Foo-chow-foo, and were now on their
way to Hongkong and India.   They had taken
with them an ample supply of the implements in
use in those districts for the purpose of manufacturing the leaves, and thus one of the chief
objects I had in view in coming to China, after
many delays and difficulties, had been successfully
accomplished.

Mr. Brooke Robertson, Her Majesty's Consul at Shanghae, had also been unceasing in his efforts to assist me in procuring manufacturers for the Indian plantations. Through his influence nine men, natives of the province of Kiangse, were now induced to engage themselves to go to India. The tea districts in this province, which border the Poyang lake, have risen into great importance within the last fifty years. Moning and Ning-chow * teas are all produced in this part of the country, and are largely exported to Europe and America.

During the days of the East India Company's Charter all the best black teas were produced in the province of Fokien. The towns of Tsin-tsun and Tsong-gan in the vicinity of the far-famed Woo-e hills were then the chief marts for the best black teas exported by the Company. At that period the districts about Ning-chow, in the Kiangse province, were known only for their green teas. Now, however, and for many years past, although the Fokien black teas are, and have been, largely exported, those produced in the Ning-chow districts have risen in public estimation, and, I believe, generally fetch very high prices in the English market.

If there is any one now who still clings to the old idea that green teas can be made *only* from the plant called *Thea virides*, and black ones *only*

---

* Names of districts well known to merchants engaged in the tea trade with China.

from *Thea bohea*, he will find a difficulty in giving credit to the account I have to give of the manner in which the Ning-chow districts have changed their green teas into black. But, however difficult it may be to get rid of early prejudices, " facts are stubborn things," and the truth of what I have to state may be fully relied upon.

Many years ago a spirited Chinese merchant who, no doubt, saw well enough that black and green teas could be made easily enough from the same plant, had a crop of *black* teas made in the Ning-chow district and brought to Canton for sale. This tea was highly approved of by the foreign merchants at that port, and was bought, I believe, by the great house of Messrs. Dent and Company, and sent to England. When it got home it found a ready sale in the market, and at once established itself as a black tea of the first class. Year by year after this the demand for this tea steadily increased and was as regularly supplied by the Chinese. At the present time the Ning-chow districts produce black teas only, while in former days they produced only green. If proof were wanting, this would appear sufficient to show that black or green teas can be made from any variety of the tea plant, and that the change of colour in the manufactured article depends entirely upon the mode of manipulation.*

From the high character these Ning-chow teas

* A full description of this will be found in my ' Journey to the Tea Countries,' to which I beg to refer those interested in the matter.

had acquired in foreign markets I was well-
pleased in being able to engage the services of
manufacturers from that district.   An engagement was drawn up in English and Chinese by
Mr. Sinclair, interpreter to the Consulate, which
was signed by the men and by myself; an advance of one hundred dollars was given to each
man for the support of their families during their
absence, and they were desired to hold themselves
in readiness to sail by the first steamer.   An old
mandarin with a white button, a native of Kiangse,
and head of the Kiangse hong in Shanghae, attended with the men at the Consulate, and became
security for them at the time that each man received his advance of wages.

The steamer destined to convey these inland
Chinamen from the shores of their native land
was advertised to sail on the 10th of August 1855.
I had given them timely notice of this, and desired
them to meet me in front of Mr. Beale's house, at
least two hours before the hour appointed for
sailing, for I knew well how Chinese procrastinate,
and anticipated some difficulty in getting them all
on board in time.   It was some time after the
appointed hour before any of them made their
appearance, and I began to fear they would draw
back and object to embark at the last moment,
even after they had had a liberal advance of
wages and after their passage-money to Hongkong had been paid.   At last, however, all except
one made their appearance with their beds, trunks,

and many other necessaries which they supposed would be required on the voyage. The old white-buttoned mandarin who had become security for them, accompanied them to see them safely away, and very anxious he seemed to be to get them off, and thus get rid of the responsibility which he had taken upon his shoulders, and for which he, no doubt, took care to be well paid.

But now another difficulty presented itself in the shape of a creditor who came down and seized one of the men for debt. In the noise which accompanied and succeeded this seizure it was quite impossible to understand the nature of the case, and to interfere in the matter would only have made things worse. There was nothing to be done except to wait as patiently as possible and allow the contending parties to settle the matter themselves. The business was arranged in some way at last, and as a boat was alongside the jetty, we got them into it and sculled off to the steamer, which was lying in the middle of the river with her steam up and ready for sea.

As the ninth man did not make his appearance, I told the old mandarin with the white button that he would have to return me the hundred dollars I had advanced and the amount of the man's passage-money, should it not be refunded by the agents of the Peninsular and Oriental Company. This he acknowledged was perfectly just, but at this moment another man came on board and offered to go as a substitute for the runaway. On inquiry I ascertained this man was also a black-tea maker from Kiangse, and as all the others affirmed him to be a first-rate workman, I consented to accept him in lieu of the other. By the time we had concluded this arrangement the vessel's anchor was at the bows, and we steamed away rapidly down the river and out to sea.

My difficulties, in so far as these men were concerned, were now over, and I was heartily glad that my efforts had thus been crowned with complete success. As all these men were from a district several hundred miles inland, and had never been to sea in their lives, I was most anxious that nothing should happen to make them disgusted with the voyage, and took measures to have them kindly treated while at sea. When we reached Hongkong, Mr. Pereira, of Messrs. Dent and Company, was good enough to get his compradore to give them quarters and feed them until an opportunity arrived of sending them on to India.

In a few days the two sets of men—those from Fokien as well as those from Kiangse — were shipped in the steamer " Chusan " for Calcutta, and, after having numerous adventures, which they related to me afterwards with great glee, they all arrived in safety and good health at their destination in the Himalayas.

It was now necessary for me to return once more to the north, in order to settle my accounts

with the Chinese in various parts of the tea districts, and to inform them that I would not require
their assistance any longer in making collections
of seeds and plants. On our way up the coast,
when a few miles south of the Chusan islands, we
fell in with Her Majesty's brig "Bittern," Captain
Vansittart, at this time busily employed in putting
down the hordes of pirates that infested the whole
line of coast from Hongkong to the Gulf of Pee-
che-lee. A stoppage had almost been put to the
native coasting trade by these marauders, and
foreign vessels had also been attacked on various
occasions. A few weeks before the Rev. Mr. Russell, of the Church Missionary Society at Ningpo,
and some other friends, were plundered on their
way from that place to the island of Poo-to.
While at anchor at a place called Sing-kei-mun,
on the south-east end of Chusan, waiting for the
tide, their boat was attacked by a number of
armed men, and stripped of everything of the
slightest value; some of their clothes even were
taken away from them. It was useless to resist a
force of this kind, and no resistance was offered.

These Chinese pirates when unresisted are not
generally cruel or bloodthirsty. In some instances they are extremely polite, and even kind,
and quite rival our highwaymen of Hampstead
Heath and Hounslow in bygone times. In the
present instance they expressed great delight with
Mr. Russell's watch, which, they said, would be
highly appreciated by their commodore. In the

course of the evening one of them brought it
back, not for the purpose of returning it to the
owner, but to take lessons from him in winding it
up! Having kept the missionaries close prisoners
all night, they put them into a small boat next
morning and sent them away; but before this a
box of tea was sent to them as a present from the
leader of the band! For all this kindness and
politeness a heavy recompense was awaiting them.

It soon became known that the rendezvous of
the pirate fleet was at a place called Shie-poo,
a few miles south from Chusan; and in this place
the "Bittern" found them a few days after the
robbery of the missionaries. The brig was accompanied by the steamer "Paou-shan," a vessel
bought by some Chinese merchants for the protection of their junks a short time before. The
pirates, who had watches on every headland, and
runners all along the coast, were fully aware of
the intentions of our men-of-war. But they had
upwards of twenty vessels, all heavily manned
and armed, and, as the entrance to the bay in
which they were at anchor was extremely narrow,
it appeared to them impossible for a vessel like
the "Bittern" to attack them with the slightest
chance of success. Their own authorities on shore
were treated with supreme contempt, and the
people in the towns and villages adjoining were
told of the fate which awaited the foreign ship of
war, should her commander be foolhardy enough
to make an attack upon them. And certainly,

looking at the number and size of their junks, their heavy armament, and the position they occupied, there seemed little chance for a ten-gun brig. The first broadside from the junks, properly directed, would have disabled or sunk her and rendered all future efforts of her crew of no avail. But Captain Vansittart and his brave officers and crew were not alarmed by the apparent strength of the enemy. With consummate skill the "Bittern" was towed by the steamer into position, and so near the junks that the shower of shot with which she was received mostly passed over her hull and through her rigging. The steamer after performing this service was directed to fall back out of range, in order to be ready for any emergency which might happen.

It was now the "Bittern's" turn, and her first broadside must have astonished the pirates. Every shot told upon the unfortunate fleet with fearful precision; junk after junk was disabled or sunk; the men panic-stricken rushed into the water or to their boats and fled to the shore, and hundreds were killed on board or drowned in an attempt to escape. In a very short space of time there was scarcely a junk in all the fleet—apparently so powerful and confident a few hours before—but what was sunk or disabled.

Every hill and headland on the shore, from which a view of the action could be had, was crowded with people, who must have been surprised with the extraordinary results which they

witnessed. Some of these persons were no doubt
pirates themselves or friends of those who were on
board of the fleet, which had just been dispersed,
but the greater part were respectable inhabitants
who were thankful their coasts had thus been rid
of a most intolerable nuisance.

About two or three hundred of the pirates who
had escaped to the shore kept together for their
safety and protection. Had they not done so the
authorities and people would soon have fallen
upon them and destroyed them. These infatuated
men fled to an enclosed piece of ground on the
side of a hill, and dragging up some guns with
them endeavoured to place them in position for
their defence.

When the mandarin on shore saw the turn
things had taken he pretended to be greatly
alarmed, and informed Captain Vansittart that in
so far as he, the mandarin, was concerned matters
were now worse than before. "For," said he,
" the pirates were then at sea, and would have
left us in a short time, but now you have driven
them on shore where they will commit all kinds of
atrocities, and I am unable to control them." But
it was not the intention of the English commander
to leave things in this state. As soon, therefore,
as the piratical fleet had been taken, orders were
given to land a sufficient number of men to attack
the stronghold on shore.

The Chinese do not understand the art of war
—either at sea or on shore. They like what they

call fair fighting, that is, for the attacking party
to come manfully up in front and receive a broadside from guns which are all ready loaded to
receive them. Before Chusan was taken the
second time, during the last year, the Chinese had
a strong battery thrown up, which commanded the
whole of the harbour. They naturally thought
that our ships would come quietly into this place,
one by one, and be sunk without much resistance.
But the commanders of the expedition did not
view things in this light, and, although brave
enough, did not see the necessity of exposing the
lives of their men unnecessarily. Orders were,
therefore, given to land the troops in a bay to the
westward and march them over a hill there, which
thus brought them in the rear of the enemy instead of in his front. The immense battery of the
Chinese was thus rendered useless, and the troops
behind it were thrown into confusion at once,
and fled from the field. In aftertimes, when we
were at peace with China, the natives used often
to tell me about this manœuvre; and although
they laughed heartily at it, yet they shook their
heads, and said it was not fair to fight in that
way.

The Shiepoo pirates, as ignorant of the art of
war as the Chusan mandarins, appear to have expected that the crew of the "Bittern" would be
foolish enough to attack them in front, and placed
all their guns accordingly. As soon as this arrangement was observed orders were given to

avoid attacking in front. The men therefore scrambled up the hill-side, and thus were enabled to gain a position where the guns of the pirates could not be brought to bear upon them. This manœuvre was perfectly successful, the pirates fled from their stronghold in confusion, many of them were shot by our seamen and marines, while those who escaped from them were captured by the natives and the mandarins. And thus ended one of the boldest and best-managed expeditions against pirates on the Chinese coast. In an attack of this kind it could scarcely be expected that the " Bittern " could come out without some disaster. The master, an excellent officer, was killed while on the bridge of the steamer engaged in towing the brig into position, and three of the crew who were working a gun were severely wounded by a shot which had been better aimed than the rest, and struck the bulwarks.

In coming up the coast in one of the Peninsular and Oriental Company's steamers we met the " Bittern " with the steamer " Paou-shun " and a captured junk coming out of the Shiepoo Bay. The brig hoisted signals, and inquired whether we would take the wounded men on board and convey them to Shanghae, to which we were bound direct. Captain Jamieson, the master of the steamer, readily agreed to do what he was requested by Captain Vansittart; the poor fellows were brought on board in charge of Dr. Gordon, the surgeon of

2 E

the brig, and we conveyed them tenderly and safely to our destination.

But little more of this story remains to be told. The Ningpo missionaries got back their boat and a portion of the property which had been stolen from them by the pirates. The guild of Chinese merchants at that place—to their honour be it recorded — subscribed a handsome sum for the support of the relatives of the master of the " Bittern " who fell in action, as well as for those who had been wounded.

Nor were the English merchants behind their Chinese brethren in showing how highly they appreciated the conduct of Captain Vansittart on this occasion. A handsome subscription was raised to be presented to him in the manner most agreeable to his feelings. The generous-hearted sailor, although he appreciated highly the kindness thus shown to him, wanted nothing for himself, but suggested that the sum might be expended in the erection of an ornamental stained-glass window in the church of his native village.

CHAPTER XXI.

Return to the interior — Curious superstition — Adventures with a priest — Journey in search of new trees — Mountain scenery — New Rhododendron — Valley of the nine stones — Fine trees — Yew and golden pine — Curiosity of the natives — A dark and stormy night — We lose ourselves amongst the mountains — Seek shelter in a hut — Alarm of the inmates —Morning after the storm — Return to Ningpo — A fine new plant discovered — Adieu to the north of China — Engage scented-tea makers, &c., at Canton — Sail for India — Complimentary letter from Lord Dalhousie — Ordered to visit the tea-plantations in the Himalayas and Punjab — Return to England.

On reaching Ningpo I lost no time in proceeding onward to the interior of the country, in order, as I have already said, to wind up matters with the natives in various parts who had been assisting me in procuring supplies of plants, seeds, and other objects of natural history.

In going up one of the rivers at this time I observed the effect of a curious superstition which both amused and surprised me at the time. Every one knows that nearly all the junks and boats of China have eyes carved or painted in the bows. I had observed them on all parts of the coast, and had often heard the reason said to be given by the Cantonese, namely, "Suppose no got eye, how can see?" but I did not imagine that any one was so

2 E 2

superstitious or ignorant as to fancy that these
junks or boats really could see with the eyes which
had been given to them. It seemed, however,
that I was mistaken. As I was sailing slowly
onwards one of my boatmen seized his broad hat,
and, rushing past me to the bows of the boat,
placed it over one of the eyes. Several other
boats in company were also blinded in the same
way; some with hats, others with coats, cloaks,
or anything that came readiest to hand. I did
not understand this proceeding at first, but soon
found out the cause. A dead body was floating
up the stream with the tide, and if the boat is
allowed to see an object of this kind some evil is
sure to happen to the passengers or crew before
the voyage is over. Such is one of the superstitions of the Chinese, and hence the reason for
covering up the eyes of the boats in order that
they might not see.

About the end of October I found myself once
more in front of the old temple of Tsan-tsing,
which I have already noticed in these pages, and
met there the same priests and the same travelling
tailor. The priests here seemed to me the most
ignorant, lazy, and imbecile I had ever met with
in any part of China. They spend their days in
perfect idleness, sitting for hours at a time basking
in the sunshine, or under the verandah of their
dwellings when the sun's rays are too powerful to
be thus exposed. They seemed to be in a kind
of dreamy, mesmeric state; their eyes indeed are

open, but apparently they see nothing that is going on around them.

On my arrival the tailor was working in the room which I had formerly occupied. The high-priest was sitting on a bed adjoining looking at him, but it seemed doubtful from his appearance if he saw either the tailor or his needle. For hours he remained in the same position, and then fell sound asleep until dinner-time. Several other priests were reclining on chairs, or wandering list-lessly about the verandahs or courts of the temple. The only beings who seemed to have life in their veins were the tailor, the cook, two boys, and several ugly-looking dogs.

And thus the priests in this temple go on from day to day—from childhood to youth and from youth to old age—until the "last scene of all" takes place, when they sink into the grave, having as they believe accomplished the object for which they were sent into the world.

Buddhism must surely have greatly degenerated since the days when it was first promulgated. It could not be by the exertions of men such as these that this form of religion was extended over half the world and obtained such a footing in a country like China, where even the Christian faith with its many able and zealous preachers can find so few converts.

The room which I occupied was furnished with two bedsteads, a small table, and three or four chairs. Behind it was another room, which could

only be entered through the one I occupied, and
which was the bed-room of the high-priest. I had
just finished dinner about eight in the evening,
when this gentleman presented himself, and politely informed me he wanted to go to bed. To
this arrangement, as a matter of course, I had no
objection, being very tired, and therefore anxious to
get rid of him for the night. I therefore rose from
my seat in order to allow him to pass on to his own
room. When he got to his door he found it locked,
and commenced looking in every conceivable place
for the key. He held in his hand two strips of bamboo, which he used instead of a candle, and which
gave out a large body of flame accompanied with
smoke, and soon filled the room, and rendered the
atmosphere very disagreeable. To make matters
worse, every now and then he snuffed the ends of
the bamboo with his fingers and threw the red-hot
charcoal on the floor. After he had looked in
every drawer and in every odd corner of the room
three or four times over, muttering to himself
while he did so something about the loss of his
ya-za (key), he left me for the purpose of looking
for it outside in some other part of the building.

In about half-an-hour he returned and told me a
second time he wanted to go to bed. "Have you
found your key, then?" I asked him. No, he had
not found his *ya-za*; and then he commenced the
search in the same places and in the same listless
and stupid manner as before. I began to think
he would fall into a state of somnambulism and go

on with his search all night long.   Again my
room was filled with smoke, again the floor was
strewed with burning charcoal, and as I was thinking of retiring to rest, this state of things was far
from being either pleasant or agreeable.   I therefore ventured to remonstrate with him and to call
his attention to the fact that as he had searched
all these places several times already, it was a loss
of time to search there again.   His only reply to
my remonstrance was uttered in a doleful, dreamy
tone—" My ya-za ! my ya-za ! I have lost my
ya-za ! "

At last he seemed to awake all at once from his
dream, and turning round to me with a good-humoured smile upon his countenance, he said, " Well,
I cannot find my key ; but, never mind, there are
two beds in this room, and as you can only occupy
one of them, I shall take the other."   This propo-
sition, although perfectly fair, and one that I could
scarcely object to, was far more reasonable than
agreeable to my feelings.   I therefore put in one
or two objections in as mild a form as possible.
" There are no bedding or clothes in that bed, and
you will surely suffer greatly from the cold."   This
had no effect ; he assured me he had plenty of
clothes upon him, and that he would sleep very
comfortably on the bare bed.   " Well but," said I,
laughing, " are you not afraid to sleep in the same
room with a pah kwie-tze (white devil) ? "   It may
be remembered that this was the man who appeared to dread me so much on our first acquaint-

ance. All his old fears seemed instantly to return, the smile left his countenance, and he gave me a look which told plainly enough that I had struck the right chord in order to gain my object, and that he would be as averse to sleeping in my company as I was to his. " Ah ! " said he, " my ya-za ! I have lost my ya-za ! " and commenced the search as before.

It was now getting very late, and as I had a long journey in view for the following day, my patience was completely exhausted. I therefore rose from my chair, and, putting my hand on his shoulder, said, " Come with me and I shall find you a bed for the night." Leading him out of my room, we proceeded across the hall to one occupied by another priest, at whose door we now knocked, and who readily admitted us. " Here is your superior," said I ; " he has lost the key of his bedroom ; pray give him a bed in yours, and make him as comfortable as you can until the morning." Leaving the two Buddhists to explain matters in their way, I returned to my own room, bolted the door, and went to bed. Nothing occurred during the succeeding part of the night to disturb my slumbers.

It was now the end of October, and the weather was cool and pleasant. When I awoke at daybreak on the following morning I found the atmosphere clear, and the sky without a cloud ; everything gave promise of one of those glorious days which are common in the north of China at this season, particularly amongst the mountains. My

servants and myself were early astir, having a
long journèy in prospect for the day.   The object
I had in view was to obtain various kinds of seeds,
more particularly those of the " golden pine-tree "
(*Abies Kœmpferi*), which I have already noticed in
these pages, and which I had searched for in the
previous season without success.

Taking an early breakfast, we ascended the
pass behind the temple, and soon reached the vale
of Poo-in-chee and the little village of that name.
Here I observed for the first time two very fine
yew-trees, which apparently were quite new.   They
evidently belonged to the genus *Cephalotaxus*—a
genus perfectly hardy in England, and very highly
prized.   They were too young to have seeds upon
them, and too large to dig up and carry away.
While my servant and myself were looking at
them, the person to whom the garden belonged
came out and very kindly gave us their name and
history.   He told us he had received the seeds
from a place about ten or fifteen miles distant
amongst the mountains, where the trees grew to a
great size and produced seeds annually in considerable abundance.   It is called Fee-shoo by the
natives, and its seeds are to be found in a dry state
in all the doctors' shops in Chinese towns.   They
are considered valuable in cases of cough, asthma,
and diseases of the lungs or chest.   I am not aware
that their seeds are known to English doctors in
China, or if they are considered by them of any
value.

Being very anxious to procure vegetating seeds of this fine tree, I offered a considerable sum to one of the villagers of Poo-in-chee providing he would go with us and act as our guide through the mountains. The person who had been giving us the information above intimated his readiness to accompany us, but suggested that instead of starting then it would be better to put off the journey until the following day, when we could start by daylight. But the day was yet early and fine, and I was determined to proceed at once. By a little coaxing our guide was induced to swallow a hasty meal and accompany us on our journey.

Our road led us over the highest ridges of the mountains, which are here fully three thousand feet above the level of the sea. The tops of these mountains are so cold in winter that nothing but an alpine vegetation can exist;—the strange tropical-looking forms, such as the bamboo, the Chusan palm, and plants of that kind met with at a lower elevation, give place to wiry grass, gentians, spiræas, and other hardy plants of a like description. Here and there on our journey we came upon fine examples of the golden pine-tree (*Abies Kœmpferi*) growing a little way down on the mountain-slopes. *Cephalotasus Fortunei* and *Cryptomeria japonica* were also found at high elevations.

In a romantic glen through which we passed on our journey I came upon a remarkably fine-looking rhododendron. A species of the genus (*R. Championæ*) had been discovered on the Hongkong hills, but none had previously been met with to the northward, although the azalea is one of the most common plants on the mountains of Chekiang, I therefore looked upon the present discovery as a great acquisition, and as the plants were covered with ripe seeds, I was able to obtain a good supply to send home. All the Chinese in that part of the country agreed in stating that the flowers of this species are large and beautiful, but as all rhododendrons have this character, it is impossible to predict what this one may turn out to be until we have an opportunity of seeing its flowers. Mr. Glendinning, of the Chiswick nursery, to whom I sent the seeds, has been fortunate enough to raise a good stock of young plants, which are now growing vigorously, and which will soon determine the value of the species.

Our journey was long and toilsome; sometimes we were on the top of the highest ridges, and at other times we seemed to go down and down until we were nearly on a level with the sea. But the views of scenery, which were ever shifting as we went along, were grand in the extreme, and richly rewarded us for all our toil. While on the tops of the highest ridges we looked round upon barren mountains, which lay about us like the waves of a stormy sea, and here and there we got glimpses of the distant and fertile plain of Ningpo stretching far away to the eastward. At other times our way led us through pleasant and secluded valleys, each of which looked like a little world of its own, shut in by rugged mountains, and having no connexion with the great world outside.

Although the tops of the mountains here were generally barren and uncultivated, yet I observed crops of Indian corn growing to a very considerable elevation, and it was now ripe. Down in the valleys the land was very rich, and nearly all under cultivation. The natives of these districts prefer living in the valleys, which are sheltered by the surrounding mountains from cold and cutting winds. Many temporary huts were met with at high elevations, but these were merely used in the summer-time and while the crops of Indian corn were ripe. No one appeared to think of living in such places during the winter.

The natives with whom we came in contact during our journey seemed a hardy, industrious race, and hospitable and kind in their habits. We were often asked to enter their cottages, when we were presented with tea, roasted Indian corn, or anything they might chance to have for themselves.

About four o'clock in the afternoon we reached the " Valley of the Nine Stones," to which we were bound. Here we found a pretty little town situated on the banks of a small stream which takes a winding course through the mountains to the eastward, and eventually falls into one of the branches of the Ningpo river. Our guide pointed with great satisfaction to numerous fine trees of the new yew or *Cephalotaxus*, which were growing on the sides of

the hill above the town. Many of them were from
sixty to eighty feet in height with fine round heads,
and altogether had a striking and ornamental appearance. There were no seeds to be seen on any
of them, but our guide informed us they had been
lately gathered, and were still in the town, where
we could purchase them. Some noble trees of the
" golden pine " were also met with here, and, to
my delight, were loaded with ripe cones. When
ripe, these cones have a rich yellow hue, which
probably suggested the name by which this fine
tree is known amongst the Chinese. I look upon
this tree as the most important of all my Chinese
introductions. It grows rapidly, produces excellent timber, and will eventually become a striking
and beautiful object in our English landscape.

While engaged in making observations upon
these trees I was on the hill-side above the town,
and consequently fully exposed to the natives.
The news of a stranger and foreigner being in
this secluded place seemed to fly from house to
house with the rapidity of lightning; in less time
than I can describe it every door, verandah, and
window was crowded with anxious faces gazing
intently up to where I was standing. Some few,
more impatient than their neighbours, came running up the hill in order to have a nearer view,
and several respectable-looking persons in the
crowd asked me to go to their houses and drink
tea. Every one treated me with marked civility
and even kindness.

But the day was now far spent, and my servants and guide knowing better than I did the difficulties of our homeward journey by night, begged me to look after the seeds without delay. They also pointed out a man who owned a number of trees, and who had a large quantity of the seeds for sale. We therefore followed this man to his house, and found he had just commenced to clean and dry these seeds for the Ningpo market. It was difficult to strike a bargain as to price, but this was done satisfactorily at last, and the owner engaged to deliver them at Ning-kong-jou in three days. Large quantities of the seeds of the "golden pine" were also contracted for in the same way; these are now growing in Mr. Glendinning's nursery at Chiswick. Upon the whole I was highly satisfied with the results of our visit to the "Valley of the Nine Stones."

After drinking a cup of tea with the hill farmer —for such he was—we made our adieus to the crowds of villagers and turned our faces homewards. But it was now nearly five o'clock in the afternoon, and being the end of October it was almost dark. The day too, which had been hitherto so fine, was now overcast; a thick mist came rolling down the sides of the hills, and it began to rain. Onward we trod for many a weary mile, sometimes missing our way, and having to retrace our steps, while at other times we proceeded with painful uncertainty as to our being in the right road. At last our guide came to a dead stand, and confessed he did not know where he was; nor was this to be wondered at in the thick mist and darkness which surrounded us. What to do next was now a most serious and anxious question, and one most difficult to answer. Our guide recommended us to remain where we were, and suggested that the thick mist might possibly clear away and enable him to make out some familiar landmark. We were far above the level of any of the villages which are scattered over these hills, and had no hope of obtaining shelter unless we could stumble upon one of those temporary summer huts erected by the farmers, who cultivate Indian corn on the higher lands. Drenched to the skin, and cold, we now endeavoured to obtain shelter from the wind and rain on the lee side of a large projecting granite rock, and remained in this comfortless position for more than an hour.

As the mist chanced to lift a little, our guide, who was anxiously looking out, fancied he discerned a light at no great distance. This soon became more clearly visible, and we gladly moved on towards it. It turned out to be shining from a miserable hut, such as I have already noticed, and was occupied temporarily by an old woman and a boy, for the purpose of getting in their crop of Indian corn. But "any port in a storm;" and I looked on this miserable hovel with more thankfulness than I had done on many a snug and comfortable inn at home.

In order to alarm the inmates as little as possible, our guide went first, and the rest followed close behind him, in order to get in before the door was shut and barred in our faces, a proceeding which we thought not improbable if those inside became alarmed. The guide knocked at the door, told his name, and said he was a native of Poo-in-chee, who had lost his way amongst the mountains, and sought shelter from the wind and rain. When the door was opened we took care that it should remain so until the fears of the inmates were quieted. The moment the old woman saw a foreigner she manifested the greatest signs of alarm, and retreated to the farthest corner of the building, at the same time pulling her little boy along with her. In vain I seconded my guide and servants in their efforts to convince her that she had nothing to fear; I was a "white devil," and that seemed to be the only idea she would allow to take possession of her mind.

In other circumstances I would have gone away and left the old lady to recover her composure; but this was at present almost impossible. After, therefore, assuring her for the last time that she had nothing to fear, we drew near to the fire and gladly warmed ourselves. In a little while the boy began to be more friendly, and eventually the old woman herself came out of the corner and threw some fresh wood on the fire. The "ice was now broken," and our friendship was further cemented by the present of a few cash, which were thankfully received, and which tended to raise us not a little in the estimation of our hostess and her child.

The air of the mountains, cold and damp as it was, had given us an appetite, and we were all ravenously hungry. We therefore suggested to the old woman the propriety of selling us some heads of her Indian corn. These we roasted at the fire, and enjoyed our simple fare with greater zest than we had ever done a most sumptuous dinner. When our dinner was over, we collected a quantity of dry straw, which the hut afforded, and spread it thickly down before the fire. Tired and weary as we were, it was not necessary that we should seek repose on a bed of down. Dry straw was a luxury in our present circumstances, so we lay down and soon forgot all our cares in the land of sleep and dreams.

When we awoke on the following morning, broad daylight was streaming in upon us through the sides and roof of our temporary dwelling. The storm of the preceding night had passed away, the sky above head was clear, and every-thing gave promise of a beautiful day. The view from the door of our hut was grand in the ex-treme. We were high up on the side of a moun-tain; on the opposite side, to the westward, there was another mountain of equal height, while between the two lay a deep and richly cultivated valley, with a small stream gliding smoothly onward down its centre. A misty cloud hung

2 f

here and there lazily on the sides of the hills, which only had the effect of making the sky look more clear and the scene around and below us more grand and lovely.

We now gave our hostess and her boy a small present for the inconvenience we had put them to, and amidst their best wishes we resumed our journey, which we had been obliged to abandon the evening before. Without having any further adventures of interest, we arrived in safety at the old temple of Tsan-tsing.

On the day following I went down to the plains and onward to Ningpo. In the garden of an old Chinese gentleman here, I met with a beautiful new herbaceous plant, having rich blotched or variegated leaves, which has since been named by Dr. Lindley, *Farfugium grande*. It was growing in a neat flower-pot, and was evidently much prized by its possessor, and well it might, for it was the most striking-looking plant in his garden. He informed me he had received it from Peking the year before, and that at present it was very rare in Ningpo, but he thought I might be able to procure a plant or two from a nurseryman in the town to whom he had given a few roots. I lost no time in paying a visit to the nursery indicated, and secured the prize. It has reached England in safety, and will shortly be a great ornament to our houses and gardens.

I had now brought my work in China to a successful termination. Many thousands of tea-plants, obtained in the finest districts, had reached their destination in the Himalayas, and had been reported in good condition by Dr. Jameson, the superintendent of the Government plantations; abundant supplies of implements used in these districts had also been sent round, and two sets of first-rate black-tea manufacturers from Fokien and Kiangse had been engaged, and were now on their way to the north-west provinces of India. In accordance with instructions received from the government of India, I had also introduced many of the useful and ornamental productions of China, such for example as timber and fruit-trees, oil-yielding plants, dyes, &c. These things were sent partly to the Government gardens and partly to the Agricultural and Horticultural Society.

I now bade adieu to many kind friends in the north of China and sailed for Hongkong and Canton. With the assistance of Messrs. Turner and Co., I succeeded in engaging some scented-tea men and lead-box makers, and took them on with me in the steamer "Lancefield," to Calcutta, where we arrived on the 10th of February, 1856. Here I had the pleasure of receiving a despatch from Mr. Beadon, Secretary to the Government of India, containing the following paragraph:—" I am directed to acknowledge the receipt of your letter No. 25, dated the 11th instant, and to state that the Most Noble the Governor-General in Council entirely approves of your proceedings, and considers the results of your mission to China to be very satisfactory." I need scarcely say that a compliment of this kind from Lord Dalhousie was most grateful to my feelings; for next to the pleasure which one feels who has accomplished a difficult object is that of knowing that his exertions are appreciated.

Having thus terminated the Chinese part of my labours, I was requested by the Government of India to proceed once more to the North-west Provinces and the Punjab, for the purpose of inspecting the various tea-plantations there, and to make a report upon their present condition and future prospects. This report, which was sent in to the Government in October 1856, shows the tea-plantations in the Himalayas and Punjab to be in a very satisfactory condition, and likely at no distant day to prove of great value to the natives of India.

On the 9th of November I left India in the Peninsular and Oriental Company's ship "Bentinck," Captain Caldbeck, and reached Southampton on the 20th of December, having been absent from England exactly four years.

CHAPTER XXII.

Dispute with the Chinese about the lorcha "Arrow" — Lorchas and
their crews — Abuse of the English flag — Right of entrance into
the city of Canton — The Chinese outwit us in diplomacy — True
causes of our position in Canton — We have ourselves to blame —
The policy which ought to be pursued — The city of Canton must
be opened — Foolish restrictions on foreigners and their trade ought
to be abolished — Direct communication with the court of Peking
— Method of carrying out these views — Remarks on the climate
with reference to the health of our troops — Conclusion.

THE narrative of my travels in China ends with
the last chapter, and in ordinary circumstances
that chapter would have been the last in this
work; but since I left Hongkong a disturbance
has broken out at Canton of a most serious kind,
which day by day assumes a more important
aspect, the end of which is most difficult for those
even who are best acquainted with China and the
Chinese to foresee.

It is not my intention in this place to attempt a
history of the original cause of the dispute in so
far as the unfortunate lorcha "Arrow" is concerned, or to express my opinions on a subject
upon which the highest legal authorities in England cannot agree. It is sufficient for me to refer
the reader to the despatches of the English and
Chinese authorities in China, and to the speeches

which have been delivered in Parliament for information upon this subject. But whether we may be right or wrong in a legal point of view I doubt much whether it be good policy to allow such vessels as this "Arrow" to fly the English flag. Every one who has travelled much on the coast of China knows well what the majority of these "lorchas" are. And here, perhaps, I had better endeavour to give some information on this point to those who have not had an opportunity of seeing and judging for themselves.

Lorchas are not English vessels, as some people appear to imagine, and are rarely owned or sailed by Englishmen. They are Portuguese vessels, and were originally built at Macao, although of late years a few have been built at Ningpo and some of the other ports on the east coast. They fly the Portuguese flag, have Portuguese papers, and are numbered and registered by the government of Macao. They are manned, almost without exception, by Chinese—natives of Macao, Canton, and adjacent ports in the south of China. Nominally they are commanded by Macao-Portuguese, but the Chinamen always seemed to me to have the chief control of the vessels. The few owned by Englishmen, which fly the English flag and have English papers, are sailed just in the same way, the only difference being that the latter may boast of an English "captain."

A few of these lorchas are common traders on the coast, particularly in the south, about

Macao, Canton, Hongkong, and Amoy, but by far the greater number have been engaged of late years in convoying Chinese junks from port to port and protecting them from pirates. When I was last in China a fleet of them was chartered by the mandarins and sent up the Yang-tse-kiang to attack the rebels at that place and Nankin, but in this instance they did not seem very successful. They have often been accused of committing acts of piracy on the coast, and stringent measures have been taken by the Macao government at various times to keep them in order. Generally they are very heavily armed, and have a most formidable-looking appearance.

These vessels, whether in convoying or in simple trading, do not confine themselves to the five ports at which foreigners are permitted by treaty to trade, and are well known both to the Chinese government and to foreigners as inveterate smugglers. Oftentimes the peaceful inhabitants in the little towns on the coast have complained bitterly to me of the lawless and tyrannical acts of their crews.

Such, then, is the class of vessels to which the "Arrow" belongs. Is it right that they should be allowed to sail under the English flag without our government having means to control the lawless acts of their crews? These vessels, as I have already shown, visit and trade at hundreds of places on the coast where bona fide English ships are not allowed. Are these crews to be allowed to commit all sorts of offences against their own government and people and then point to the flag of England—that flag which as Englishmen we proudly look up to as the emblem of liberty and justice—as their protection and as their warrant? This may be in accordance with treaty rights—it may be the law of the case—but it scarcely accords with what reason suggests or common sense. It therefore appears to me to be bad policy on the part of the local government of Hongkong to grant permission to fly the English flag to lorchas or native boats manned by Chinese over whose actions, when away from that port, it has no control.

But as we watch the dispute in question the scene suddenly changes, another act commences, and the lorcha falls into the back-ground. It is no longer satisfaction for the insult offered by the government of China, or rather Commissioner Yeh, to the English flag only which is demanded. It is now discovered that this is a good opportunity for insisting upon our treaty-right of entering the city of Canton. There can be no doubt that we are fully entitled to this privilege, and have been so since the Treaty of Nankin was signed, at the close of the last China war, but it is extremely doubtful that his Excellency Yeh had the power to grant a right, without a reference to the Court of Pekin, which had been allowed to stand so long in abeyance.

It has often been remarked that in everything

the Chinese are exactly the reverse of European
nations, and here is a fresh proof that the remark
is, to a certain extent, a just one. As a nation
they cannot fight, but they are first-rate diploma-
tists; on the other hand, we can win our battles
and then allow ourselves to be outwitted by the
diplomacy of a nation whom we despise in the
field.

In 1842, after taking most of the important
maritime cities of China, from Hongkong as far
north as Nankin, we made peace with the government upon condition that five ports, namely, Canton, Amoy, Foo-chow, Ningpo, and Shanghae,
should be opened to foreigners of every nation for
the purposes of trade. Scarcely was this treaty
signed before the right of entrance to the city of
Canton was disputed by the Chinese, and then we
committed our first and greatest mistake in not
enforcing it. Some years afterwards the demand
was made again by Sir John Davis, who in order
to enforce it destroyed many of the forts in the
river with the fleet then at his disposal in the
Chinese waters. But the Chinese Commissioner
of that day did by clever diplomacy what he
found impossible by force of arms. He induced
Her Majesty's Plenipotentiary to put the evil day
off for two years on account of the prejudices of
the people; at the end of that period our countrymen would be received with open arms by the
loving Cantonese! The Imperial Commissioner
knew well enough that at the end of two years

the difficulty would just be the same as it was then, but ere that time another officer would have to deal with it, and he himself would get the credit of duping the English out of the city of Canton.

I must confess that the arrangement we made at that time took me completely by surprise. Having a pretty good knowledge of the Chinese character I knew perfectly well that at the end of two years we would be as far from the city of Canton as ever we had been, and the events which have taken place since that time have proved the correctness of the opinion which I then formed.

Not only have we allowed ourselves to be out-witted by Chinese commissioners but we have suffered much in the eyes of the people of China by first making these demands and then allowing them to be evaded. It may be all very well to say that we did so from compassion for a weak power, or semi-civilized nation; the Chinese, full to the brim of self-conceit, put it down to fear. With a nation like the Chinese our demands should be well considered before they are made, but once we have made them they ought to be enforced.

Were the city of Canton open to-morrow few persons would ever visit it except for the purpose of calling upon the officers of government. The finest streets and shops are all outside the walls, and the city itself, from all accounts, possesses but few attractions. But although this is the case the vexed question has assumed an importance not its own, and it is really absolutely necessary now that we force a compliance with our demands if we mean that the lives and property of our country-men should be safe and commerce go on.

Had we enforced our treaty-rights at first all this would have been avoided, much blood would have been spared, and the Canton Chinese would have treated us with more civility and respect. When the port of Foo-chow-foo, the capital city of Fokien, was opened to foreign trade, an effort was made by the authorities there to prevent us from having a footing in the city. Our consul, the late Mr. Lay, alone and unaided, forced his way through the gates and took up a temporary resi-dence in a joss-house within the walls. The man-darins, finding *one man* determined to secure our treaty-rights, gave up the point, and never after-wards objected to our having the consulate in the city. Had a little of such spirit and determination been shown at Canton, and supported by a suffi-cient force, this vexatious question might have been settled long ago.

In making treaties with a nation like the Chinese we ought not to look upon them as we do upon the more civilized nations of the west. They cannot appreciate our motives of clemency or consideration. During the last war we spared Canton when it lay entirely at our mercy, and the Cantonese to a man gave it as their opinion that we were afraid to attack it. Again, according to them, it was fear which prevented us from insisting upon our treaty-rights as regards free admission within their city walls.

It would appear, therefore, that we have ourselves to blame for much of the barbarous treatment we have received at the hands of the Canton Chinese.

But putting on one side the case of the unfortunate lorcha " Arrow," about which our " doctors differ," there seems to be little doubt that our relations with the Cantonese were upon a most unsatisfactory footing, and that sooner or later the " good understanding " existing between us would have been disturbed. It was only a question of time, and it has been decided somewhat prematurely, perhaps, by this supposed insult to the English flag and infraction of treaty-rights. Our relations with the people and government of Canton can never be considered on a satisfactory footing until we have a full and complete understanding with each other. They must be taught to look upon us as a nation as highly civilised and as powerful as themselves. Until this is accomplished we may have a disturbance at any time; our commerce may be stopped, and what is of far more importance, the lives of our countrymen living in this remote region may be placed in imminent danger.

Whether we were right or wrong, therefore, at the commencement of this unfortunate dispute, it is now absolutely necessary for us to carry it through until our relations are placed upon a firm and satisfactory basis. It may seem fair and plausible for persons ignorant of the Chinese character to talk of justice and humanity—fine sounding words no doubt—but totally inapplicable to the present state of things. Suppose we were now to go down on our knees to Commissioner Yeh, acknowledge our fault, crave forgiveness for the past, and promise to behave better for the future, what would be the result? Is it to be supposed for one moment that this worthy functionary would view such conduct in a proper light, or that the thousands of Chinese under his rule would give us credit for the feelings by which we were actuated? Most assuredly not. The "barbarians," or the "foreign devils," would be again accused of fear, or, what is worse, of cringing to the Cantonese in order that our trade might be allowed to be carried on. By such a proceeding we should place ourselves upon the top of a mine which might be sprung at any time. There would be no security for life or property in Canton, and eventually a war would be forced upon us more disastrous than what may happen at the present time.

In order, therefore, to be humane in the strictest sense of the term, to prevent future war and bloodshed, to give the Cantonese a true estimate of our character, to render the lives and property of our countrymen secure, and to prevent those vexatious interruptions to our commerce, we must carry out what we have begun with a firm and determined hand. With a nation like the Chinese, particularly about Canton, this is true humanity and mercy.

But the question " What do we want from the Chinese ? " naturally presents itself, and what points in a new treaty ought to be insisted upon in order to guard against and if possible prevent, future disturbances between us and them. We must have free entrance into the city of Canton, however unimportant this may be ; and not for our officials only, *as they themselves have suggested*, but for our merchants, missionaries, or any one who chooses to go, just as we have at the other five ports which are now open to our trade. Our officials must be received by Chinese officers of equal rank on all occasions when any important business is to be transacted.

If possible, and I do not see anything to prevent it, all those prohibitory regulations as regards our trading at certain ports only, and going only a certain distance into the country, ought to be swept away. These regulations appear to have been framed upon the supposition of our being a barbarous race, foreign devils, and wild animals, which it is necessary to cage up to secure the safety of the civilized Chinese. The sooner such regulations are abrogated the better it will be both for the Chinese and ourselves.

And, lastly, means ought to be taken to have

direct communication with the court of Peking, either by means of an ambassador or occasional resident. The Chinese cannot remain much longer isolated from the rest of the world, nor does it seem desirable that they should be so. With the Russians stretching eastward on the banks of the river Amoor, the Americans in California, ourselves in India, and fleets of steamers traversing the sea which washes the shores of this vast empire, isolation for any length of time seems out of the question.

To bring the Chinese within the pale of nations, to extend our commerce, and to open up the country to missionary labour and scientific research, are objects worthy of the earnest consideration of statesmen, not only in England but also in France, America, and in other civilized European countries who are interested in the welfare of mankind.

Supposing that the present time is suitable for the consideration of this important subject, the question as to how it ought to be commenced and carried out naturally presents itself. That the Government of China will offer many objections to the plan may easily be predicted; but the same force which it will be necessary to employ to place our relations on a temporary footing will be sufficient to gain these most desirable results, providing we do not allow ourselves to be outdone *once more* in diplomacy.

If we are ever to have a permanent peace with

the Cantonese, if our trade is to be carried on peaceably, and if the lives and property of our countrymen there are to be secured, the pride of the Chinese officials must be humbled, and the rabble mob in that city must be taught that they cannot insult us with impunity. In the last war this guilty city escaped, while we punished the unoffending inhabitants of the cities to the north, such as Amoy, Ningpo, and Shanghae. We can scarcely commit such an error a second time. If we must punish it seems but just that the chief part of that punishment should fall upon the guilty.

It appears to me to be useless, and only a waste of time to attempt negociations with a man like Commissioner Yeh. Even if he had the will to agree to our terms he has not the power. We must communicate directly with the Court of Peking; and to have influence there we must be backed with an imposing force to compel a compliance with our demands.

The best and easiest way to accomplish the object in view would be to reoccupy the island of Chusan. This island might be taken without much loss, and while the city of Ting-hae and the adjoining suburbs would afford shelter to our troops, our fleet might rendezvous in its beautiful and commodious harbours. This island is more healthy than Hongkong or any other of the northern ports, and this fact is one of very great importance to the welfare of our troops. It has always been found in our wars with China that the climate has been much more fatal to our soldiers than the guns of the Chinese.

With a force in Chusan we could easily communicate with the Government of Peking. In the south-west monsoon, from May to the end of September, vessels of large draught can run up to the gulf of Pee-che-lee and anchor at no very great distance from the capital. Later in the year, when the north winds are blowing, this could not be done owing to the shallowness of the gulf.

During the last Chinese war the most vulnerable point attacked was the city of Chin-kiang-foo, a few miles below Nanking. Here the most important inland trade of the empire is carried on by means of the grand canal. But this city has been occupied for some years by the insurgents, and any attack upon it would only serve the ends of the Imperial government. Nor would it serve any good end to meddle with the ports of Amoy, Foo-chow, Ningpo, and Shanghae, providing the inhabitants at these places do not mix themselves up in our quarrel.

It would seem, therefore, that our operations should be directed principally to Canton in the south, and to the capital and towns adjacent in the north. And as these operations are likely to last for some time, I can point to no better place than Chusan as the head-quarters for our troops. They are likely to suffer less here from

2 G

the effects of climate than anywhere else, and will have little difficulty in obtaining an abundant supply of fresh provisions.

It is not my intention in these pages to offer any suggestions to the commander of the Chinese forces as to his mode of action.—I know nothing of the art of war,—but as the whole coast of China from Canton to Shanghae, and much of the inland, is well known to me, any information I give is entitled to consideration.

I have already remarked that the climate of the country is much more to be dreaded than the armies of the Chinese, and I shall draw these remarks to a close by giving a description of what that climate is. In all parts of China where I have been, the hottest months in the year are July and August. In the north the heat is very oppressive from the middle of June to the end of August. About Hongkong and Canton the oppressive heat commences a little earlier and lasts longer, although it is not quite so intense as it is further north. My registering thermometer during July and August at Hongkong frequently stood as high as 90°, and one day reached 94° in the shade. In Shanghae and Ningpo the same thermometer used to stand sometimes for days at 100°.

But the hottest months are not the most unhealthy, at least we have not so much sickness then as we have a little later in the season. In September, when the monsoon begins to change, and when the northerly winds come down, causing a sudden depression of temperature, natives as well as foreigners suffer much from fever and dysentery. The excessive summer heat seems to weaken the constitution, and thus renders it more easily affected by the sudden changes of temperature which occur at this period of the year. *The rivers of China are particularly unhealthy at this season*, a fact which ought to be kept in view by the commanders of our ships of war.

When the monsoon is fairly set in, in October, the climate of Shanghae and Ningpo is as healthy as that of any part of the world. Although the sun is hot during the day at this time, the air is cool and bracing and the nights are cold. In the end of October the thermometer sometimes sinks as low as the freezing point. December, January, and February are the coldest months of the year, the cold then being quite as severe as it is in England. Snow frequently falls, but the sun is too powerful to allow it to lie long upon the ground. Ice of a considerable thickness is formed annually upon all the lakes and canals.

About Canton the winters are much warmer than they are at the more northern ports ; the thermometer rarely falls to the freezing-point, and ice and snow are of very rare occurrence. But the climate here, although perhaps not so bracing to a European constitution, seems perfectly healthy during the winter and spring months.

For eight or nine months out of the twelve,

then, it would appear that the climate of China, both in the north and also in the south, is healthy to Europeans, and no doubt these are the proper months for the prosecution of military operations with English troops.

The monsoons in the China sea are not so decided as they are in India, but generally the prevailing winds from the end of April to the middle of September blow from the south-west. During the remainder of the year, northerly and easterly winds prevail. Thus what is called the south-west monsoon blows in summer, and the north-east in winter. Sailing vessels from Europe or India, bound for Hongkong or Chusan, or any of the northern ports, are almost certain to have a fair wind up the China sea from April to September, and *vice versâ*, a fair wind down during the other season. During the months of May, June, July, and August, a fleet of sailing vessels could easily rendezvous at Chusan, or any other point on the Chinese coast, and if necessary come down to Hongkong or Canton in three or four days, in the end of September, when the monsoon changes. But if these same vessels wanted to get from Canton to Chusan at that period, they would find considerable difficulty in reaching their destination.

From the information I have thus given it would appear safe to arrive at the following conclusions. 1st. It is useless to attempt to negociate with a man like Commissioner Yeh : we must have communication with the Court of Peking.

2nd. The island of Chusan is the most suitable point from which we can conduct our negociations, both on account of its position, and as it is the most healthy part of China for our troops. 3rd. If the lives and property of foreign merchants and others are to be safe in Canton, the mandarins and mob must be taught to treat us with more respect.   4th. The other four ports ought to be respected providing they do not mix themselves up in our quarrel with the Cantonese. 5th. China ought to be opened, and all those foolish restrictions imposed by the last treaty on our trade should be swept away.   6. In conducting our operations the nature of the climate ought to be carefully considered with a view to preserve the lives of our soldiers and sailors.

In conclusion let us hope that the day is not far distant, when this large and important empire, with its three hundred millions of human beings, shall not remain isolated from the rest of the world.   The sooner this change takes place the better will it be for the Chinese as well as for ourselves.   Trade and commerce will increase to a degree of which the most sanguine can form but a very faint idea at the present time.   The riches of the country will be largely developed, and articles useful as food, in the arts, or as luxuries, at present unknown, will be brought into the market. It cannot be true that a vast country like China, where the soil is rich and fertile, the climate favourable, and the teeming population industrious and ingenious, can produce only two or three articles of importance, such as silk and tea, for exportation. There must be many more, and these will be brought to light when the country is fairly and fully opened to the nations of the west.

But when this is accomplished a boon of far greater value will be conferred upon the Chinese than anything connected with the extension of their commerce. The Christian missionary will be able, without fear or restriction, to proclaim the "glad tidings of great joy" to millions of the human race who have never yet heard the joyful sound.

Objects such as these—the placing of our relations on a firm and satisfactory basis, the prevention of unequal wars where much blood is necessarily shed, the extension of trade and commerce, and the free and unrestricted dissemination of the Gospel of Christ—are worthy of the consideration of the highest statesmen and greatest philanthropists of our time.

THE END.